From
**Grassroots
Activism** to
Disinformation

The ISEAS – Yusof Ishak Institute (formerly Institute of Southeast Asian Studies) is an autonomous organization established in 1968. It is a regional centre dedicated to the study of socio-political, security, and economic trends and developments in Southeast Asia and its wider geostrategic and economic environment. The Institute's research programmes are grouped under Regional Economic Studies (RES), Regional Strategic and Political Studies (RSPS), and Regional Social and Cultural Studies (RSCS). The Institute is also home to the ASEAN Studies Centre (ASC), the Singapore APEC Study Centre, and the Temasek History Research Centre (THRC).

ISEAS Publishing, an established academic press, has issued more than 2,000 books and journals. It is the largest scholarly publisher of research about Southeast Asia from within the region. ISEAS Publishing works with many other academic and trade publishers and distributors to disseminate important research and analyses from and about Southeast Asia to the rest of the world.

From Grassroots Activism to Disinformation

Social Media in Southeast Asia

EDITED BY
Aim Sinpeng • Ross Tapsell

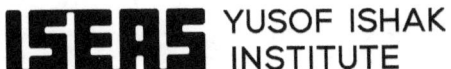 YUSOF ISHAK INSTITUTE

First published in Singapore in 2021 by
ISEAS Publishing
30 Heng Mui Keng Terrace
Singapore 119614

E-mail: publish@iseas.edu.sg
Website: <http://bookshop.iseas.edu.sg>

All rights reserved. No part of this publication may be reproduced, stored in a retrieval system, or transmitted in any form or by any means, electronic, mechanical, photocopying, recording or otherwise, without the prior permission of the ISEAS – Yusof Ishak Institute.

© 2021 ISEAS – Yusof Ishak Institute, Singapore

The responsibility for facts and opinions in this publication rests exclusively with the authors and their interpretations do not necessarily reflect the views or the policy of the publisher or its supporters.

ISEAS Library Cataloguing-in-Publication Data

Name(s): Sinpeng, Aim, editor. | Tapsell, Ross, editor.
Title: From grassroots activism to disinformation : social media in Southeast Asia / edited by Aim Sinpeng and Ross Tapsell.
Description: Singapore : ISEAS – Yusof Ishak Institute, 2021. | Includes bibliographical references.
Identifiers: ISBN 978-981-4951-02-9 (paperback) | 978-981-4951-03-6 (PDF)
Subjects: LCSH: Social media—Political aspects—Southeast Asia. | Disinformation—Political aspects—Southeast Asia. | Communication in politics—Southeast Asia.
Classification: LCC JA85.2 A9F93

Cover photo: Ray Yen
Typeset by International Typesetters Pte Ltd

CONTENTS

About the Contributors		vii
1.	From Grassroots Activism to Disinformation: Social Media Trends in Southeast Asia *Aim Sinpeng and Ross Tapsell*	1
2.	Curing "Patient Zero": Reclaiming the Digital Public Sphere in the Philippines *Pamela Combinido and Nicole Curato*	19
3.	The Political Campaign Industry and the Rise of Disinformation in Indonesia *Muninggar Sri Saraswati*	43
4.	Disinformation as a Response to the "Opposition Playground" in Malaysia *Niki Cheong*	63
5.	Social Media, Hate Speech and Fake News during Myanmar's Political Transition *Nyi Nyi Kyaw*	86
6.	Securitizing "Fake News": Policy Responses to Disinformation in Thailand *Janjira Sombatpoonsiri*	105
7.	Cambodia: From Democratization of Information to Disinformation *Mun Vong and Aim Sinpeng*	126

8. Social Media's Challenge to State Information Controls in Vietnam 145
   Dien Luong

9. Social Media and Changes in Political Engagement in Singapore 167
   Natalie Pang

10. Democratic Backsliding and Authoritarian Resilience in Southeast Asia: The Role of Social Media 192
    Marco Bünte

Index 213

ABOUT THE CONTRIBUTORS

Marco BÜNTE, Professor, Institute of Political Science, Friedrich-Alexander University, Erlangen Nuremberg, Germany

Niki CHEONG, Lecturer, School of Media and Performing Arts, Coventry University, UK. Formerly Postdoctoral Researcher, Department of Cultural, Media and Visual Studies, University of Nottingham, UK

Pamela COMBINIDO, Independent Researcher, The Philippines

Nicole CURATO, Associate Professor, University of Canberra

Nyi Nyi KYAW, Visiting Fellow, ISEAS – Yusof Ishak Institute, Singapore

Dien LUONG, Visiting Fellow, ISEAS – Yusof Ishak Institute, Singapore

Natalie PANG, Senior Research Fellow, Institute of Policy Studies, Lee Kuan Yew School of Public Policy; and Senior Lecturer, Department of Communications and New Media, National University of Singapore

Muninggar Sri SARASWATI, Deputy Head, Communication Studies Department, Swiss German University, Indonesia

Aim SINPENG, Lecturer, Government and International Relations, University of Sydney, Australia

Janjira SOMBATPOONSIRI, Assistant Professor, Faculty of Political Science, Thammasat University, Thailand

Ross TAPSELL, Senior Lecturer, College of Asia and the Pacific, The Australian National University

Mun VONG, PhD candidate, School of Government and International Relations, Griffith University, Australia

1

FROM GRASSROOTS ACTIVISM TO DISINFORMATION: SOCIAL MEDIA TRENDS IN SOUTHEAST ASIA

Aim Sinpeng and Ross Tapsell

When the Hanoi city administration announced a plan to cut some 6,700 trees from the city's boulevards in 2015, the authorities did not anticipate it would trigger a large-scale grassroots movement online. A Facebook page "6,700 people for 6,700 trees" quickly gathered more than 55,000 likes. Protests in the capital city subsequently ensued as civil society groups and ordinary citizens hit the streets. Within days, the central government immediately halted the plan to cut the trees, and launched a further investigation. In a one-party Communist state like Vietnam, whose regime has a tight grip on traditional media and criticism of the government is largely repressed and frequently punished, that an online movement could trigger a widespread backlash and force authorities to scrap its plan was extraordinary. As one of the most repressive regimes in the world, grassroots online activism was rising in Vietnam and a more politically engaged citizenry seemed to be an inevitable result.

Elsewhere in Southeast Asia, social media's positive impact on promoting grassroots issues seemed similar. In Indonesia, Joko Widodo was elected as president in 2014 partly through a powerful social media presence as a "new" kind of grassroots-driven politician, supported by much of Indonesia's civil society and pro-democracy activists. In Malaysia, the Bersih "Clean Elections" movement used social media to coalesce reformists, and enabled mass street protests against a corrupt semi-authoritarian regime. In Myanmar, one of Southeast Asia's most conservative societies, LGBT communities flourished on Facebook when Colours Rainbow Yangon was established to advocate for gay rights. Even in Thailand, reformists were making important gains. The Thai government planned to consolidate internet traffic through the creation of a single gateway, causing internet rights and media civil society groups to fight back. Internet advocacy groups created online petitions on change.org that elicited more than 500,000 signatures and heated conversations across a number of Thai web board communities. A Facebook group, พลเมืองต่อต้าน Single Gateway เพื่อเสรีภาพและความยุติธรรม ["Citizens against the Single Gateway for Freedom and Justice"], garnered more than 200,000 likes and generated much grassroots pressure on the government's controversial plan. Eventually, the Thai government backed off from the single gateway proposal.

The emergence of the internet in the late 1990s and early 2000s coincided with the flourishing of democracy in much of Southeast Asia. As internet penetration expanded, and as social media sites became central to citizens' information society, there was hope for "liberation technology" to have a significant effect in both democratic and authoritarian states in Southeast Asia (Diamond and Plattner 2012). Social media was empowering ordinary people to speak out, increase political participation, expand the space for civic activism and provide new avenues for independent media (Norris 2011; Stoycheff and Nisbet 2014). Some scholars noted the power of social media in reducing entrenched socioeconomic inequalities by lowering information asymmetries and costs of political engagement (Earl and Kimport 2011; Castells 2012). Studies from around the 2013–15 years espoused a positive correlation between social media use, civic action and political participation across both democratic and authoritarian political systems (Bennett and Segerberg 2012; Hyun and Kim 2015). According to the Global Database of Events, Language and Tone (GDELT), which tracks protest events around the world since 1979, the majority of Southeast Asian states experience a significant increase in the number of reported protests once internet penetration rate surpasses 10 per cent of the population.

Initially, much scholarly literature was dedicated to examining the role of new media technologies in providing alternative spaces and reforms in a region with an increasingly vibrant online public sphere (Liow and Pasuni 2010). The rise in offline protest events is most notable among authoritarian states in the region, such as Vietnam, Singapore, Thailand, and Malaysia, and is likely underestimated as online contentious actions are not included. A study by Fergusson and Molina (2019) draws on contentious events and value survey databases from 2006 to 2016 in 194 countries, and demonstrates that 14–26 per cent fewer protests would have occurred without Facebook. Their findings conclude that Facebook has a positive and robust effect on citizen protests, especially in countries experiencing economic downturns and/or whose citizens have few opportunities to oppose authorities (low freedom of expression and assembly, opposition repression). They argue that Facebook accounts for a 10 per cent increase in individual's perception of freedom to express their thoughts, join organizations and voice political opinion.

But the optimism was short-lived. By the mid to late 2010s, scholars were more concerned about the negative or hindering role social media was playing in democracies and around issues pertaining to universal human rights (Deibert 2015; Sunstein 2018), while at the same time the diversity and vibrancy of online platforms has seemingly reduced. With increasingly repressive and manipulative use of social media tools undertaken by governments, there is widespread concern that social media is fuelling anti-democratic elements of society, rather than grassroots reformists (Freedom House 2019). Some scholars even regard social media as a key driver of authoritarianism and repression (King, Pan and Roberts 2013).

Scholars are now most concerned with the role of "disinformation" and "fake news" production, and governments are creating laws which attempt to address this trend, ultimately limiting the freedom in which people can interact and engage with each other online (Bennett and Livingston 2018; Freelon and Wells 2020). Disinformation here is defined as "all forms of false, inaccurate, or misleading information designed, presented and promoted to intentionally cause public harm or for profit" (EU Commission 2018). While disinformation itself is not new, social media is regarded as "weaponizing" it to a new level, with its global reach and speed unmatched by previous and existing media platforms. Disinformation production via social media enables greater distrust in political and media institutions, and widening polarization (Iyengar and Westwood 2015). The Computational Propaganda Research Project reports in its 2019 Global Inventory of Organised Social Media Manipulation that there is evidence that at least one political party or a government agency in seventy countries has launched disinformation campaigns to shape domestic public opinion—an increase of 150 per cent in the last two years (Bradshaw and Howard 2019). The Association of Southeast Asian Nation (ASEAN) has recognized the growing peril of online falsehoods and issued a Declaration on a Framework to Minimise the Harmful Effects of Fake News in 2018 to promote socially responsible online behaviour.

This edited volume asks: what went wrong? It answers this question in the context of country specific chapters in Southeast Asia. In identifying trends in these Southeast Asian states, and situating them within the global context, the authors pay particular attention to the specific local contexts of each country that contribute to a deeper understanding of how social media has impacted state-society relations. We have covered eight countries in the region, but do recognize that more work needs to be conducted in smaller, less studied countries of Laos, Brunei and East Timor, and more opportunities for scholars in these countries who are not included in this volume. All of the authors are locally-based Southeast Asian scholars. They are not only experts in their field, with many having completed a PhD thesis on social media in their country, but they have also lived through the past ten years by engaging in social media platforms themselves. Rather than solely going back on existing literature to study earlier years, they are in many ways reflecting on their own lived experience of how they felt the "shift" personally.

The research grows out of a concern over mounting online disinformation worldwide, despite early optimism of the benefits social media could bring towards grassroots activism. This volume examines this global shift, but in the context of Southeast Asia, by asking three main questions:

1) How has social media evolved to become a platform used predominantly for reform to a space of increasing deception and manipulation?
2) Who were the main actors in this transition: governments, citizens or the platforms themselves?
3) Finally, we challenged the authors to find a "light at the end of the tunnel" by asking how Southeast Asian reformists might "reclaim" the digital public sphere?

This book advances the argument that social media has contributed to genuine expansion of grassroots activism in the early stages of its inception in Southeast Asia. That digital activism has been able to take hold in the region, in varying times, was made possible largely because Southeast Asian states had left the online space alone. Slow and reluctant state interventions in the cyberspace had provided political opportunities for existing civic groups to expand and new ones to emerge. Once these states recognized the threats social media could pose to the political security of the governing parties, they in turn have begun to exploit social media affordances to manipulate public opinion for their gains.

A key element of this book is the ability of each author to identify a key "turning point" in social media production in each country. The turning points occurred at different times in each Southeast Asian country, but they tended to correspond to national elections where either the incumbents experienced a decline in electoral support or opposition parties have been able to gain important electoral leverage online. Online disinformation tactics along with increased surveillance and attempts at censorship have been deployed to suppress, discredit and drown out political opposition as well as to co-opt virtual publics.

Given the rising prominence of the smartphone in Southeast Asia, we should look to this region to see what these new "communities" look like, and how society is changing. The fields of political science and media studies, and social media studies in particular, have become excited by the possibilities big data analytics can bring. Quantitative studies of politics and social media are, as a result, plentiful in Western universities. But we need a wide range of scholarly fields to engage more deeply with the subject, not only through an analysis of big data algorithms. The rise of closed groups also negates the potential for big data analysis. This means that the type of research and analysis that has dominated the digital research industry—notably data obtained largely from Twitter—is likely to be less relevant in understanding politics and societies. Rather, empirical and ethnographic research by scholars who have access to these communities and understand their needs and identities, can provide deeper insights on the impact of social media in the Southeast Asian region. This was our premise as we set out to choose authors and research methodologies for contributing chapters.

This book contributes to a crucial issue of the growing autocratization of the internet and social media, shaped by both domestic politics and external forces. While there remain real democratic benefits of social media, their overall impact on the politics and society of these states are uneven, in various pockets and are becoming overshadowed by rising cyber restrictions. Yet, the benefits social media bring exists in serious tension with the expanding information controls by governments. The result is an attack on transparency, freedom of expression and quality of journalism. Finding our way out of this tangled web of disinformation and state crackdowns will be crucial for democracy, human rights and good governance as we move further into the "digital era".

SOUTHEAST ASIA'S DIVERSE SOCIAL MEDIA LANDSCAPE

No other region experiences both the fortunes and misfortunes of social media's impact than Southeast Asia. Southeast Asia is one of the most social media active regions in the world and one of most politically diverse. Measuring internet access and social media usage, however, is not a simple task in Southeast Asia. Surveys show that, for example, some 64 per cent of Indonesians, 65 per cent of Filipinos and 75 per cent of Malaysians have regular access to the internet. But these statistics are often beset with erroneous conclusions—for example, many citizens answer "yes" to having Facebook, but "no" to having internet access when taking part in professional surveys (Jurriens and Tapsell 2017). These percentages also do not tell us the disparity *within* internet usage. The millions of Southeast Asians on the "digital divide", who have minimal access to the internet, are generally understudied. This group has grown considerably because of the massive expansion of the smartphone market through cheap, Chinese-made Android handsets. As such, the majority of Southeast Asians access the internet only by mobile phones (estimated at 70 per cent of internet users in the region).

A mobile phone for internet usage changes the way citizens read, watch and participate in social media. Long articles, therefore, are far less likely to be read, while content that is available for short, one- to two-minute videos is easy to consume. We need to think more about the limited access that Southeast Asians have to the broader domains of the internet that do not adhere to such mobile phone usage formats. Internet speed matters too, because it means that internet access is more likely to be for the use of platforms that require slower internet speeds for effective usage, such as Facebook's "free basics" in the Philippines, Myanmar and Indonesia, and other simple messenger sites like WhatsApp in Malaysia and Indonesia, and LINE in Thailand. Thus, many of these citizens are not loading full websites, reading lengthy news stories, let alone spending time going through fact-checking sites, which various government and civil society organizations increasingly urge them to do.

It is common to read about how younger millennial Southeast Asians are driving this new information society in the region. There is of course much truth to this overall argument. Seventy per cent of Indonesia's online population is under the age of 35, most of whom are using social media sites on a daily basis. Around 47 per cent of internet users in Malaysia are aged between 20 and 29, and another 25 per cent between 30 and 39, while 31 per cent of Filipino Facebook users are aged between 18 and 34 (Tapsell 2020). However, at the same time, older generations in semi-rural areas of Southeast Asia are for the first time accessing the internet via a mobile phone, and it is generally they who are understudied and underrepresented in mainstream media accounts of rising internet access and social media uptake. Younger Southeast Asians are usually the first to complain of their parents or extended family members spreading false information on family WhatsApp groups, suggesting the drivers of information (and misinformation) are not always millennials.

Within Southeast Asia, there is some disparity in the use of platforms. For example, Filipinos use Facebook Messenger regularly and connect with people who are not "friends" on the platform. Messenger sites like WhatsApp are growing rapidly in neighbouring Malaysia and Indonesia. In Thailand, the Japanese platform, LINE, is the most popular. In the Philippines, Facebook's ubiquity is its greatest strength. Facebook's ubiquity in some Southeast Asian countries, such as Indonesia and Singapore, can be its greatest weakness, as citizens move towards more "closed group" spaces where they can post away from the prying eyes of older generations, wider friendship groups and even government monitoring. Thus for some Southeast Asians, Facebook is becoming less popular for younger urban people because of its ubiquity—they see their parents, extended family members, and other people they have never met, all on the home page and therefore seek a more "exclusive" site where they can post material meant for their friends. This view explains the rise of social media platform Path in the early 2010, and subsequently the rapid popularity of Instagram amongst Indonesian urban youths. Scholarship in Indonesia and Malaysia has shown the growing importance of Instagram celebrity Muslim preachers, and thus how Instagram is increasingly crucial in shaping political discourse (Slama and Barendregt 2018), including the rise of "click farming" (Lindquist 2018).

Scholars and analysts tend to focus their findings from Twitter analyses in disinformation studies. They do so largely because data are much more easily available for big data mining and analysis. But in Southeast Asia, Twitter's role seems to be declining and is generally used by older, urban elites. For example, 64 per cent of Malaysians gather news from Facebook, and 54 per cent from WhatsApp, far higher than from Twitter, at 25 per cent (Tapsell 2020). This is not to say that Twitter is unimportant. It is still widely used by elite actors and media professionals, and their comments can generate mainstream media articles and wider public discussion. Furthermore, public relations companies who provide social media data to companies and governments in Southeast Asia often rely greatly on Twitter data, suggesting its discourse has a significant effect on how elites view "public attitudes". But this discourse is likely to be slanted towards urban, middle-class usage. Thus, social media usage in Southeast Asia is not uniform, and much depends on what device citizens use to access the internet with, which social media platform they use regularly and therefore potentially trust more, and what internet speeds they endure in order to receive and share various forms of political and other materials.

THE RISE OF DISINFORMATION

"Negative campaigning" has long been a feature of election campaigns, but digital technologies have exacerbated the spread and impact of slanderous or libel materials. Political parties and candidates are increasingly hiring professional online campaigners to produce "hoax news" about their opponents, which includes an increasing prevalence of terms like "black campaign", "weaponized" social media and "fake news". In each country, certain social media campaigners are identified through local terms: "trolls" in the Philippines, "buzzers" in Indonesia, and "cybertroopers" in Malaysia, for example. Numerous investigative journalism reports and academic research have outlined large swathe of online campaigners creating and disseminating disinformation. Disinformation in the Philippines, for example that of the Oxford Internet Institute (Bradshaw and Howard 2017), shows a rising trend of "bots" and paid fake accounts via Twitter.

Globally, internet freedom has been on a decline since 2010 and social media has been the main culprit for the growing restrictions in cyberspace. Revelations of the Russian fake news campaigns in the 2016 US election and the 2016 Brexit referendum have prompted the World Economic Forum to identify digital disinformation as among the top ten greatest perils to society (Stroppa and Hanley 2017). Governments of all stripes have caught on to the benefits of social media—an inexpensive platform to shape public opinions and deliver political messaging. The Freedom House estimates that 59 per cent of internet users live in countries where authorities have employed disinformation tactics online. In their seminal article, "The Disinformation Order: Disruptive Communication and the Decline of Democratic Institutions", Bennett and Livingston (2018) argue that online disinformation proliferates in environments of legitimacy crisis, such as when there is a declining trust in democratic and press institutions. Combined with a belligerent and untrustworthy digital culture, social media is charged with damaging free and fair elections—a key tenet of any liberal democracy.

Political disinformation campaigners range from high-end million-dollar advertising companies to mid-range companies who hire young university students casually to young sole traders and entrepreneurs who understand the digital realm and strategically create and pay Facebook to boost disinformation content.

A recent report published by NATO's StratCom Centre of Excellence shows that the "disinformation industry" is growing in Southeast Asia (Ong and Tapsell 2020). Almost all candidates—from presidential to local mayors and councillors—see the importance in social media campaigning. Increasingly, they feel the need to hire a social media team that can counter "black campaigning" against them. These groups often end up producing "black campaign" material against their employer's opponents. The reality is that the changes platforms are making are not keeping up with the dynamic, innovative and also insidious new disinformation as well as the social media "black campaign" industry.

Tech companies will say that their growth is central to the emerging digital economy, which will create jobs and therefore provide more potential for innovation and thus greater growth. The ability of tech companies to microtarget customers, including by ethnic or religious group, is why they are valued so highly, not just for present purposes, but also for future gains, as their algorithms become more advanced at locating—geographically and sociopolitically—and selling to specific people and groups. Of course, this is true of locally-based apps as well as the global behemoths like Facebook and Google. But as this book will show through critical examples in a number of countries in Southeast Asia, it is no longer enough for big tech companies, or other global social media platforms, to espouse the virtues of economic growth in the United States, and not be held responsible for damages caused locally elsewhere.

While there is diversity in platform usage regionally, Facebook continues to dominate as a monopoly in many Southeast Asian countries, not only in social media interactions but also as "the internet" for many citizens who have only recently bought a smartphone for the first time. In the early 2010s, Facebook CEO Mark Zuckerberg was one of the most popular guests of Southeast Asian politicians, with his visits attracting thousands of onlookers eager to get a photo. This would not be the case today; Facebook is derided by governments, activists, civil society and journalists, seen to be undermining trust in institutions and ultimately hindering the democratic system. In short, social media is seen as a tool which divides and polarizes Southeast Asian communities rather than assisting in its diversity and vibrancy.

Many working in big tech companies think that society's problems with social media can be resolved by the very industry in Silicon Valley which created the platforms in the first place. That is, manipulation of social media platforms simply needs computer scientists with better and faster algorithms to counteract bad actors. But each time an algorithm is created, disinformation producers find new ways to get around it. When citizens move away from Twitter due to too many buzzers and prefer Instagram instead, for example, campaigners sack their buzzers and begin to hire Instagram "click farmers". The challenges are many, but given the ubiquitous use of social media platforms, there is no reason Southeast Asia cannot lead the world in finding solutions to these complex problems.

However, the Southeast Asian "solution" has been for governments to introduce new laws to (ideally) crack down on hoax news peddlers and disinformation producers. When these laws become politicized or are used inappropriately, citizens will be increasingly cautious of what they say publicly on social media platforms. They will revert to the safety of closed groups, in trust that their information will not be distributed. This trend has the potential for even greater echo chambers and filter bubbles of information, which scholars have previously identified as an important impact for social media.

As such, this book argues that the reformists and activists need to "reclaim" the social media space in Southeast Asia, and urges authors of each chapter to try to examine how this might be possible. Social media has given the voice to the previously disengaged and disenfranchised and massively expanded avenues for activism and new ways to strengthen civic society. It has provided new repertoires for participation and contestation on public issues to ordinary citizens where they were not previous afforded. Governments at all levels are under increasing public scrutiny over their affairs and are held to more accountability and transparency. As such, this book is also a reminder that social media can and has promised a more open, tolerant and liberal society which should translate into some positive impacts on democratic development in these states.

THE ARGUMENTS OF THIS BOOK

The increasing use of social media to manipulate public opinion has emerged as one of the greatest threats to democracy in recent years. Each chapter in this book addresses this phenomenon within their national context. For most analyses, the key "turning point" was an election, where the ruling government either increased their own activities (including disinformation production) on social media campaigning, or the government introduced and began to implement harsh laws and crackdowns on the social media space.

Elections

In Indonesia, Muninggar Sri Saraswati argues that despite many commentators and scholars believing in "bottom up" social media campaigning driven by grassroots actors, the seeds of disinformation began to be sown as early as 2012. Saraswati asserts that "the rise of disinformation via social media is new, but is part of a long history of engineering consent and manipulation by elite political and economy forces in the country". The 2012 governor's election which brought local politicians Jokowi (Joko Widodo) and Ahok (Basuki Tjahaja Purnama) to the national stage witnessed for the first time extensive and professional use of social media campaigning, and the beginning of what is now well entrenched in the Indonesian digital sphere—"buzzers". The political campaign industry has expanded ever since, and Jokowi's ascendency through to two election victories in both 2014 and 2019, included these campaigners and their staff and supporters.

In Malaysia, Niki Cheong points to the 2013 general election as a turning point because the ruling coalition, the Barisan Nasional, amplified and professionalized existing practices due to the "pervasiveness of new communication technologies" amongst opposition forces. It was around this time that the Barisan Nasional established teams of "cybertroopers", a strategy which ultimately failed them in the 2018 election—the first time Malaysia experienced a change in government in sixty years. In many ways, new digital technologies in Malaysia remained the "opposition playground". As citizens move towards closed group discussions on WhatsApp and Facebook, it rendered state-sponsored "cybertroopers" initiatives outdated. For Malaysia, the challenge is to make sure all political parties understand the difficulties these new campaign tactics bring to democracy and political discourse, as the country's political elite struggle to consolidate gains made by civil society, in what Hutchinson and Lee (2019) describe as a "complicated democracy".

In the Philippines, Pamela Combinido and Nicole Curato examine the 2016 election victory of Rodrigo Duterte, and how the Philippines was described as "patient zero" for disinformation. They argue that Duterte's victory was "a turning point in the amplification of hateful comments and disinformation". The authors also point out that his election campaign of drugs and crime "resonates to public anxieties, and fits with architectures of communication that sustain public life in contemporary Philippines", and shows how various groups on online forces need to be examined beyond simply describing them as "trolls". Since Duterte became the president, disinformation has become "entrenched" and increasingly "multifaceted". Only a reimagining of the digital public sphere in the Philippines will transform politics in the country.

In Cambodia, Mun Vong and Aim Sinpeng posit that the 2013 national elections served as a turning point as the ruling Cambodian People's Party (CPP) and its long-time leader, Hun Sen, nearly lost power. Up until then, Cambodia experienced a moderately open cyberspace that had allowed for an emergence of a very small, but active, blogosphere, and burgeoning forms of social media activism. Regime critics, civil society organizations and opposition figures were the digital entrepreneurs and first movers when it came to leveraging digital media affordances for activism. Since the 2013 elections, the CPP took social media seriously and began to use it as a tool to suppress and co-opt critics for their own gains. Social media has also become a key domain for the ruling party to manipulate public opinion to shore support for the regime. With the main opposition party now largely eliminated, the challenge for social media activism for Cambodians is how to use the platform to counter state abuse of power and hold the ruling party accountable.

Laws and Crackdowns

For Singapore, Natalie Pang argues that the 2011 election and its immediate aftermath are the key turning point due to the way in which new media technologies "inspired the awakening of 'political consciousness'". After this election, the Singapore government began to regulate the online space more forthrightly. In 2013 the Broadcasting

Act was expanded to include a law requiring online sites that "report regularly on Singapore and have a significant reach" (Gov.sg, 2013) to apply for a media licence as individual entities, followed later by the Network Enforcement Act where problematic content had to be taken down completely. Under this law, licensees need to put up a $50,000 performance bond, and comply with taking down offensive content within twenty-four hours. In 2019, Singapore created the Protection from Online Falsehoods and Manipulation Act, known as POFMA. Pang concludes by making the important point that "legislations alone will not be sufficient" and that we need to recognize that in Southeast Asia and elsewhere, misinformation and disinformation campaigns threaten various sectors of society, particularly minority groups who are most vulnerable to hegemonic group actions and state crackdowns.

In Thailand, Janjira Sombatpoonsiri argues that prolonged political conflict and polarization prompted the political establishment to securitize disinformation in order to mobilize public opinion in their favour. Social media emerged during a time of intense political crisis and had been used by both pro- and anti-establishment forces. Both groups build contrasting versions of "truths" to mobilize grassroots support for each feuding side. The coups d'état in 2006 and 2014 served as turning points in this war on "truths" and provided the military—and the political establishment—the upper hand in securitizing the digital realm. Through a suite of new laws and institutions in the cyber arena, the establishment has sought to control the narratives of online information and to marginalize opposing voices. As long as Thailand remains politically divided, social media would remain an intensely divisive space.

In Myanmar, social media arrived in the midst of the country's greatest political transformation in contemporary history. As Myanmar embarks on its unprecedented political transition from decades of military dictatorship towards an electoral democracy, Nyi Nyi Kyaw argues that social media has become a weapon of hate speech and falsehoods with devastating results. Social media is a contributing factor to the worsening humanitarian crisis with regards to the Muslim and Rohingya minorities, which has led to sustained offline communal violence. Social media has become a readily available tool for hate speech and disinformation partly because the state—especially the military—condones radical voices against Muslims and the Rohingyas online for their own political gain. Despite the coming to power of the political opposition, their implicit support for such hate speech and falsehoods against the targeted minorities means that a resolution is not foreseeable in the near future.

In Vietnam, Dien Luong argues that the ruling communist party had sought to control online information early on, especially on social media, but such measure was ineffective. Civil society organizations and critics of the government were able to continue using social media as a platform for activism, despite repressive internet controls. As social media grew rapidly in Vietnam, the ruling party saw an opportunity instead to engage in disinformation campaigns to silence dissent and manipulate the public to bolster its legitimacy. But as more netizens find their voices online and become more politically active, Vietnam is headed for a more tolerant and repressive internet regime. Grassroots activism on digital media would continue as long as there is sufficient space for online advocacy.

The concluding chapter is written by Marco Bünte, who provides an important comparative discussion on the role of social media across political regimes in Southeast Asia. Does social media help or hinder democratization in the region? Bünte argues that the overall impacts of social media on Southeast Asian politics has been one of autocratization. While acknowledging the liberalizing contributions social media has made in empowering activism and increasing civic engagement, social media has contributed to autocratizing both democratic and authoritarian regimes in the region. For electoral democracies like Indonesia and the Philippines, social media has facilitated democratic regression, while for authoritarian regimes in Vietnam, Cambodia and Thailand, social media has helped embolden the ruling power.

In conclusion, we hope this edited volume provides an important and timely analysis of the ways in which social media impacts state-society relations and the politics of Southeast Asia. The strengths of this book lie in its emphasis in chronicling social media contributions to politics from inception to the present as well as its attention to the local contexts. We recognize that one cannot fully examine the role social media plays in society without understanding the political and societal structures in each locality in which social media first came into contact. Social media arrived and expanded in each Southeast Asian country in different ways and at varying speeds, and such variations matter to understanding its individual impact in each country. Furthermore, we recognize that social media is not used the same way in each country and any serious examination of how social media impacts societies must pay attention to the local specificities. Our volume therefore contributes much needed empirical analysis of the role social media plays in the politics of all eight Southeast Asian nations. While the dynamics of social media on politics in the region follows the global pattern of increasing information controls, the unprecedented impacts that social media has in empowering grassroots activism even in the most repressive regimes serve as an optimistic caution to such a depressing global trend. Reflecting on the original gains, as well as seeing where things went wrong, allow us to think about how citizens can "regain" the digital public sphere to promote reforms for democracy, human rights and a fairer and more equitable economic system.

REFERENCES

Bennett, Lance W. and Alexandra Segerberg. 2012. "The Logic of Connective Action: Digital Media and the Personalization of Contentious Politics". *Information, Communication & Society* 15, no. 5: 739–68.

Bennett, Lance W. and Steven Livingston. 2018. "The Disinformation Order: Disruptive Communication and the Decline of Democratic Institutions". *European Journal of Communication* 33, no. 2: 122–39.

Bradshaw, Samantha and Philip Howard. 2017. "Troops, Trolls and Troublemakers: A Global Inventory of Organised Social Media Manipulation". Working Paper 12. Oxford, UK: Project on Computational Propaganda. http://comprop.oii.ox.ac.uk/wp-content/uploads/sites/89/2017/07/Troops-Trolls-and-Troublemakers.pdf (accessed 20 May 2020).

―――. 2019. "The Global Disinformation Order: 2019 Global Inventory of Organised Social Media Manipulation". Working Paper 2. Oxford, UK: Project on Computational Propaganda.https://comprop.oii.ox.ac.uk/wp-content/uploads/sites/93/2019/09/CyberTroop-Report19.pdf.

Castells, Manuel. 2012. *Networks of Outrage and Hope*. Cambridge: Polity.

Deibert, Ronald. 2015. "Authoritarianism Goes Global: Cyberspace under Siege". *Journal of Democracy* 26, no. 3: 64–78.

Diamond, Larry and Marc F. Plattner, eds. 2012. *Liberation Technology: Social Media and the Struggle for Democracy*. Baltimore, MD: John Hopkins University Press.

Earl, Jennifer and Katarina Kimport. 2011. *Digitally Enabled Social Change: Activism in the Internet Age*. Cambridge, Massachusetts: MIT Press.

EU Commission. 2018. "Final Report on the High Level Expert Group on Fake News and Online Disinformation", 21 March 2018. https://ec.europa.eu/digital-single-market/en/news/final-report-high-level-expert-group-fake-news-and-online-disinformation%20 (accessed 20 May 2020).

Fergusson, Leopoldo and Carlos Molina. 2019. "Facebook Causes Protests". *Documento CEDE*, no. 4. https://papers.ssrn.com/sol3/papers.cfm?abstract_id=3553514 (accessed 20 May 2020).

Freedom House. 2019. "Freedom on the Net 2019". https://freedomhouse.org/sites/default/files/2019-11/11042019_Report_FH_FOTN_2019_final_Public_Download.pdf (accessed 20 May 2020).

Freelon, Deen and Chris Wells. 2020. "Disinformation as Political Communication". *Political Communication* 37, no. 2: 145–56.

Hutchinson, Francis E. and Lee Hwok Aun. 2019. *The Defeat of Barisan Nasional: Missed Signs or Late Surge?* Singapore: ISEAS – Yusof Ishak Institute, 2019.

Hyun, Ki Deuk and Jinhee Kim. 2015. "The Role of New Media in Sustaining the Status Quo: Online Political Expression, Nationalism, and System Support in China". *Information, Communication & Society* 18, no. 7: 766–81.

Iyengar, Shanto and Sean Westwood. 2015. "Fear and Loathing across Party Lines: New Evidence on Group Polarization". *American Journal of Political Science* 59, no. 3: 690–707.

Jakarta Post. "Indonesia has 171 Million Internet Users: Study Finds", 19 May 2019. https://www.thejakartapost.com/life/2019/05/18/indonesia-has-171-million-internet-users-study.html (accessed 28 May 2020).

Jurriens, Edwin and Ross Tapsell. 2017. "Challenges and Opportunities of the Digital 'Revolution'". In *Digital Indonesia: Connectivity and Divergence*, edited by Edwin Jurriens and Ross Tapsell, pp. 1–17. Singapore: ISEAS – Yusof Ishak Institute.

King, Gary, Jennifer Pan and Margaret Roberts. 2013. "How Censorship in China Allows Government Criticism but Silences Collective Expression". *American Political Science Review* 107, no. 2: 326–43.

Lindquist, Johan, 2018. "Illicit Economies of the Internet: Click Farming in Indonesia and Beyond". *Made In China: To The Soil*. https://madeinchinajournal.com/2019/01/12/illicit-economies-of-the-internet-click-farming-in-indonesia-and-beyond/ (accessed 20 May 2020).

Liow, Joseph and Afif Pasuni. 2010. "Debating the Conduct and Nature of Malaysian Politics: Communalism and New Media post-March 2008". *Journal of Current Southeast Asian Affairs* 29, no. 4: 39–65.

Norris, Pippa. 2001. *Digital Divide: Civic Engagement, Information Poverty, and the Internet Worldwide*. Cambridge: Cambridge University Press.

Ong, Jonathan and Ross Tapsell. 2020. "Mitigating Disinformation in Southeast Asian Elections: Lessons from Indonesia, Philippines and Thailand". Latvia: NATO Strategic Communications Centre of Excellence. https://www.stratcomcoe.org/mitigating-disinformation-southeast-asian-elections (accessed 20 May 2020).

Slama, Martin and Bart Barendregt. 2018. "Introduction: Online Publics in Muslim Southeast Asia". *Asiascape: Digital Asia* 5, no. 1–2: 3–31.

Stoycheff, Elizabeth and Erik Nisbet. 2014. "What's the Bandwidth for Democracy? Deconstructing Internet Penetration and Citizen Attitudes about Governance". *Political Communication* 31, no. 4: 628–46.

Stroppa, Andrea and Michael Hanley. 2017. "How We Can Defeat Fake News". World Economic Forum. https://www.weforum.org/agenda/2017/02/how-can-we-defeat-fake-news-automate-the-right-to-reply/ (accessed 21 May 2020).

Sunstein, Cass R. 2018. *# Republic: Divided Democracy in the Age of Social Media.* Princeton: Princeton University Press.

Tapsell, Ross. 2020. *Deepening the Understanding of Social Media's Impact in Southeast Asia.* Trends in Southeast Asia, no. 4/2020. Singapore: ISEAS – Yusof Ishak Institute. https://www.iseas.edu.sg/wp-content/uploads/2020/02/TRS4_20.pdf.

2

CURING "PATIENT ZERO": RECLAIMING THE DIGITAL PUBLIC SPHERE IN THE PHILIPPINES

Pamela Combinido and Nicole Curato

"Patient zero" was how Facebook executive Katie Harbath (2018) described the Philippines in a public talk in Germany, on the topic of "protecting electoral integrity on Facebook". "That was the beginning", she argued, referring to the election of Philippine President Rodrigo Duterte in a country that prided itself to be one of Asia's oldest democracies. "A month later it was Brexit, and then Trump got the nomination, and then the US elections", she added. Describing the Philippines as "patient zero" both illuminates and obscures the role of digital technologies in shaping democratic politics. It is illuminating insofar as it exposes the pathologies associated to strategies of digital campaigning that brought illiberal strongmen to power. In 2016, journalists, academics, civil society groups and even the Roman Catholic Church of the Philippines called out the toxic incivility and proliferation of fake news on Facebook. The Philippines' Commission on Human

Rights was alarmed with the growing extent of cyberbullying and harassment of citizens who posted critical views of President Duterte on social media. Female journalists were often targeted, particularly those who published unsavoury reports about the Duterte campaign (Rodriguez 2016). Meanwhile, 81 per cent of Filipinos reported having read fake news on social media according to a recent national survey (Pulse Asia Research Inc. 2018). These trends have led to international headlines about Duterte's "paid trolls" or "keyboard armies" who spread disinformation and amplify hate speech (Palatino 2017; Syjuco 2017; Williams 2017). For Rappler founder and CEO Maria Ressa (2016)—Time Magazine's Person of the Year for her work on press freedom—the "weaponization" of social media spells the death of democracy in the Philippines. The contagion of fake news and hate speech resulted in a series of proposed "cures" of patient zero. These include fact checking, promoting digital literacy, and anti-fake news laws.

The spread of digital disinformation is indeed a pathology that compromises the integrity of democratic politics. However, describing the Philippines as "patient zero" obscures the longer history of inequalities in economic and political power that created conditions for the proliferation of digital disinformation. In this chapter, we argue that digital disinformation is firmly embedded in the longer history of enduring structures of economic inequality, uneven distribution of political power, and prominence of the Philippine diaspora, that defines the character of Philippine society today. We are arguing against diagnoses that Duterte's quick rise to presidency is a result of "technological alchemy" that manipulated Filipinos to vote for a man who "would be happy to slaughter" the drug addicts (BBC News 2019) along with human rights defenders (Observatory for the Protection of Human Rights Defenders 2019). While Duterte's campaign can be considered a turning point in the amplification of hateful comments and disinformation, we also argue that what is being amplified resonates to public anxieties, and fits with architectures of communication that sustain public life in contemporary Philippines. We conclude this chapter by examining the extent to which existing proposals to curb disinformation can "cure" patient zero and putting forward our own recommendations that respond to the deeper history of disinformation in the country.

A LONG AND BROAD VIEW OF DISINFORMATION IN THE PHILIPPINES

The Philippines is called the "social media capital" of the world for the past three years (We Are Social 2019). Internet penetration is 71 per cent, but Filipinos online spend the longest time on social media in the world with an average of four hours and twelve minutes per day (We Are Social 2019). Facebook is the most popular platform (97 per cent of Filipino internet users reported using this platform), followed by YouTube (96 per cent), Facebook Messenger (89 per cent), and then Instagram (64 per cent) (We Are Social 2019). Internet speed is 15.05 MBPS, slower compared to other Southeast Asian countries like Malaysia or Thailand, meaning sites like Facebook are popular because they do not require a lot of bandwidth to communicate. The availability of low-cost internet services makes it possible for many lower-middle class Filipinos to connect on digital platforms. Mobile operators, for example, bundle their data promotions with free access to Facebook, encouraging economically disadvantaged groups to stay on Facebook and not explore other platforms or pages which would use up data (Soriano, Cao and Sison 2017). Market innovations like *Pisonet* allows for one peso five to seven minutes of online access in internet portals widely available from urban slum communities to remote villages in the archipelago. Additionally, smartphones, which is the primary way that Filipinos access social media sites, can now be bought at more affordable costs (Soriano, Cao and Sison 2017; We Are Social 2019). Filipinos can buy budget smartphones for as low as 2,000 pesos (US$40) from local smartphone brands such as Cherry Mobile.

This is not to say Facebook is the only source of media for all Filipinos. Television remains the top source of news and information (Bautista 2019), leading some to down play the decisive role of social media in electoral success (Philippine Centre for Investigative Journalism 2019). Many Filipinos may be regularly on social media, but users with a strong internet connection remain concentrated in Metro Manila, particularly among upper- and middle-income families (Pulse Asia Research Inc. 2018). Indeed, the Philippines has a long way to go in enforcing universal access to the internet, especially those in rural areas where even phone signal is non-existent (Barela et al. 2018). However, the steady rise of internet penetration and social media usage demonstrate that social media is increasing its importance in information-gathering and political discourse. It is crucial to recognize this trend, especially in a context where Filipinos are growing distrustful of traditional media outlets. Recent polling data finds that Filipinos with internet access trusted social media more (87 per cent) than the mainstream media (73 per cent), such as television, radio and newspapers (Philippine Trust Index 2017).

How has the Philippines become a "testbed" (Ong and Cabañes 2019, p. 7) for producing digital disinformation? We answer this question by taking a long and broad view. We focus on two factors—political economy and political culture—as crucial factors that allow digital disinformation to flourish.

Political Economy

There are two economic transformations that created conditions for the Philippines to be a trailblazer in the use of digital technologies. The first is the export of Filipino migrant labour, and the second is the rise of local tech-savvy digital workers. We argue that by focusing on labour, we are able to understand both the capacity and vulnerabilities of Filipinos when engaging in digital communication.

The Philippines places ninth among the top ten biggest exporting countries of migrant labour in the world, behind only much bigger countries like India and Mexico (McKinsey Global Institute 2016). 2.3 million Filipinos are documented to work overseas, with top destinations including Saudi Arabia and United Arab of Emirates (Philippine Statistics Authority 2019). Having a migrant worker in the family is no longer an exception but a characteristic of what it means to be a Filipino family today. Naturally, digital technologies play a central role in mitigating the effects of physical distance. Through Skype conversations and Viber chat groups, Filipino families can maintain a semblance of family order or "doing family" (Madianou 2016, p. 199), despite the time difference and geographic separation (Cabañes and Acedera 2012; Madianou and Miller 2011; Paragas 2009). A generation of young Filipinos have been accustomed to "parenting at a distance" (Madianou and Miller 2011). Filipinos working overseas have learnt to make their presence felt, albeit virtually, during family rituals. Graduations and funerals are now livestreamed, while festivities like Christmas are celebrated by posting thoughtfully curated collages of family photos on Facebook

(Cabalquinto 2018). Parents engage surveillance of their children on social media (Madianou 2016, p. 198), scrutinizing their children's whereabouts and their children's friends by the photos they are tagged on their online profile. That the Philippines is now the social media capital of the world is no surprise, for it is the same country once described as the "texting capital of the world" due to the demands of connectivity with migrant labour. What emerges from these every day practices of mediated family relationships is a nation highly reliant on digital technologies and a citizenry growing to be confident consumers and creators of online content (Cabañes and Acadera 2012; Madianou and Miller 2011).

The affordance of social media, however, has not only made it possible for overseas Filipino workers (OFWs) to keep in touch with their families. They are also used to build diasporic communities in places where they work. Facebook groups, for example, are useful for OFWs to get invitations to attend gatherings, acquire information about investment opportunities and legal assistance, and crowdsourcing donations for, say, disaster survivors (Curato 2019). These civic relationships are proto-political in the sense that they begin to develop characteristics that can be tapped for electoral support or mass mobilization. In Facebook groups, for example, OFWs exchange and affirm each other's grievances and "latent anxieties" about political developments at home (Cabañes, Anderson and Ong 2019; Curato 2016). OFWs are thus a market ripe for political engagement. For example, maids working in Saudi Arabia, Hong Kong or United Arab of Emirates, have regular access to internet, and a life which is largely restricted in where they can physically go but largely unrestricted in how they engage with social media content from home. Evenings are regularly spent alone, in their small room, on their phone, on Facebook (Madianou 2016).

The Philippines is also one of the major suppliers of digital workers in the global economy. In the past decade, the country has become the prime site of business-process outsourcing work, surpassing India as the world's call centre hub (Bajaj 2011; Mercurio 2018). Additionally, Filipinos are among the most highly qualified yet the cheapest paid labour force in the world (Graham et al. 2017), providing online freelance services such as data analytics, web design and social media content moderation (Roberts 2016). The Philippine government actively promotes the potential of digital work in addressing unemployment. So promising is this industry that the government now confers the label "modern heroes" and "world-class workers", previously attributed to OFWs, to Online Freelance Workers or what is now known as the OFW 2.0 (Soriano and Cabañes 2019).

Not only did this industry bring significant revenues to the country, it also created a generation of tech-savvy workforce who have the skills to support various innovations, including disinformation production online. Filipinos' distinct suite of skills suitable to the demands of the digital economy, such as English proficiency, digital literacy, deference to authority, and entrepreneurial spirit (David 2015; Soriano and Cabañes 2019), were proven useful in operations of political campaigns (Ong and Cabañes 2018). The need for entrepreneurial spirit, for example, allows workers to market their ideas to industry patrons while juggling multiple "gigs" or side projects with political clients to boost their income. The common arrangement is creative workers working full time in a boutique advertisement agency while moonlighting with political clients who need their "crisis management work" to save them from an exposed scandal. This fluid work arrangement demanding Filipinos to be self-entrepreneurs, in addition to keeping the wage of digital work low (Graham et al. 2017; Soriano and Cabañes 2019), makes them precarious and vulnerable to "slipping into the digital underground" (Ong and Cabañes 2018, p. 66). Graham et al. (2017) find that Filipino online freelancers provide the cheapest rate to clients, competing with online workers from India. As Ong and Cabañes (2018) reveal, digital campaign operators utilize their skills learnt from this field to do insidious work for political clients, most profitable during election periods. What emerges is a highly connected, creative yet precarious digital workforce used as "a stockpile of digital weapons" to be used and discarded for different political ends (Ong and Cabañes 2018, p. 31).

Political Culture

We cannot understand the rise of disinformation in the Philippines without understanding the role political culture plays in furthering its production. Unlike many democratic countries, the Philippines has no viable political parties. Parties are not stable organizations but are "nebulous entities that can be set up, merged with others, split, resurrected, regurgitated, renamed, repackaged, recycled, or flushed down the toilet any time" (Quimpo 2007, p. 277). In place of parties are political personalities whose command for loyalty and star power shape electoral outcomes. President Duterte is a beneficiary of this system, where televisual performances of melodrama and personal charisma helped him build an emotional connection with voters (Pertierra 2017). While some populist politicians like the action star Joseph Estrada made his way to presidency through his performances of compassion to the poor (Garrido 2017), Duterte established his connections through emotions of fear, manifest in his dystopian narrative of the Philippines as a narco-state (Evangelista and Curato 2016). His "war on drugs" was blended with appeals to hope for Philippines to be "safe" from "drug lords", manifest with his campaign slogan "change is coming".

There are various ways in which communication technologies give oxygen to this political culture. It is common practice for broadcast media and in some cases film producers to bankroll biopics that portray the heroic lives of politicians. Campaign paraphernalia often come in the form of comic books that create a larger-than-life mythology of candidates. Celebrity endorsements have been powerful political tools, especially in drawing crowds for campaign rallies. Political culture in the Philippines, in other words, has long blurred the boundaries between politics and showbiz. As Pertierra (2017, p. 222) argues, the "integration of popular media and populist politics" creates a "televisual politics that assumes both the political leaders and their audiences of viewer-voters are adept at embracing the emotional elements of melodrama that figure centrally in both the entertainment and the electoral mode".

The emotive character of political culture takes a different turn with the use of digital technologies for political campaigns. While politicians still use the elements of melodrama, they connect to audiences more directly. "Facebook Live" broadcasts allow politicians to develop their own viewership without editorial input from the mainstream media. Social media allows for politicians to appear more "authentic" and connect to audiences in a direct and personalized manner. While some countries consider social media as a gamechanger with the way candidates run their campaigns (Lalacente and Raynauld 2017), our argument here is that in the Philippines, social media has served as a natural extension to the way politics is conducted.

This section has presented two main arguments. First, technologies used to sustain social ties and support financial needs are the same technologies that sustain political disinformation. Second, the use of social media for political purposes is a natural extension of the Philippines' personalistic and celebrity-driven political culture. But if the Philippines has been using these technologies for a long time, why did disinformation seemingly explode in the 2016 presidential election? What critical junctures have taken root in this period that led many to consider the Philippines no longer just the social media capital but the "patient zero" of disinformation?

DISINFORMATION IN THE 2016 PHILIPPINE ELECTIONS

We find two turning points for why disinformation emerged more prominently in the 2016 elections. By calling them "turning points", we do not mean to suggest that these trends are particularly novel or that they abruptly shifted the trajectory of Philippine politics. As we emphasized earlier, the rise of digital disinformation is firmly embedded in long-term and widespread trends in Philippine society. They are "turning points" insofar as they render the pathologies of Philippine politics evident, and, in turn, provoked responses from the government, industry and civil society.

Amplification of Coarse Political Discourse

The first turning point, we argue, is the amplification of coarse political discourse in the national scene. Politicians using gutter language are nothing new in the Philippines. When he was mayor in Davao City (1988–98), Duterte was notorious for bragging about his murderous track record. He "always cursed", recalled one pioneering journalist from Davao, "that was just the standard fare" (Canuday 2017, p. 131). This political style is not unique to Duterte. Provincial warlords are known for their gangster-like behaviour resembling the mafia (Sidel 1999). What distinguished the 2016 presidential race is the normalization of such behaviour in the national political discourse. What was once an open secret among citizens—that local politicians are uncouth, sexist, and violent—is now brandished as part of the package of an authentic, iron fisted, straight shooting leader. This, we argue, is part of the global wave of populism, where bad manners and coarse political language have become a standard component in the populist playbook (Moffitt 2016). Some argue that Duterte's vitriol against journalists, human rights activists, members of the opposition, and other critics have unleashed a flood of emotions coming from many sectors of society, whether it is Evangelical Christians who justified the call to kill drug addicts using the language of redemption (Cornelio and Medina 2019) to OFWs who feel neglected by political elites and the "biased" liberal media (Combinido 2019). Bello (2017) finds that Duterte's approach sends a signal to his supporters that in a country at war, citizens need to defend the nation by disempowering traitors through public shaming and harassment. The current Vice President Leni Robredo, for example, has been the target of shaming and threats for speaking with United Nations bodies about Duterte's drug war (Aning 2017). She has been branded as the country's traitor, with some urging her impeachment for "betraying public's trust" (*Thinking Pinoy* 2017, n.p.).

Aside from the normalization of hatred in the national political scene, what sets 2016 apart is the normalization of political lies in mainstream politics. While black propaganda, smear campaigning, and bribing journalists are not new electoral campaign strategies, Duterte's blatant lies in public speeches, both as a candidate and elected President of the Republic reset the boundaries of acceptable political speech. Among his most blatant lies include declaring a veteran journalist critical of his regime to have cancer (she does not have cancer), accusing members of the International Critical Court as paedophiles, and naming a list of personalities involved in an unverified plot to oust him from presidency, and, of course, the inflated number of drug users in the country. In 2017, Duterte slammed two successive Dangerous Drug Board chiefs for disputing the president's statistics on drug war. Duterte claims that there are four million drug users in the country when the agency only reported 1.8 million (Romero 2020). "You do not contradict your own government", he warned former DDB Chief Benjamin Reyes. Unfortunately, the list of Duterte's contradicting "facts" goes on (Nery 2019; Ranada 2019).

These lies are amplified in social media by both organic supporters and networks of disinformation. While these stories can easily be dismissed as the president propagating "fake news", it is important to underscore the argument we made earlier about the emotive character of Philippine politics. Fake news spreads not because people are easily manipulable but because these lies form a part of a "deep story" or stories that feelings tell (Cabañes, Anderson and Ong 2019). The proto-political character of OFW Facebook groups for example, is a fertile ground for such lies to be amplified, given the deeply held suspicion of OFWs against elites who are rigging the system against their favour. Our previous ethnographic study about overseas Filipinos in the UK (Combinido 2019) reveal that these Filipino communities share Duterte's accusation of certain media agencies as "fake news" and journalists as corrupt and media companies owned by oligarchic elites, in the business of selling news to the highest bidder (Hofileña 1998). This media distrust led OFWs to seek news and content from sources considered as hyperpartisan such as pro-Duterte YouTube channels and social media influencers to counter "fake news" from mainstream media (Combinido 2019). The same can be said about the factual lies against drug addicts—whether it is about the extent of drug use in the country, the false scientific claims that drug users are beyond rehabilitation, or the accusation that the neophyte senator who led the investigation about the Duterte's Death Squads is involved in the anti-narcotics trade. These may be factually challenged but for citizens who have deep-seated anxieties against drug addicts who threaten their families and the future of their children, Duterte was simply engaged in "real talk".

Professionalization of the Disinformation Industry

The 2016 election also presented a wide array of online disinformation services within the reach of political candidates. In Ong, Tapsell and Curato's study (2019) on digital disinformation and the 2019 midterm elections, they find that the digital arm of electoral campaigns in the Philippines is starting to receive substantial spending allocation. Some of these funds are for above board campaigns, like maintaining a candidate's Instagram page, uploading vlogs or responding to comments on Facebook. Others are for underground operations, where candidates have plausible deniability in case networks of disinformation spreading lies get exposed. This combination of approaches is best represented by the international expose of the company, Cambridge Analytica. Before taking down their marketing pitch on their website, Cambridge Analytica claimed to have harvested online data in the Philippines which revealed voters' preferences for a tough talking decisive leader (Robles 2018). Beyond issues on the breach of data privacy, what we see here is the professionalization of the disinformation industry. While earlier versions of disinformation take the form of bribing journalists to write a fluff piece and paying radio pundits to spread rumours and attack political opponents, the micro-targeting techniques of disinformation today transformed campaigning to a more precise, if not scientific, voter-information gathering enterprise.

The professionalization of the disinformation industry, as we underscored earlier, would not have been possible without a steady supply of tech-savvy digital workers. Ong and Cabañes' study (2018) on the *Architects of Networked Disinformation* demonstrated the elaborate structure of political trolling and production of fake news. There are chief disinformation architects, the high-powered executives working in public relations firms. They are digital strategists who keep a day job in advertising with household brands, corporate clients, and politicians. They conceptualize campaigns but do not do the grunt work of crafting memes and slogans that make the internet toxic. And then there are the digital influencers, the microcelebrities of Instagram, those who cultivate a digital profile attracting 50,000 to two million followers who then monetize their influence by endorsing political candidates. In the Ong, Tapsell and Curato (2019) research, they tracked influencers who post photos of cats, latte art, bible quotes and fitness tips on Instagram but in between these posts are staged photographs of influencers reading the biography of a senator running for elections, or uploads of digital campaign posters of party list groups. Combining the supply of precarious digital workers with microcelebrity influencers and high-powered advertising executives create a highly professionalized network of disinformation with its own logics, hierarchies and paygrades (Silverman, Lytvynenko and Kung 2020). It is not a simplification to say that digital disinformation exists because it pays. Disinformation is now a lucrative industry for public relations professionals and advertising companies, and for younger, tech-savvy Filipinos looking for an injection of employment revenue during an election campaign.

The amplification of coarse political discourse and the professionalization of the disinformation industry are turning points for the Philippines. They set the new rules of the game as far as tolerable political behaviour is concerned, and, without meaningful and coordinated responses from the regulatory agencies, industry and civil society, disinformation practices will continue to prosper.

DISINFORMATION BEYOND ELECTIONS

Since Duterte took power in the Philippines, practices of digital disinformation have flourished. In this section, we identify three examples in the spheres of politics, history and public health of how disinformation campaigns have evolved. We selected these examples to demonstrate the growing breadth of disinformation networks and the precise consequences of seeding divisive and anti-democratic political content.

Cyber-*Tokhang*

The term *"tokhang"* has been synonymous to Duterte's brutal anti-narcotics campaign. It is a shorthand for police operations where cops knock on doors (*toktok*) and plead (*hangyo*) for drug suspects to surrender. In popular parlance, however, *tokhang* is associated with violence where drug suspects are either shot by unidentified motorcycle-riding gunmen, killed by the police execution-style, or kidnapped, tortured, killed and then dumped in the streets to serve as example to others, similar to the way public executions were held in the past (Coronel 2017; Rafael 2019).

The practice of *tokhang* is not limited to physical encounters. *Tokhang* also takes place in the digital public sphere. Just like violence inflicted on drug suspects, critics of the Duterte regime are subject to dangerous personal attacks using tactics of harassment, shaming, sexualization, and, in many cases, direct threats. What makes cyber-*tokhang* peculiar, however, is not just its toxic quality but the coordinated manner in which it is performed. Just like police operations with a game plan, cyber-*tokhang* involves systematic attempts to game the system, with generals organizing the battle plan at the digital war room where the attacks are planned (Hapal 2016). In 2016, one of the Duterte's supporters called Mr Riyoh posted a Facebook video declaring war against the "Yellow Army", which refers to the supporters of the Liberal Party. Mr Riyoh is an OFW in Saudi Arabia, posting online contents to his 340,000 followers on Facebook and 132,000 subscribers on YouTube.

"Let's go all out", he told his viewers, and go after "yellow garbage". A private group was created where Duterte's self-identified cyber-warriors plot their missions, collaborate with programmers, hackers and tech experts (Hapal 2016). The strategy involves "mass reporting" of pages and Facebook posts of the administration's critics as well as "special ops" such as hacking. Silent No More—a page for citizens who wish to speak up against the Duterte regime—is an example of cyber-*tokhang*'s casualty. Facebook suspended the page after a deluge of reports to Facebook about their violation of community standards (Hapal 2016). Opposition Senators Leila de Lima and Antonio Trillanes, as well as blogger Jover Laurio and performance activist Mae Paner were also subject to similar attacks. Journalist Raissa Robles (2016), herself a target of cyber-*tokhang* describes the group as a "digital mob" where a group of Duterte supporters, with the aim of protecting the president from critics' attacks are instructed to block and report the journalist's libellous articles. In a publicly available document, Robles exposed the group's conversations through screen grabs. Some asked for step-by-step instructions on how to report, others asked how the operation can be carried out in a mobile phone, while some others report "done" to the group (Robles 2016).

And, "just as the real-world killings include innocents, the online assassinations have proven similarly indiscriminate" (Syjuco 2017). Online assassinations or cyber-*tokhangs* have resulted in opposition members getting their accounts shut down by Facebook due to mass reporting, while there are worries that legitimate news reports could be taken down by Facebook because of these coordinated attacks. Just like police operations against drug suspects, cyber-*tokhang* sends a "chilling effect" message to critics of the Duterte regime. It "outs" anonymous critics and leaves them vulnerable to attacks.

Organic community of supporters of Duterte also play an important role in making cyber-*tokhang* work. Once influencers such as Mr Riyoh encourage supporters to go "all out" against Liberal Party or to report Silent No More Facebook page, Duterte supporters mobilize by simultaneously reporting these Facebook accounts, their behaviours akin to online spamming. A major part of this strategy is the mobilization of loyal Duterte supporters who feel empowered to defend the president from what they consider to be a "war" for the future of the nation. The hyper-emotional and personalistic character of Philippine politics resonates here once again, for it is through appeals to protect their beloved "Daddy Duterte" (*Tatay Digong*) at all costs where cyber-*tokhang* gains traction.

Historical Revisionism

If history is written by victors, then winning political battles in the Philippines today are certainly not the vanguards of the liberal order. In a hugely controversial event for the country, on 18 November 2016, the body of the late dictator Ferdinand Marcos was moved from a refrigerated crypt in his hometown in Ilocos Norte to the Heroes' Cemetery in Manila, a decision the Supreme Court declared to be legal only in 2016. Since the Philippines ousted Marcos in 1986, the predominant historical narrative is one of democratic restoration, led by democracy icon Corazon Aquino and a coalition of supporters from the church, social movements, and business groups. The Marcos family, meanwhile, have faced numerous charges of plunder in Philippine and foreign courts, and faced a government agency specifically mandated to recover the Marcos family's ill-gotten wealth and sequester their assets. As cases continue to be tried, and assets slowly being recovered, there is a counter-narrative being created by the Marcos family. It is a narrative built on historical revisionism—the malicious reworking of collective memory to serve political ends (McPherson 2003).

Social media played a key role in the Marcos family's and their supporters' attempt to rewrite history. Months before the late dictator's burial in the Heroes' Cemetery, there were noticeable organized campaigns on Facebook and Twitter that promoted positive messages of healing, moving on and unity (Ong and Cabañes 2018). Pro-Marcos Facebook pages and Twitter accounts seeded the hashtags #NotoHate #YestoHealing and #IlibingNa (#BuryHimNow) alongside videos, graphics and life quotes that revolved around the themes of *bayanihan* (or community spirit) and religiosity. For example, some pages posted a barrage of memes and life quotes about the value of forgiving. "Forgiving yourself and others for mistakes done in the past does not mean the damage never existed", a pro-Marcos page called Marcos Cyber Warriors posted on Facebook on 20 September 2016 (Marcos Cyber Warriors 2016). "It just means the damage no longer controls your life", the caption added. Marcos loyalists shared these posts in their Facebook networks and in pro-Marcos Facebook groups, and circulated an online petition aimed at getting one million signatures to persuade the Supreme Court to rule in their favour (*Rappler* 2016). The narratives that circulated online were consistent with the messages of political figures supporting it. "He was a great president and he was a hero", Duterte openly claimed during his campaign in Ilocos, adding that the burial would bring "national healing" (Ranada 2016).

The campaign to revise history exposes several strategies of digital disinformation. One facet is to overclaim achievements while downplaying the costs of an authoritarian regime. Speaking about Marcos regime's achievements is not an outright lie. It can indeed be verified that during the Marcos era, the longest bridge in the Philippines was constructed. Similarly, Imelda Marcos indeed funded the construction of numerous theatres, galleries and hospitals. What is malicious about promoting these achievements online is the decontextualization of how these infrastructure projects were completed. The impact of foreign debt to the Philippine economy, as well as the cover-up of human rights violations are invisible in this sanitized narrative, often appearing in memes and short films. When carried to the level of public conversation, the overemphasis of achievements elides outright lies made by Marcos' children. When asked about human rights violations, daughter of the late dictator and now Senator Imee Marcos deflects the conversation to positive stories about Martial Law (*CNN Philippines* 2018). When asked about ill-gotten wealth, son Ferdinand (Bongbong) Marcos Jr. maintains claims of innocence, despite courts already deciding in the Philippine government's favour (*ABS-CBN News* 2020). Like Duterte, they too say outright lies, like claiming to graduate in prestigious universities without evidence that they have done so (Cepeda 2019). This is what makes the historical revisionist tactic particularly clever in promoting disinformation. The Marcos family and their public relations firms masterfully blend truths (infrastructure achievements) and untruths (did not steal) making them indistinguishable, and sowing seeds of doubt from audiences about what they know about the Martial Law.

The tactics of disinformation are also of note. Both Imee and Bongbong Marcos are active in curating their digital profile, especially in YouTube where they regularly upload sleekly produced videos that portray them as fun, relatable and action-oriented politicians. They are clearly trying to reach out to millennials and Gen Z voters—the generation that has not experienced the authoritarian regime and its immediate aftermath first hand. Negotiating historical legacies means crafting new stories and making these stories trend through tactics of boosting posts, seeding hashtags and securing the services of micro-influencers and pop culture accounts.

What can be learned from the strategies of historical revisionism? Compared to the case of cyber-*tokhang*, the Marcoses' style works in smoother, less visible operations, where their patrons are portrayed in a positive light. The goal is not necessarily to harass or silence as in the case of cyber-*tokhang*, but to confuse and normalize admiration for the Marcos family. These tactics are powerful because they are insidious and have serious consequences for securing the legacies of a revolution that ousted a brutal regime.

Health Disinformation

Disinformation is increasingly impacting discussions on public health. Specifically, we find that health disinformation fuels the public's scepticism of immunization practices in the Philippines. In April 2016, over 700,000 children enrolled in public schools all over the country received dengue vaccines as part of the Department of Health's immunization programme (Bonalos 2016). Considered a public health milestone, the 3.5 billion pesos (or around US$69 million) spent to purchase Dengvaxia (*Interaksyon* 2017) is supposed to curb the country's dengue epidemic affecting thousands of Filipinos every year, with recorded 1,546 deaths as of November 2019 (World Health Organization 2019). Until 2017, we witnessed a dramatic turn of events when Sanofi Pasteur, the vaccine's manufacturer, released their study's finding that those vaccinated with Dengvaxia but have not been infected with dengue before could be at risk of a more severe form of the disease (Sanofi in the Philippines 2017).

What was thought as a promising solution suddenly became the cause of mass hysteria among parents, who were worried for the safety of their children. The government attempted to diffuse the public's panic by opening a direct hotline where they could reach the Department of Health for their questions and queries (Department of Health 2017). What was more difficult to address, however, were the anxieties exchanged online in light of the deaths of children who were injected with vaccine (Alimario 2017). Parents were alarmed after the Public Attorney's Office (PAO) published their autopsy reports claiming that there is a conclusive relationship between Dengvaxia and the death of fourteen children despite an independent investigation led by forensic pathologists from the Philippine General Hospital disputing it. Pro-Duterte influencers such as RJ Nieto offered his platform to the publication and interpretation of PAO's forensic report (*Thinking Pinoy* 2018a). Meanwhile, the comment section of these influencer pages as well as closed Facebook groups became a space for mothers, in the Philippines and those working abroad, to exchange their grievances. For example, some parents commented on *Thinking Pinoy*'s Facebook post that they were not even informed that their children received the vaccine (*Thinking Pinoy* 2018b).

As the story developed, the crisis was framed due to the corruption and mismanagement of the past administration (Punongbayan 2019). Online, people ridiculed the former health secretary Janette Garin and her beginner track record in health practice. Some urged that former President Benigno Aquino should face the death penalty. This is one of the reasons why the sensationalized antics of PAO, formerly headed by Persida Acosta, spoke well given the deep-seated issues of the public against the previous administration (Lasco and Curato 2019). However, they opened another can of worm altogether because since the Dengvaxia scandal, the Philippines' Health Department reported a sharp decrease in Filipino's use of basic immunization services, paving way to the outbreak of measles, and now the resurgence of polio.

CONCLUSION

The digital public sphere in the Philippines has witnessed the "rhetorical cycle of hateful confrontation" (Ong and Cabañes 2018, p. 12). What was once declared as the texting and social media capital of the world is now known as "patient zero" in the global disinformation epidemic. In this chapter we demonstrated how exactly the pathologies of disinformation take root, by situating it in the longer and broader context of Philippine society. We argue that seemingly novel manifestations of digital disinformation are firmly embedded in political economy and political culture, as well as shaped by the turning points of the 2016 presidential race that brought Duterte to power. We also mapped the legacies of the 2016 race through three illustrative examples, each of which demonstrates the multifaceted character of digital disinformation.

Media companies, civil society organizations, the Roman Catholic Church, and the Philippine Senate have stepped in to propose practical solutions. This ranged from listing websites that contain "fake or unverified content" (Villegas 2017), to creating a web plug-in that alerts readers of fake news content appearing on their Facebook feeds (Gonzales 2017), to fact-checking initiatives (Magsambol 2018). Senator Joel Villanueva proposed to criminalize the sharing of false information on social media (Senate of the Philippines 2017). In Senate Bill 1492, he proposed that offenders should be charged a fine of 100,000 to five million pesos and be jailed for one to five years. Facebook, meanwhile, encourages responsible digital citizenship among Filipino students through its "Digital Discernment" workshop launched in February 2018. The aim is to teach students how to decipher credible information from falsehoods and show respect and empathy to diverse opinions (Inquirer.net 2018).

While we welcome prospects for reforming digital communication, we argue that these discreet proposals are not enough. As with any pathology, there needs to be a holistic approach to cure "patient zero". As Ong, Tapsell and Curato (2019) argue, disinformation networks are as much a labour issue as it is a communication issue. With tech-savvy freelancers constantly struggling to get fair wages, the allure of joining disinformation campaigns remains. The proposals mentioned above mostly focus on the "demand side" of disinformation and places the burden on consumers and eventual sharers of content. Our view is that the supply side is equally important and this cannot simply be resolved without recognition of the inequalities in digital work.

Disinformation production in the Philippines is now entrenched as a crucial election campaign practice and a lucrative industry. The affordances of social media that made the Occupy Wall Street, Arab Spring and Hong Kong protests happen are the same affordances that allow disinformation to unfold. The question is no longer whether digital technologies are good for democratic politics but a question on how digital technologies can serve as tools for transformative politics. We need to reimagine the digital public sphere beyond disinformation, and for this the Philippines has become known internationally as a central case study to sound the alarm.

REFERENCES

ABS-CBN News. 2020. "Bongbong Marcos Wants to Revise Textbook Version of Dad's Strongman Rule; Critics Raise Howl", 11 January 2020. https://news.abs-cbn.com/news/01/11/20/bongbong-marcos-wants-to-revise-textbook-version-of-dads-strongman-rule-critics-raise-howl.

Alimario, Anjo. 2017. "Families Claim Their Children Died Due to Dengvaxia". *CNN Philippines*, 19 December 2017. https://cnnphilippines.com/news/2017/12/19/Dengvaxia-dengue-vaccine-death.html.

Aning, Jerome. 2017. "Duterte Supporters Slam Robredo for 'Wild Accusations' on War vs Drugs". *Philippine Daily Inquirer*, 2 April 2017. https://newsinfo.inquirer.net/885849/duterte-supporters-slam-robredo-for-wild-accusations-on-war-vs-drugs.

Bajaj, Vikas. 2011. "A New Capital of Call Centers". *New York Times*, 25 November 2011. https://www.nytimes.com/2011/11/26/business/philippines-overtakes-india-as-hub-of-call-centers.html.

Barela, Mary Claire, Josephine Dionisio, Kurtis Heimeri, Manuel Sapitula and Cedric Angelo Festin. 2018. "Connecting Communities through Mobile Networks: The VBTS-CoCoMoNets Project". In *Global Information Society Watch 2018: Community Networks*, pp. 209–13. USA: Association for Progressive Communications (APC) and International Development Research Centre (IDRC).

Bautista. Jay. 2017. "TV Remains King in the Philippines – Kantar". *Kantar SEA Insights*, 16 March 2017. https://sea.kantar.com/tech/tv/2017/tv-remains-king-in-the-philippines/.

BBC News. 2019. "Profile: Duterte the Controversial 'Strongman' of the Philippines", 22 May 2019. https://www.bbc.com/news/world-36659258.

Bello, Walden. 2017. "Rodrigo Duterte: A Fascist Original". In *A Duterte Reader: Critical Essays on Rodrigo Duterte's Early Presidency*, edited by Nicole Curato, pp. 77–91. Quezon City: Ateneo de Manila University Press.

Bonalos, Pia. 2016. "DOH Starts Dengue Vaccination Program". *CNN Philippines*, 4 April 2016. https://cnnphilippines.com/news/2016/04/04/doh-starts-dengue-vaccination-program.html.

Cabalquinto, Earvin Charles. 2018. "'We're Not Only Here But We're There in Spirit': Asymmetrical Mobile Intimacy and the Transnational Family". *Mobile Media & Communication* 6, no. 1: 7–52.

Cabañes, Jason, C.W. Anderson and Jonathan Corpus Ong. 2019. "Fake News and Scandal". In *The Routledge Companion to Media and Scandal*, edited by Howard Tumber and Silvio Waisbord. London: Routledge.

Cabañes, Jason and Kristel Anne Acedera. 2012. "Of Mobile Phones and Mother-Fathers: Calls, Texts, Messages, and Conjugal Power Relations in Mother-Away Filipino Families". *New Media & Society* 14, no. 6: 916–30.

Canuday, Jose Jowel. 2017. "Conversations on the Global South". *Social Transformations* 5, no. 1: 121–36.

Cepeda, Mara. 2019. "FALSE: Imee Marcos 'Earned Degree from Princeton'". *Rappler*, 20 January 2019. https://www.rappler.com/newsbreak/fact-check/221395-false-imee-marcos-princeton-degree.

CNN Philippines. 2018. "Imee Marcos: We Will Never Admit Faults Under My Father's Rule", 31 August 2018. https://cnnphilippines.com/news/2018/08/31/imee-marcos-admit-faults-martial-law.html.

Combinido, Pamela. 2019. "The Everyday Reality of Fake News: An Ethnographic Study of Filipino Communities in the UK". MPhil dissertation, University of Cambridge.

Cornelio, Jayeel and Erron Medina. 2019. "Christianity and Duterte's War on Drugs in the Philippines". *Politics, Religion & Ideology* 20, no. 2: 151–69.

Coronel, Shiela. 2017. "Murder as Enterprise: Police Profiteering in Duterte's War on Drugs". In *A Duterte Reader: Critical Essays on Rodrigo Duterte's Early Presidency*, edited by Nicole Curato, pp. 167–98. Quezon City: Bughaw and Ateneo de Manila University Press.

Curato, Nicole. 2016. "Politics of Anxiety, Politics of Hope: Penal Populism and Duterte's Rise to Power". *Journal of Current Southeast Asian Affairs* 35, no. 3: 91–109.

———. 2019. *Democracy in a Time of Misery: From Spectacular Tragedies to Deliberative Action*. Oxford, UK: Oxford University Press.

Curato, Nicole and Jonathan Corpus Ong. 2018. "Who Laughs at a Rape Joke? Illiberal Responsiveness in Rodrigo Duterte's Philippines". *Ethical Responsiveness and the Politics of Difference* 65.

David, Emmanuel. 2015. "Purple Collar Labor: Transgender Workers and Queer Value at Global Call Centers in the Philippines". *Gender & Society* 29, no. 2: 169–94.

Department of Health, Republic of the Philippines. 2017. "DOH Task Force Addresses Concerns on Dengvaxia", 8 December 2017. https://www.doh.gov.ph/node/12025.

Evangelista, Patricia and Nicole Curato. 2016. "The Imagined President". *Rappler*, 19 February 2016. https://www.rappler.com/nation/politics/elections/2016/121124-the-imagined-president.

Garrido, Marco. 2017. "Why the Poor Support Populism: The Politics of Sincerity in Metro Manila". *American Journal of Sociology* 123, no. 3: 647–85.

Gonzales, Gelo. 2017. "PH Media Groups Release Facebook Fake News Blocker". *Rappler*, 8 June 2017. https://www.rappler.com/technology/news/172310-fake-news-blocker-facebook-philippines-nujp-cmfr-fakeblok.

Graham, Mark, Vili Lehdonvita, Alex Wood, Helena Barnard, Isis Hjorth and David Peter Simon. 2017. *The Risks and Rewards of Online Gig Work at the Global Margins*. Oxford: Oxford Internet Institute.

Hapal, Don Kevin. 2016. "Oplan Cyber Tokhang on Facebook: 'Extrajudicial Killing Reporting'". *Rappler*, 1 December 2016. https://www.rappler.com/newsbreak/investigative/154099-oplan-cyber-tokhang-facebook-security.

Harbath, Katie. 2018. "Protecting Election Integrity on Facebook", 23 June 2018. Presented at 360/OS, Berlin, Germany, 27 May 2015. https://www.youtube.com/watch?v=dJ1wcpsOtS4.

Hofileña, Chay. 1998. *News for Sale: The Corruption of Philippine Media*. Quezon City: Philippine Center for Investigative Journalism.

Interaksyon. 2017. "Risa Says Sanofi Must Pay Over Dengvaxia Mess; DOJ Orders Probe of PNoy Gov't's P3.5-B Vaccination Drive", 4 December 2017. http://www.interaksyon.com/breaking-news/2017/12/04/111480/risa-urges-govt-to-create-database-of-children-given-dengvaxia-says-sanofi-must-shoulder-needs-of-affected-pinoys/.

Lalacentte, Mireille and Vincent Raynauld. 2017. "The Power of Political Image: Justin Trudeau, Instagram, and Celebrity Politics". *American Behavioral Scientist* 63, no. 7: 888–924.

Lasco, Gideon and Nicole Curato. 2019. "Medical Populism". *Social Science and Medicine* 221: 1–8.

Madianou, Mirca. 2016. "Ambient Co-Presence: Transnational Family Practices in Polymedia Environments". *Global Networks* 16, no. 2: 183–201.

Madianou, Mirca and Daniel Miller. 2011. "Mobile Phone Parenting: Reconfiguring Relationships Between Filipina Migrant Mothers and Their Left-Behind Children". *New Media & Society* 13, no. 3: 457–70.

Magsambol, Bonz. 2018. "Facebook Partners with Rappler, Vera Files for Fact-Checking Program". *Rappler*, 12 April 2018. https://www.rappler.com/technology/social-media/200060-facebook-partnershipfact-checking-program.

Marcos Cyber Warriors. 2016. Facebook page (accessed 14 January 2020).

McKinsey Global Institute. 2016. "People on the Move: Global Migration's Impact and Opportunity". New York: McKinsey & Company.

McPherson, James. 2003. "From the President: Revisionist Historians". *Perspectives on History*, 1 September 2003. https://www.historians.org/publications-and-directories/perspectives-on-history/september-2003/revisionist-historians.

Mercurio, Richmond. 2018. "Philippines Remains World's Center Capital – CCAP". *Philippine Star*, 31 May 2018. https://www.philstar.com/business/2018/05/31/1820097/philippines-remains-worlds-call-center-capital-ccap.

Moffitt, Bejamin. 2016. *The Global Rise of Populism: Performance, Political Style, and Representation*. Stanford: Stanford University Press.

Nery, John. 2019. "Why Does the President Lie?" *Philippine Daily Inquirer*, 11 June 2019. https://opinion.inquirer.net/121904/why-does-the-president-lie.

Observatory for the Protection of Human Rights Defenders. 2019. "Philippines: I'll Kill You Along with Drug Addicts – President Duterte's War on Human Rights Defenders in the Philippines". *OMCT SOS-Torture Network*, 28 February 2019. https://www.omct.org/human-rights-defenders/reports-and-publications/philippines/2019/02/d25257/.

Ong, Jonathan Corpus and Jason Vincent A. Cabañes. 2018. *Architects of Networked Disinformation: Behind the Scenes of Troll Accounts and Fake News Production in the Philippines*. The Newton Tech4Dev Network.

———. 2019. "Politics and Profit in the Fake News Factory: Four Work Models in Political Trolling in the Philippines". Latvia: NATO Strategic Communications Centre of Excellence.

Ong, Jonathan Corpus, Ross Tapsell and Nicole Curato. 2019. *Tracking Digital Disinformation in the 2019 Philippine Midterm Election*. Canberra: New Mandala.

Palatino, Mong. 2017. "Beware Duterte's Troll Army in the Philippines". *The Diplomat*, 18 November 2017. https://thediplomat.com/2017/11/beware-dutertestroll-army-in-the-philippines/.

Paragas, Fernando. 2009. "Migrant Workers and Mobile Phones: Technological, Temporal, and Spatial Simultaneity". In *The Reconstruction of Space and Time: Mobile Communication Practices*, edited by Rich Ling and Scott Campbell, pp. 36–66. New Brunswick, USA: Transaction Publishers.

Pertierra, Anna. 2017. "Celebrity Politics and Televisual Melodrama in the Age of Duterte". In *A Duterte Reader: Critical Essays on Rodrigo Duterte's Early Presidency*, edited by Nicole Curato, pp. 219–30. Quezon City: Bughaw and Ateneo de Manila University Press.

Philippine Centre for Investigative Journalism. 2019. "PCIJ Audit: Candidates on Social Media", 14 February 2019. https://pcij.org/article/1391/pcij-audit-candidates-on-social-media.

Philippine Statistics Authority. 2019. "Total Number of OFWs Estimated at 2.3 Million", 30 April 2019. https://psa.gov.ph/statistics/survey/labor-and-employment/survey-overseas-filipinos.

Philippine Trust Index. 2017. "The Philippine Paradox: Growing Trust in a Time of Growing Uncertainty". https://www.scribd.com/document/357522203/Philippine-Trust-Index-2017-Executive-Summary.

Pulse Asia Research Inc. 2018. "September 2018 Nationwide Survey on Social Media Use". http://www.pulseasia.ph/september-2018-nationwide-survey-onsocial-media-use/.

Punongbayan, JC. 2019. "[Analysis] Dengvaxia Scare: How Viral Rumors Caused Outbreaks". *Rappler*, 16 January 2019. https://www.rappler.com/thought-leaders/221087-analysis-dengvaxia-scare-how-rumors-caused-viral-outbreaks.

Quimpo, Nathan Gilbert. 2007. "The Philippines: Political Parties and Corruption". In *Southeast Asian Affairs 2007*, edited by Daljit Singh and Lorraine Carlos Salazar, pp. 277–94. Singapore: Institute of Southeast Asian Studies.

Rafael, Vincent. 2019. "The Sovereign Trickster". *The Journal of Asian Studies* 78, no. 1: 141–66.

Ranada, Pia. 2016. "Duterte in Ilocos Norte: I Will Allow Marcos' Burial in Heroes' Cemetery". *Rappler*, 19 February 2016. https://www.rappler.com/nation/politics/elections/2016/123061-duterte-marcos-burial-libingan-bayani.

———. 2019. "'The President Does Not Lie' – Panelo". *Rappler*, 2 May 2019. https://www.rappler.com/nation/229508-panelo-says-president-duterte-does-not-lie.

Rappler. 2016. "Marcos Loyalists to SC: Hero's Burial for National Healing, Unity", 27 September 2016. https://www.rappler.com/nation/147431-marcos-loyalists-signature-campaign-supreme-court-hero-burial.

Ressa, Maria. 2016. "Propaganda War: Weaponizing the Internet". *Rappler*, 3 October 2016. https://www.rappler.com/nation/148007-propaganda-war-weaponizing-internet.

Roberts, Sarah. 2016. "Commercial Content Moderation: Digital Laborer's Dirty Work". In *The Intersectional Internet: Race, Sex, Class and Culture Online*, edited by Safiya Umoja Noble and Brendesha M. Tynes. New York: Peter Lang Publishing.

Robles, Raissa. 2016. "How Duterte Supporters Conduct 'Cyber Tokhang' on Facebook". *Raissa Robles*, 18 December 2016. https://www.raissarobles.com/2016/12/18/how-duterte-supporters-conduct-cyber-tokhang-on-facebook/.

———. 2018. "UK Firm Specializing in Managing Elections Claims It Helped Duterte Win in 2016". *Raissa Robles*, 4 April 2018. https://www.raissarobles.com/2018/04/04/uk-firm-specializing-in-managing-elections-claims-it-helped-rodrigo-duterte-win-in-2016/.

Rodriguez, Fritzie. 2016. "Election-Related Human Rights Violations Rampant Online – CHR". *Rappler*, 18 April 2016. https://www.rappler.com/nation/politics/elections/2016/129909-online-human-rights-violations-elections.

Romero, Segundo. 2020. "Fuzzy Drug War Facts and Figures". *Philippine Daily Inquirer*, 13 January 2020.

Sanofi in the Philippines. 2017. "Sanofi Updates Information on Dengue Vaccine in the Philippines", 4 December 2017. https://www.sanofi.ph/-/media/Project/One-Sanofi-Web/Websites/Asia-Pacific/Sanofi-PH/Home/press-room/Sanofi-updates-information-on-dengue-vaccine-in-Philippines.pdf?la=en.

Senate of the Philippines. 2017. "Anti-Fake News Act of 2017". https://www.senate.gov.ph/lis/bill_res.aspx?congress=17&q=SBN-1492.

Sidel, John. 1999. *Capital, Coercion, and Crime: Bossism in the Philippines*. Stanford: Stanford University Press.

Silverman, Craig, Jane Lytvynenko and William Kung. 2020. "Disinformation for Hire: How a New Breed of PR Firms is Selling Lies Online". *Buzzfeed News*, 6 January 2020. https://www.buzzfeednews.com/article/craigsilverman/disinformation-for-hire-black-pr-firms.

Soriano, Cheryll and Jason Cabañes. 2019. "Between 'World-Class Work' and 'Proletarized Labor': Digital Labor Imaginaries in the Global South". In *The Routledge Companion to Media and Class*, edited by Erika Polson, Lynn Schofield Clark and Radhika Gajjala. New York: Routledge.

Soriano, Cheryll, Ruepert Jiel Cao and Marianne Sison. 2017. "Experiences of ICT Use in Shared, Public Access Settings in Philippine Slums". *Development in Practice* 28, no. 3: 358–73.

Syjuco, Miguel. 2017. "Fake News Floods the Philippines". *New York Times*, 24 October 2017. https://www.nytimes.com/2017/10/24/opinion/fake-newsphilippines.html.

Thinking Pinoy (blog). 2017. "Inside Leni Robredo's International Propaganda Machinery", 6 January 2017. http://www.thinkingpinoy.net/2017/01/oustduterte-inside-leni-robredos.html.

―――. 2018a. "DOH and Sanofi's Secret: Dengvaxia® May Cause Multiple Organ Failure". *Facebook*, 8 February 2018a. https://web.facebook.com/notes/thinking-pinoy/doh-and-sanofis-secret-dengvaxia-may-cause-multiple-organ-failure/1000433603437076/?_rdc=1&_rdr.

―――. 2018b. "The Dengvaxia Scandal in Ten Simple Sites". *Facebook*, 9 February 2018b. https://web.facebook.com/TheThinkingPinoy/posts/the-dengvaxia-scandal-in-ten-simple-stepslet-me-explain-part-of-the-dengvaxia-sc/1000804520066651/?_rdc=1&_rdr.

Villegas, Socrates B. 2017. "Consecrate them in the Truth". *CBCP News*, 21 June 2017. http://cbcpnews.net/cbcpnews/consecrate-them-in-the-truth/.

We Are Social. 2019. "Digital in 2019". https://wearesocial.com/global-digital-report-2019.

Williams, Sean. 2017. "Rodrigo Duterte's Army of Online Trolls". *The New Republic*, 4 January 2017. https://newrepublic.com/article/138952/rodrigo-dutertes-armyonline-trolls.

World Health Organization. 2019. "Update on the Dengue Situation in the Western Pacific Region". Dengue Situation Update 584, 19 December 2019. https://www.who.int/docs/default-source/wpro---documents/emergency/surveillance/dengue/dengue-20191219.pdf?sfvrsn=b42cfbd0_22.

3

THE POLITICAL CAMPAIGN INDUSTRY AND THE RISE OF DISINFORMATION IN INDONESIA

Muninggar Sri Saraswati

Disinformation production has become a prominent fixture in recent electoral campaigns in Indonesia, leading to fears of "divisive" political discourse that affect not only online debates, but also have real-life consequences for violence (Heriyanto 2019). Social media platforms are often blamed both for the spread of disinformation and for "polarizing" the nation. This article argues that social media disinformation is an extension of the expanding political campaign industry, whose significance increased, and is being used by political elites to maintain their power. The rise of disinformation via social media is new, but is part of a long history of engineering consent and manipulation by elite political and economy forces in the country.

My research in Indonesia has shown that the production of disinformation via social media campaign teams could be observed since as early as the 2012 Jakarta gubernatorial election, an election which saw the victory for Joko Widodo (hereafter Jokowi), who would become Indonesia's president two years later. The 2012 election witnessed for the first time the extensive and professional use of social media campaigning, although much of this activity went unnoticed by scholars and the mainstream media. The industry continued to develop in the 2014 Indonesian presidential election, grew substantially in the 2017 Jakarta gubernatorial election, and grew even more in the 2019 presidential election. During these elections, social media was increasingly used for disinformation production, pitting supporters of candidates against each other. It was driven by the emergence of increasing campaign funds directed towards social media management, production and manipulation of social media discourse.

This chapter will examine the political-economic context which allowed for the growth of disinformation production in Indonesia. It will begin by examining the early use of social media campaigning, examine a "tipping point", and identify the growing players behind the disinformation production in the social media sphere. In doing so, it highlights a Gramscian argument that the power holders control the masses (particularly in democracy) through committing repression but also by gaining their consent.

EARLY USE OF SOCIAL MEDIA IN INDONESIA

Social media engagement in Indonesia began positively for reformists, and was largely seen as activities considered to be supportive of democracy. This optimistic perspective of social media production follows on from the positive role that new, internet-based technologies played in assisting Indonesia's democracy movement in the late 1990s (Ahmad and Popa 2014; Hameed 2007). Earlier studies saw the internet in Indonesia as a "democratic innovation" or even a "technology of freedom" (Hill and Sen 2000; Hill and Sen 2005; Nurhadryani, Maslow and Yamamoto 2009). The internet in Indonesia was seen as a facilitator of "the space where frustrations and aspirations excluded from state and commercialized platforms—not all political, and certainly not all 'democratic' could be expressed" (Hill and Sen 2005, p. 34). Indonesian pro-democracy activists, journalists and politicians used the internet as a tool for activism and as an alternative political channel to the highly-controlled mass media under the rule of Suharto's authoritarian government (Bräuchler 2003; Hill 2003; Lim 2003; Steele 2005).

In their early years of being adopted by Indonesians, social media platforms showed vitality in enabling an alternative activism space for its users (Lim 2013; Nugroho and Syarief 2012). Two success stories of social media activism are the cases of Prita Mulyasari and the Indonesian Anti-Corruption Commission (KPK). The first case involved Mulyasari, a housewife, which engaged in a legal battle with an affluent private hospital in Jakarta in 2009. Mulyasari was found guilty for defaming the hospital's doctors, following her complaints of the services of the hospital to her network of family and friends through an email, which went viral. The mother of two was subsequently detained during the judicial process, found guilty and ordered to pay Rp204 million in fine by the Tangerang High Court. The verdict provoked Indonesian activists to initiate a social media campaign by the name of "Coins for Prita" to raise money to help pay her fine. The Facebook and Twitter campaign turned into a bigger offline movement as the story was made headlines in the mainstream media, resulting in around Rp825 million (around SG$80,000) in donation and the hospital dropping one of the lawsuits. Prita was found guilty, but was given a probationary sentence by the Supreme Court, suggesting that the public sentiment driven by social media discourse played a role in lightening her sentence, and was hailed as a victory by her supporters.

The second early significant case of social media activism involved the KPK, following the arrests of their deputy chairpersons, Bibit S. Riyanto and Chandra Hamzah, by the National Police in 2009. Their arrests, widely interpreted as a plot to weaken the KPK, which is seen one of the most respected products of *reformasi* in Indonesia, provoked a lecturer from Bengkulu, Sumatra to launch an online campaign by the name of "the Movement of 1,000,000 Facebookers in Support of Chandra Hamzah and Bibit Samad Riyanto". The campaign page attracted 1.4 million members (Nugroho and Syarief 2012). This online movement progressed offline with thousands of people joining rallies against their arrests in Jakarta and other cities across Indonesia, prompting the authorities to drop the charges against them. These examples show how social media was used as a political space for Indonesian activists to articulate their views and to push their agendas.

In the field of electoral contestation, scholars have observed the contribution of social media in mobilizing popular support for Jokowi, a mayor of the medium-sized city of Surakarta in Central Java, to eventually become Indonesia's president (Sefsani and Ziegenhain 2015; Suaedy 2014), winning two presidential elections in 2014 and 2019. Jokowi's victory in the 2012 Jakarta gubernatorial election is seen as evidence of the importance of social media in bringing about popular reformist candidates. As a politician from the periphery of the national politics epicentre, Jokowi defeated rivals who were mainly established and well-connected politicians, including then incumbent Governor Fauzi Bowo in 2012, and later the "oligarchic populist" Prabowo Subianto in both 2014 and 2019 (Aspinall 2015).

Social media has been a crucial aspect of his campaigns, that indeed facilitated large-scale grassroots volunteerism and participation (Ahmad and Popa 2014; Suaedy 2014). In 2012, the number of internet users in Jakarta had reached more than 3.5 million, which was 36.9 per cent of the total Jakarta population of around 9.5 million (APJII 2012; BPS 2012). Many Jakartans were active on Twitter, so much so that the city earned the title of the most active Twitter city in the world in 2012 (Semiocast 2012). The majority of these internet users were able to access social media regularly on their mobile phones (Insight 2012), and comprised mainly young people (17–35 year-old), who were educated and middle class (Utomo et al. 2013). Politics was widely discussed; one survey showed politics was second only to entertainment in gaining the attention of social media users throughout this period (Rahmawati 2014).

Social media volunteers were seen as a positive development for engaging young people in the sphere of politics (Suaedy 2014; Suwana 2018) and in allowing for new forms of discourse which usurped mainstream media agendas driven by elite media owners (Gazali 2014; Widodo 2011). Furthermore, social media's increasing politicization was seen as a positive development for reform, decentralization, and the emergence and promotion of younger leaders with a track record of governance prior to running for president. Jokowi's campaign seemed to be driven more by popular sentiment. Indeed, post-authoritarian technological transformations meant significant changes for electoral campaigning practices.

However, while social media was undoubtedly a force for activism in Indonesia in the early years of its adoption, scholars and analysts generally ignored or were unable to see the "underground" forces that began to be present in the political campaign industry. Post-authoritarian dynamics in both the economic and political spheres were no less significant in facilitating online political campaigning practices. In other words, social media campaigning is not independent of political and economic developments in the country. The use of social media for electoral campaigning in Indonesia is shaped significantly by the political economy of election campaigning, involving key actors such as candidates, political parties, and campaign donors. In the next section we will see how the grassroots online volunteers were in fact the start of the professionalization of social media campaigning, driven in large part by elite money with ties to the campaign industry.

THE DISINFORMATION INDUSTRY AND POLITICAL BUZZERS

The success stories of social media campaigning described in the previous section overshadow the fact that the very same campaigning techniques resulted in the emergence of disinformation production. The political campaign industry was often overlooked in the discussions of social media campaigning despite its important role in shaping online narratives. This chapter understands the political campaign industry as a distinct business based on "the cross-development of political and commercial persuasion techniques in the Twentieth Century" (Stockwell 2002, p. 3). The political campaign industry includes communication and marketing, public relations, advertising and opinion polling businesses, which formed clusters as shown in Figure 3.1.

Each cluster is not exclusive. Indeed, polling agencies may provide political consultancy while a big data company may join forces with a digital marketing agency to provide campaign services for their clients. The whole clusters essentially provide "a full range of services needed to secure the victory of a candidate—from strategic planning, to conceptualizing a candidate's 'vision and mission', from campaigning door to door and designing and organizing media campaigns to providing poll monitors on election day" (Qodari 2010, p. 132). The political campaign industry's ability to develop social media campaigning as a new mode of campaigning is enabled by social media's inter-connected networks of users who are able to engage in the production, distribution and consumption of political texts (Steinfield et al. 2009). Thus, social media campaigning should be seen

FIGURE 3.1
Political Campaign industry

- Big data analytics
- Polling agencies
- Digital marketing agencies
- Individual operators
- Marketing communication agencies
- Political consultants
- Printing companies (outdoor publication)

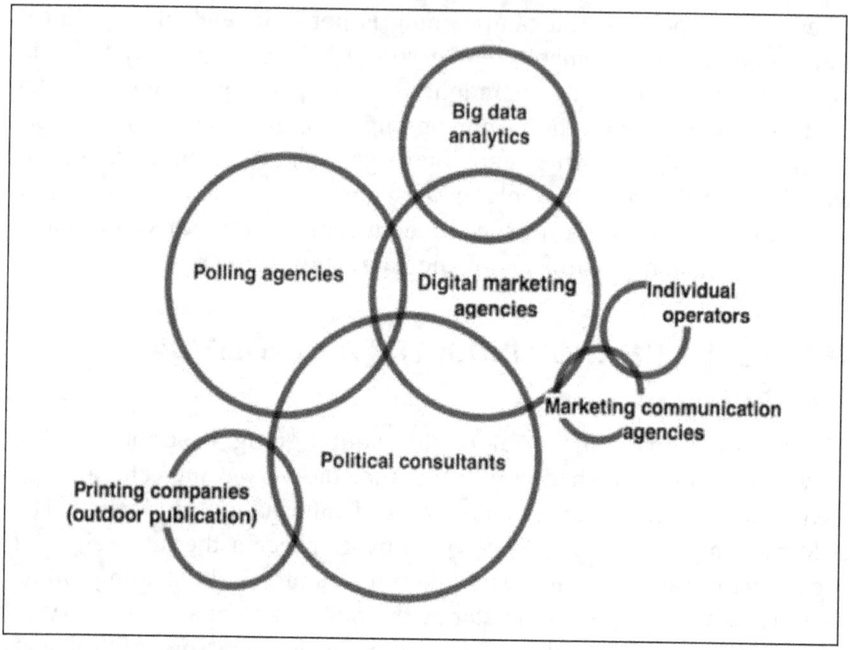

Source: Rakhmani (2019).

as mediated predominantly by the political campaign industry, funded by political elites, in order for them to mobilize popular support for their politicians and policies.

Contemporary election campaign teams cannot avoid employing basic social media campaigning strategies. Generally, "teams" comprise of three layers of campaign narrative-making. The first is positive campaigning, referring to the production and distribution of campaign narratives that highlighted the achievements of the candidate. The second is negative campaigning, referring to the production and distribution of campaign narratives that highlighted the candidate's political opponent(s)'s professional flaws. The third is the so-called "black campaigning" that deals with the creation of narratives of the candidate's political opponent(s)'s professional and personal life, much of which is untrue. This third narrative-making strategy is what we now acknowledge as disinformation, and has grown exponentially since this 2012 election.

Jokowi's campaign teams began to employ social media campaigning in the time when Facebook, Twitter, YouTube and other social media have attracted a greater number of users, and were able to take advantage of this new form of political discourse. His professional campaigners were able to aptly develop and implement marketing strategies to improve his personal political brand in Jakarta (Ahmad and Popa 2014, p. 98). Portraying himself as a "commoner" with no connection to the Suharto's New Order government in his campaign, he was able to attract lower and certain sections of middle class Indonesians, but more importantly, he was able to get many influential activists to join in his campaign bandwagon, including pro-democracy and human rights activists. Jokowi's campaigning in the 2012 Jakarta election was indeed characterized by the emergence of volunteers, who were attracted by the reputations of both Jokowi and his deputy candidate, Basuki Tjahaja Purnama, popularly known as "Ahok" (Suaedy 2014). The groups were organized under the Jokowi Ahok Social Media Volunteers (or JASMEV), which became well-known in public for the grassroots volunteerism on social media.

In the 2012 Jakarta gubernatorial election, several industry members foresaw business opportunities enabled by social media. A key industry player was Sonny Subrata. A director of advertising and marketing agency Tridaya Nusantara Internasional and Arwuda Indonesia, Subrata joined forces with Yose Rizal, the director of big data and social media monitoring company PT Mediawave Analytics to launch the company, Politicawave, offering social media monitoring services for politics. Together with Kartika Djoemadi, the director of lobbying company Spin Doctors Indonesia, they joined in the campaign bandwagon of Jokowi in the 2012 Jakarta election.

As a candidate from the region running for the first time in the Jakarta gubernatorial election, Jokowi was in need of support from professional campaign companies, including those of Subrata, Rizal and Djoemadi. Subrata, who has a close connection with executives in Jokowi's party, Partai Demokrasi Indonesia Perjuangan (PDIP), supported Jokowi through social media campaigning, which was relatively new in the context of electoral campaigning business in Indonesia in 2012. Subrata, Rizal and Djoemadi initiated and operated

JASMEV. While the campaign teams organized by political parties mainly managed the offline and mass media campaigns, JASMEV worked on the production and distribution of social media campaign content, managing user engagement and coordinating a new form of campaign labour now known as "buzzing" in Indonesia. "Buzzing" refers to the production and distribution of campaign messages through social media by users with a large followers, and had been widely used in commercial marketing domains prior to the 2012 election (Paramaditha 2013).

In subsequent elections in Indonesia, "buzzing" has been carried out by influential social media accounts whose role is to mobilize users to engage in the production and distribution of campaign messages. Political buzzers in Indonesia are also social media campaigners commissioned by politicians, political parties and private clients to distribute pro-government or pro-party propaganda, attack political opponents and spread information to polarize public opinion (Bradshaw 2019).

Many "buzzers" are writers, journalists, copy writers, content creators and/or those in marketing communications businesses. The birth of political buzzers highlighted the "fluid" nature of the political campaign industry, which as an industry of "innovation" regularly opens to new players and ideas during campaigns (Hamburger 2001; Thurber and Nelson 2000). Among the first known buzzers in Indonesia was an anonymous Twitter account @triomacan2000, which accumulated 83,873 followers by 24 May 2012 (Tarigan 2012). This particular account focused on attacking Jokowi's personal life (Sadasri 2016). It was run by a group of individuals led by Raden Nuh, a former commissioner of state-enterprise PT Asuransi Berdikari, and Abdul Rasyid, who was the expert staff of the Coordinating Minister of Economic Affairs Hatta Rajasa, who was both chairman of the National Mandate Party and father-in-law of the youngest son of then President Susilo Bambang Yudhoyono (Yusron 2012). The account administrators reportedly threatened Ahok's campaign team that they would buzz the smear campaign team if they did not use their buzzing services of Rp1 billion, which was rejected by the team (Amri et al. 2013).

The political buzzers' approach changed to not only involve "celebrity influencer" accounts, but also began to employ teams of social media campaigners who all worked together as anonymous producers of material (Lilin, Idris and Indradie 2013; Nailufar 2019; Paramaditha 2013). This includes various techniques from making fake accounts, posting comments on social media pages, posting spam in various online forums, sharing articles from both genuine and bogus websites, using bots to multiple campaign texts, and much more. They were given funds which enabled them to buy followers, ads and sponsored posts, and "give away" prizes to attract social media users. These social media mobilization techniques aimed not only at other social media users to consume but, more importantly, re-produce and re-distribute campaign texts to follow the direction of the buzzers' narratives.

As the 2014 presidential election campaign neared, social media turned into an established mode of campaigning—a commercial service that offers more definite scope of work and goals for candidates. These commercial services represent the commodification of content, social media users (audience) and labour. In addition, it includes services of social media monitoring to trace the dynamic behaviour and preferences of social media users necessary to develop a social media campaign strategy to win the cyber campaign wars during the political campaign period. This particular service can be likened to audience ratings in the conventional media, which "demands the use of measurement procedures to produce commodities and monitoring techniques to keep track of production, distribution, exchange and consumption" (Mosco 2009, p. 141).

Consequently, the employment of political buzzers during political campaign period proliferated. Since the 2014 presidential campaign, the production and distribution of disinformation appeared to be intensified and more visible partly because the political campaign industry members and political buzzers who are involved in social media campaign, and engaged in cyber wars, have learnt and shared similar strategies in producing and distributing campaign messages (Renaldi 2018). This dynamic explained the confirmation of social media campaigning as an accepted mode of electoral campaigning. At the same time, the acceptance of the political elites of the new mode of electoral campaigning suggested their needs to claim social media as a new space for consent engineering necessary to maintain their rule. These methods not only expanded the political campaign industry but also nurtured these disinformation actors as key players in the Indonesian political landscape.

DISINFORMATION PRODUCTION GROWS

Election Disinformation Grows

The acceptance of the Indonesian political elites of social media campaigning as the new mode of campaigning was prominently shown by Jokowi, who immediately engaged a number of buzzers to the palace after he was declared the winner of the 2014 presidential election (Ismail 2014; Sani 2019). Some political campaign industry figures and political buzzers, who supported him in the Jakarta election continued their supports in the 2014 and 2019 presidential elections as well as his government policies. Among them were Subrata, Rizal, Djoemadi, Chairperson of Cyrus Network opinion polling company Hasan Nasbi, Chairperson of Cirrus Surveyor Group Andrinof Chaniago and former journalist Ulin Ni'am Yusron. In the 2014 and 2019 elections, more number of political buzzers were known to Jokowi, such as writers and self-confessed social media activists (*penggiat media sosial*) Denny Siregar, Eko Kunthadi, Permadi Arya, Fadjroel Rachman as well as former JASMEV coordinator Hariadhi.

In return for their supports, many of these political industry figures and political buzzers gained positions in various state-owned companies and the government (Asril 2015). Some noted industry figures who gained compensation after Jokowi's victory in the presidential election in 2014 were Subrata who was appointed as the commissionaire of state-owned cement company PT Semen Indonesia, Djoemadi the commissionaire of state-owned financial company PT Danareksa, and Rizal the commissionaire of telecommunication company Telkomsel, a subsidiary of state-owned telecommunication company PT Telkom. Chaniago, was made a minister briefly and a commissionaire of Bank Rakyat Indonesia (BRI), the largest state bank in Indonesia; Rachman was made the commissionaire of PT Adhi Karya state construction company and the president's spokesperson.

While Jokowi is more prominent in his links to political buzzers and social media campaigning in general, other politicians engaged with them too. In 2014, Prabowo's campaign team was known to employ Budi Purnomo Karjodiharjo, a media professional, and advertising company Think Big Indonesia. Karjodiharjo, who owns a marketing communication and media agency Indonesia Media Center, initially supported Jokowi's campaign teams in the 2012 Jakarta election.

However, he decided to jump up the wagon to support Jokowi's rival, Prabowo, in the 2014 and also 2019 presidential elections. Karjodiharjo's company was assigned to manage Prabowo's campaign team media centre and social media campaigning. Think Big Indonesia largely handled Prabowo's media and social media campaigns. Led by Prabowo's close friends Juke Sutarman, Dharmawan Ronodipuro and Ron Mueller, the company trained, managed and supervised dozens of political buzzers (*Tempo* 2014).

After the 2014 presidential election, social media campaigning and "buzzing" became more prominent, especially in the lead up to the 2017 Jakarta governor's election, which is seen as a precursor to national elections two years later. For example, Teman Ahok (Friends of Ahok), was used by Ahok and financed by Hasan Nasbi, the director of Cyrus Network opinion polling company. Teman Ahok started as a volunteer group aimed at getting public support for Ahok to run independently in the 2017 Jakarta election. While it was able to collect one million copies of voters' ID cards necessary to nominate an independent candidate in the election. As the election year began in 2017, Ahok chose to use the PDIP to run as a party-backed candidate in the election (Saragih 2016). After gaining the support from PDIP, JASMEV stepped in to support Ahok in his 2017 campaign for governor, using the banner "JASMEV2017". This time JASMEV was abbreviated to Jakarta Ahok Social Media Volunteers. Ahok was also supported by a number of buzzers (Lamb 2018) whose main job was to engage in countering negative and smear campaigns against him, especially after he criticized Islamic clerics who attempt to lure Muslim voters in Jakarta away from electing him.

The 2017 Jakarta election was the scene for the widespread use of political identity for campaigning (Lim 2017). Anti-Ahok online groups emerged more prominently during this time, described broadly as the "Muslim Cyber Army", which openly criticized Ahok on grounds of race and religion, and supported the governor candidacy of Anies Baswedan in his campaign. These groups amassed thousands of members from across the country, and engaged in a series of social media campaigns including calling on Muslims to boycott Ahok (Sulaiman 2017). The police eventually arrested some of their leaders in 2018, as President Jokowi and others in government were concerned about rising identity politics, and also undermining the president's popularity.

It is during this time that the Jokowi administration ramped up their own use of "buzzers" (Bramasta 2019). While many political buzzers tended to hide their identities in public previously, some were now opting to do the opposite. Among these are the so-called "buzzer *istana*" (the Palace's buzzers) (Nailufar 2016). Some of these buzzers include Denny Siregar and Pepih Nugraha. These buzzers identified themselves as writers or social media activists. Siregar was largely unknown in the 2012 Jakarta election social media campaign scene. Their popularity started to rise since they consistently posted their comments supporting Jokowi on social media, most notably on Twitter. Siregar's followers on Twitter reached over 700,000 in early 2020. Pepih Nugraha was better known as a *Kompas* newspaper journalist, who developed *Kompas*' citizen journalism platform Kompasiana and carved his reputation as a blogger. The presence of the government's buzzers has incited criticism for the government increasing the influence of the pro-government buzzers, which enabled them to get direct access to the president and government officials (*Tempo* 2019). The growing power of such buzzers indicated the expansion of the political campaign industry in Indonesia from 2012 to 2019. Social media campaigning has now become an established campaign service (Patrick 2019), carried out by professional operators and, more importantly, is seen by candidates as an essential part of a political campaign (Riana 2019).

Disinformation Beyond Elections

Given their now dominance in the Indonesian online landscape, political buzzers did not cease at the end of elections. Rather, their work has been found in non-electoral campaign settings, but still in the political realm. One such case is the political buzzers' works in raising the issue of radicalism within the KPK. The issue, raised among others by a "Palace's buzzer" Siregar, centred on the idea that the KPK has been infiltrated by radicals, including KPK investigator Novel Baswedan, a victim of an acid attack that left him blind in one eye in 2017, and the former KPK commissioner Bambang Widjojanto (Trianita 2019). Denny and other pro-government buzzers supported the government's controversial decision to form a committee to select KPK leadership, which eventually selected an active police general, Firli Bahuri, as KPK leader. Bahuri had previously served as the anti-corruption commission deputy of prosecution and had been tainted following an ethical misconduct case. The House of Representatives eventually approved Bahuri as the new KPK chairperson in September 2019. This and a number of others of Jokowi's policies involving KPK have met with public outcry that brought university students to the streets. Throughout this time, the pro-government buzzers played an important role in safeguarding Jokowi's unpopular policies.

A second example is disinformation around West Papua. In October 2018, Facebook issued a statement that it had identified and removed 69 Facebook accounts, 42 pages and 34 Instagram accounts over "coordinated inauthentic behavior", mostly regarding West Papua. Facebook announced in the statement that it found links to advertising agency Insight ID, which spent about $300,000 on Facebook ads behind the networks that used fake accounts to manage pages, disseminate their texts and drive people to off-platform sites (Syakriah 2019). Some reports detailed the indirect links between Insight ID and then Vice President Jusuf Kalla's campaign team (Strick and Syavira 2019; Strick and Thomas 2019). In the case of Papua riots in 2019, a "battle" occurred between pro-government buzzers and pro-Papuan activists on Facebook and Twitter, who presented alternative perspectives amid the social media campaign by pro-government buzzers (Tehusijarana 2019). It was a sign of the problems of the persistence of buzzers in non-election times, and despite using pro-government buzzers to apparently negate the controversial situation, the Indonesian government in the end was forced to slow down or cut off the internet given the worsening situation. The riots that followed a video circulated of Papuan students being racially abused in the presence of the police in Surabaya, East Java prompted the government to shut down the internet in the provinces of Papua and West Papua. The extensive use of social media campaigning operated by the political campaign industry, including the emergence of political buzzers through more complicated social media campaigning practices have demonstrated further encroachment of the political campaign industry into the field of campaign texts creation and distribution.

CONCLUSION

This chapter has detailed the roles of the political campaign industry, and the subsequent birth of buzzers, in normalizing the production of disinformation in social media in Indonesia. It argues that disinformation should not be seen merely as a by-product of campaigning tools in a democracy, but rather a crucial aspect of consent making in the political realms. Social media has ultimately proved to be an example of the power of political economic campaign industry.

Gramsci's concept of hegemony is useful to explain the significance of disinformation in the changing social political terrain in Indonesia. Based on Gramsci's argument of power (1971), the elites require more than just violence to maintain their rule, including in a democracy. They also need the consent of the people under their rule to keep them in power. In post-authoritarian democracy, money politics or political violence are not the only mechanisms to maintain the power of the elites (Hadiz 2010). The consent of the people, be it in the form of votes in elections or public opinion, is also a necessity for the elites to continue their ruling. Thus, the elites' needs to mobilize people to engage—willingly and enthusiastically—in the elections and support their agenda open the doors for the political campaign industry to play a greater role in politics. Within this line, disinformation is not seen as a "major threat" in democracy, but a requirement for the consent engineering in social media. Through the production of disinformation, driven by political buzzers, the political campaign industry contributed to the maintenance of social media interaction, albeit often pseudo interactions, to capture public attention and shape public opinion in the electoral contexts and beyond. In Indonesia, the increasing significance of political buzzers and the production of disinformation through social media have been proven to be important to help win an election and to support the policies of the elected leader. This has demonstrated the expansion and encroachment of the political campaign industry in the political realm. Ultimately, it further validated the necessity of the changing content engineering practices in the digital age to keep the ruling elites in power.

REFERENCES

Ahmad, Nyarwi and Ioan-Lucian Popa. 2014. "The Social Media Usage and the Transformation of Political Marketing and Campaigning of the Emerging Democracy in Indonesia: Case Study of the 2012 Gubernatorial Election of the Special Region of the Capital City Jakarta". In *Social Media in Politics:*

Case Studies on the Political Power of Social Media, edited by and pp. 97–125. Cham, Zwitzerland: Springer International Publishing.

Akmaliah, W. 2018. "Bukan sekedar penggaung (buzzers): media sosial dan transformasi arena politik" [Beyond Buzzer: Social Media and Political Arena Transformation]. *MAARIF Journal* 13, no. 1: 9–25.

Amri, A.B., S. Ruqoyah, R. Nurbaya, R.S. Afrisia, T.A. Wibowo, R.J. Akbar and S. Ansyari. 2013. "Memburu @TrioMacan2000" [Hunting @TrioMacan2000]. *viva.co.id*. http://sorot.news.viva.co.id/news/read/415644-memburu--triomacan2000.

APJII. 2012. *Statistik Pengguna Internet di Indonesia 2012* [The 2012 Indonesian Internet Users Statistics]. Jakarta: APJII.

Aspinall, Edward. 2015. "Oligarchic Populism: Prabowo Subianto's Challenge to Indonesian Democracy". *Indonesia* 99: 1–28.

Asril, Sabrina. 2015. "16 politisi dan relawan Jokowi jadi komisaris, bahaya menanti BUMN" [16 Jokowi's Politicians and Volunteers Appointed as Commissionaires, Danger Awaits BUMN]. *Kompas.com*, 12 April 2015. http://nasional.kompas.com/read/2015/04/12/11412621/16.Politisi.dan.Relawan.Jokowi.Jadi.Komisaris.Bahaya.Menanti.BUMN.

BPS. 2012. *Jumlah Penduduk Menurut Provinsi 2012*. Jakarta: BPS.

Bradshaw, Samantha and Philip Howard. 2019. "The Global Disinformation Order: 2019 Global Inventory of Organised Social Media Manipulation". Working Paper 2. Oxford, UK: Project on Computational Propaganda. https://comprop.oii.ox.ac.uk/wp-content/uploads/sites/93/2019/09/CyberTroop-Report19.pdf.

Bramasta, Dandy Bayu. 2019. "Benarkah Ada Bayaran Buzzer Politik di Indonesia?" *Kompas.com*, 5 October 2019. https://www.kompas.com/tren/read/2019/10/05/163800465/benarkah-ada-bayaran-buzzer-politik-di-indonesia.

Bräuchler, Birgit. 2003. "Cyberidentities at War: Religion, Identity, and the Internet in the Moluccan Conflict". *Indonesia* 75: 123–51.

Fontana, Benedetto. 2008. "Power and Democracy: Gramsci and Hegemony in America". In *Perspectives on Gramsci: Politics, Culture and Social Theory*, edited by oseph pp. 80–96. London and New York: Routledge.

Gazali, Effendi. 2014. "Learning by Clicking: An Experiment with Social Media Democracy in Indonesia". *International Communication Gazette* 76, nos. 4–5: 425–39.

Gramsci, Antonio. 1971. *Selections from the Prison Notebooks of Antonio Gramsci*. New York: International Publishers.

Hadiz, Vedi R. 2010. *Localising Power in Post-Authoritarian Indonesia: A Southeast Asia Perspective*. Stanford, CA: Stanford University Press.

Hamburger, Martin. 2001. "The Business of Political Consulting". In *Campaign Warriors: The Roles of Political Consultants in Election*, edited by James A.

Thurber and Candice J. Nelson, pp. 37–52. Washington, D.C.: Brookings Institution Press.

Hameed, Shahiraa Sahul. 2007. "Internet Deployment in the 2004 Indonesian Presidential Elections". In *The Internet and National Elections: A Comparative Study of Web Campaigning*, vol. 2, edited by Randolph Kluver, Nicholas W. Jankowski, Kirsten A. Foot and Steven M. Schneider, pp. 194–209. Milton Park, Abingdon, OX: Routlege.

Herdiansah, Ari Ganjar. 2019. "Political Participation Convergence in Indonesia: A Study of Partisan Volunteers in the 2019 Election". *Jurnal Politik* 4, no. 2: 263–96.

Heriyanto, Devina. 2019. "The Rise of 'Kadrun' and 'Togog': Why Political Polarization in Indonesia is Far from Over". *Jakarta Post*, 20 November 2019. https://www.thejakartapost.com/news/2019/11/19/the-rise-of-kadrun-and-togog-why-political-polarization-in-indonesia-is-far-from-over.html.

Hill, David T. 2003. "Communication for a New Democracy: Indonesia's First Online Elections". *The Pacific Review* 16, no. 4: 525–48.

Hill, David T. and Krishna Sen. 2000. "The Internet in Indonesia's New Democracy". *Democratization* 7, no. 1: 119–36. https://doi.org/10.1080/13510340008403648.

———. 2005. *The Internet in Indonesia's New Democracy*. Chicago: Routledge.

Insight, Markplus. 2012. "Pengguna Internet di Indonesia 55 juta" [55 millions of Indonesian Internet Users].

Ismail, Taufik. 2014. "Relawan serahkan daftar calon menteri hasil polling ke Jokowi" [Volunteers Submit the List of Opinion Polling Results of Ministerial Candidates to Jokowi]. *Tribunnews.com*, 4 September 2014. http://www.tribunnews.com/nasional/2014/09/04/relawan-serahkan-daftar-calon-menteri-hasil-polling-ke-jokowi.

Lamb, Kate. 2018. "'I Felt Disgusted': Inside Indonesia's Fake Twitter Account Factories". *The Guardian*, 23 July 2018. https://www.theguardian.com/world/2018/jul/23/indonesias-fake-twitter-account-factories-jakarta-politic.

Lilin, Anastasia Y., Umar Idris and Andri Indradie. 2013. "Klik, pundi-pundi para buzzer pun terisi" [Click, the Buzzers' Pocket Filled in]. *Kontan.co.id*, 6 November 2013. http://industri.kontan.co.id/news/klik-pundi-pundi-para-buzzer-pun-terisi.

Lim, Merlyna. 2003. "From Real to Virtual (and Back Again)". In *Asia.com: Asia Encounters the Internet*, edited by K.C. Ho, Randy Kluver, and C.C. Yang, pp. 113–42. London: Routledge.

———. 2013. "Many Clicks But Little Sticks: Social Media Activism in Indonesia". *Journal of Contemporary Asia* 43, no. 4: 1–22.

———. 2017. "Freedom to Hate: Social Media, Algorithmic Enclaves, and the Rise of Tribal Nationalism in Indonesia". *Critical Asian Studies* 49, no. 3: 411–27.

Mosco, Vincent. 2009. *The Political Economy of Communication*. 2nd ed. London: SAGE.

Nailufar, Nibras Nada. 2016. "Cerita pencalonan Ahok dan mundurnya Boy Sadikin dari PDI-P" [The Story of Ahok's Nomination and the Withdrawal of Boy Sadikin from PDI-P]. *Kompas.com*, 23 September 2016. http://megapolitan.kompas.com/read/2016/09/23/08401801/cerita.pencalonan.ahok.dan.mundurnya.boy.sadikin.dari.pdi-p.

———. 2019. "Buka-bukaan soal buzzer (1): Pengakuan Denny Siregar dan Pepih Nugraha soal buzzer Istana" [Coming Clean on Buzzer (1): The Confession of Denny Siregar and Pepih Nugraha on the Palace's Buzzers]. *Kompas.com*, 9 October 2019. https://www.kompas.com/tren/read/2019/10/09/060029265/buka-bukaan-soal-buzzer-1-pengakuan-denny-siregar-dan-pepih-nugraha-soal?page=all.

Nugroho, Yanuar and Sofie Shinta Syarief. 2012. *Beyond Click-Activism? New Media and Political Processes in Contemporary Indonesia*. Jakarta: Friedrich-Ebert-Stiftung.

Nurhadryani, Yani, Sebastian Maslow and Hiraku Yamamoto. 2009. "Democracy 1.0' Meets 'Web 2.0': E-Campaigning and the Role of ICTs in Indonesia's Political Reform Process since 1998". *Interdisciplinary Information Sciences* 15, no. 2: 211–22. https://doi.org/10.4036/iis.2009.211.

Paramaditha, Andjarsari. 2013. "In Indonesia, Buzzers are Not Heard, but Tweet for Money". Reuters, 23 August 2013. http://www.reuters.com/article/2013/08/22/net-us-indonesia-twitter-idUSBRE97L14T20130822.

Patrick, Jonathan. 2019. "Uang panas industri buzzer politik" [Dirty Money of the Political Buzzer Industry]. *CNN Indonesia*, 10 January 2019. https://www.cnnindonesia.com/teknologi/20181210015450-185-352341/uang-panas-industri-buzzer-politik.

Prasongko, Dias. 2019. "Pendiri Watchdoc Dandhy Laksono disangka melanggar UU ITE" [Watchdoc Founder Dandhy Laksono Accused of Violating ITE Law]. *Tempo.co*, 27 September 2019. https://nasional.tempo.co/read/1252892/pendiri-watchdoc-dandhy-laksono-disangka-melanggar-uu-ite.

Qodari, Muhammad. 2010. "The Professionalisation of Politics: The Growing Role of Polling Organisations and Political Consultants". In *Problems of Democratisation in Indonesia: Elections, Institutions and Society*, edited by arcusanddwardpp. 122–40. Singapore: Institute of Southeast Asian Studies.

Rahmawati, Indriani. 2014. "Social Media, Politics, and Young Adults: The Impact of Social Media Use on Young Adults' Political Efficacy, Political Knowledge, and Political Participation towards 2014 Indonesia General Election". Masters thesis, University of Twente.

Renaldi, Adi. 2018. "Ngobrol Bareng Koordinator Bot dan Buzzer, Pemicu Polarisasi Politik Makin Panas Jelang 2019" [Conversing with Bot and Buzzer Coordinator, the Trigger of Increasing Political Polarisation Head of 2019 (Elections)]. *Vice.com*, 8 November 2018. https://www.vice.com/id_id/article/vbaga9/ngobrol-bareng-koordinator-bot-dan-buzzer-pemicu-polarisasi-politik-makin-panas-jelang-2019.

Riana, Friski. 2019. "Membongkar rahasia dapur buzzer" [Uncovering the Secrets of Buzzer]. *Tempo.co*, 5 October 2019. https://nasional.tempo.co/read/1255955/membongkar-rahasia-dapur-buzzer/full&view=ok.

Sadasri, Lidwina Mutia. 2016. "Micro-celebrity: Menakar kajian ilmu komunikasi dalam media baru". In *Ilmu Sosial di Indonesia: Perkembangan dan Tantangan*, edited by Widjajanti Mulyono pp. 433–79. Jakarta: Yayasan Pustaka Obor.

Sani, Ahmad Faiz Ibnu. 2019. "Setelah politikus, Jokowi undang buzzer dan influencer ke Istana" [After Politicians, Jokowi Invites Buzzers and Influencers to the Palace]. *Tempo.co*, 5 July 2019. https://pilpres.tempo.co/read/1221350/setelah-politikus-jokowi-undang-buzzer-dan-influencer-ke-istana.

Saragih, Selamat. 2016. "PDIP dan Teman Ahok Berseberangan" [PDIP and Friends of Ahok in Opposition]. *Mediaindonesia.com*, 22 February 2016. https://mediaindonesia.com/read/detail/30095-pdip-dan-teman-ahok-berseberangan.

Sefsani, Ririn and Patrick Ziegenhain. 2015. "Civil-Society Support: A Decisive Factor in the Indonesian Presidential Elections in 2014". *ASIEN* 136: 14–33.

Semiocast. 2012. "Twitter Reaches Half a Billion Accounts", 30 July 2012. http://semiocast.com/en/publications/2012_07_30_Twitter_reaches_half_a_billion_accounts_140m_in_the_US.

Steele, Janet E. 2005. *Wars Within: The Story of Tempo, an Independent Magazine in Soeharto's Indonesia*. Jakarta: Equinox Publishing.

Steinfield, Charles W., Joan M. DiMicco, Nicole B. Ellison and Cliff Lampe. 2009. "Bowling Online: Social Networking and Social Capital Within the Organization". *C&T '09: Proceedings of the Fourth International Conference on Communities and Technologies* (June): 245–54.

Stockwell, Stephen E. 2002. "Taxonomy of the Political Campaign". Paper presented at the ANZCA 2002 Conference: Communication: Reconstructed for the 21st Century, Coolangatta, 10–12 July 2002.

Strick, Benjamin and Elise Thomas. 2019. "Investigating Information Operations in West Papua: A Digital Forensic Case Study of Cross-Platform Network Analysis". *Bellingcat.com*, 11 October 2019. https://www.bellingcat.com/news/rest-of-world/2019/10/11/investigating-information-operations-

in-west-papua-a-digital-forensic-case-study-of-cross-platform-network-analysis/.
Strick, Benjamin and Famega Syavira. 2019. "Papua: Cara kerja jaringan bot penyebar hoaks soal Papua dengan biaya miliaran rupiah" [Papua: The Procedure of the Bot Network Spreading Hoax about Papua costs billion of Rupiah]. BBC News Indonesia, 9 October 2019. https://www.bbc.com/indonesia/indonesia-49969337.
Suaedy, Ahmad. 2014. "The Role of Volunteers and Political Participation in the 2012 Jakarta Gubernatorial Election". *Journal of Current Southeast Asian Affairs* 33, no. 1: 111–38.
Sulaiman, Sultan Andiha. 2017. "Komunikasi Politik JASMEV: studi terhadap kampanye politik JASMEV 2017 sebagai buzzer di era demokrasi digital pada Pilgub DKI Jakarta 2017" [JASMEV Political Communication: A Study of JASMEV 2017 Political Campaign as Buzzers in the Era of Digital Democracy During the 2017 Jakarta Gubernatorial Election]. (Bachelor), UIN Syarif Hidayatullah, Jakarta.
Suwana, Fiona. 2018. *Digital Media and Indonesian Young People: Building Sustainable Democratic Institutions and Practices*. Brisbane: Queensland University of Technology.
Syakriah, Ardila. 2019. "We are pro-Indonesia: InsightID responds to Facebook's statement". *Jakarta Post*, 10 October 2019. https://www.thejakartapost.com/news/2019/10/10/we-are-pro-indonesia-insightid-responds-to-facebooks-statement.html.
Tarigan, Mitra. 2012. "Pengikut Triomacan2000 lampaui Benny_israel" [Triomacan2000 Followers Exceeds Benny_israel's]. *Tempo.co*, 24 June 2012. http://www.tempo.co/read/news/2012/06/24/078412556/pengikut-triomacan2000-lampaui-benny-israel.
Tehusijarana, Karina M. 2019. "She Tweeted about the Attack on Papuan Students. Now, She is State Enemy No. 1". *Jakarta Post*, 6 September 2019. https://www.thejakartapost.com/news/2019/09/06/she-informs-the-world-about-the-situation-in-papua-now-she-is-state-enemy-no-1.html.
Tempo. 2014. "Simpatisan dari seberang" [Supporter from the Other Side]. *Majalah Tempo*, 30 June 2014. https://majalah.tempo.co/read/laporan-khusus/145707/simpatisan-dari-seberang?
———. 2019. "Saatnya menertibkan buzzers" [It is Time to Curb Buzzers]. *Tempo.co.*, 28 September 2019. https://majalah.tempo.co/read/opini/158488/saatnya-menertibkan-buzzer.
Thurber, James A. and Candice J. Nelson. 2000. *Campaign Warriors: Political Consultants in Elections*. Washington, D.C: Brookings Institution Press.
Trianita, Linda Novi. 2019. "Ada Denny Siregar, Antasari Azhar tepis isu grup Taliban di KPK". *Tempo.co*, 26 June 2019. https://nasional.tempo.

co/read/1218520/ada-denny-siregar-antasari-azhar-tepis-isu-grup-taliban-di-kpk.

Utomo, Ariane, Anna Reimondos, Iwu Utomo, Peter McDonald and Terence H. Hull. 2013. "Digital Inequalities and Young Adults in Greater Jakarta: A Socio-Demographic Perspective". *International Journal of Indonesian Studies* 1: 79–109.

Widodo, Yohanes. 2011. "Citizen Journalism and Media Pluralism in Indonesia". In *Social Justice and Rule of Law: Addressing the Growth of a Pluralist Indonesian Democracy*, edited by Thomas J. Conners, Frank Dhont, Mason C. Hoadley and Adam D. Tyson. Semarang: Diponegoro University Press.

Yusron, Ulin. 2012. "Wawancara eksklusif dengan Raden Nuh, admin akun @TrioMacan2000" [Exclusive Interview with Raden Nuh, Admin @ TrioMacan2000 Account]. *Beritasatu.com*, 14 November 2012. http://www.beritasatu.com/nasional/82991-wawancara-eksklusif-dengan-raden-nuh-admin-akun-triomacan2000.html.

4

DISINFORMATION AS A RESPONSE TO THE "OPPOSITION PLAYGROUND" IN MALAYSIA

Niki Cheong

Malaysia's adoption of disinformation was part of a gradual response by the Barisan Nasional (BN) government to an online space perceived to be dominated by pro-opposition forces. The ruling Barisan Nasional coalition[1]—and by extension, the state—adopted social media as part of its communication strategy in the late 2000s. But it realized that those efforts were not sufficient to win over online sentiment in what was considered the "opposition's playground" (Leong 2019). This turn to disinformation was most evident in the 2013 General Election (GE13) campaign. In the previous general election of 2008, the pervasiveness of new communication technologies, such as online news sites and blogs, was credited as having contributed to Barisan Nasional's loss of its two-thirds majority in Parliament, only the second time[2] this had occurred since the country gained independence in 1957 (Hah 2012; Ndoma and Tumin 2011). As GE13 approached, Barisan Nasional feared similar results, and was fending off strong sentiments of distrust at the establishment pushed by the *Bersih*³ social movement calling for free and fair elections.

The wave of anti-Barisan Nasional sentiment among many urban, Peninsula social media users, alongside years of efforts by opposition parties and civil society groups to target the ruling coalition on internet platforms, led to more concerted measures from the state, including turning to disinformation practices (Ding, Koh and Surin 2013; Johns and Cheong 2019; Muhamad 2015). The BN state thus increasingly tried to control the flow of information and communicative practices on the internet, including tightening up media regulation and introduction of new laws, surveillance and threats, and censorship. Furthermore, this period saw the establishment of government-linked "cybertroopers" to counter opposition sentiment. Despite the emergence of cybertroopers, the anti-Barisan Nasional sentiment on social media continued towards the end of the 2010s, amplified by the domestic and international accusation of corruption associated with Prime Minister Najib Razak. At the next general election in 2018 (GE14), Barisan Nasional would lose power for the first time in the nation's history.

Barisan Nasional's disinformation campaigns could not hold up against two decades of the "opposition playground", bucking the trend in the Southeast Asian region where many elite ruling regimes have remained firmly in power. This chapter provides some answers as to how Malaysia became this anomaly. At a time when disinformation has spread globally, Malaysia's ruling semi-authoritarian government failed to take advantage of these practices. I argue that the ruling power's effectiveness of its disinformation campaigns was limited because: first, "outsourcing" social media sentiment to cybertroopers ultimately failed; second, closed-messaging platforms were unable to be controlled; and third, worldwide condemnation of kleptocracy could not be ignored.

SOCIAL MEDIA ACTIVISM AND OPPOSITION POLITICS

Under BN rule, Malaysian opposition parties competed in a weak electoral system stifled from media control, malapportionment, gerrymandering, and pervasive practices of money politics such as vote buying (Chan 2018; Saravanamuttu and Mohamad 2019; Weiss 2013). However, the rapid increase of internet penetration since the late 1990s—

allowed both the increasingly strong opposition force and the "vibrant" civil society to comment on and criticize Barisan Nasional (Weiss 2009, p. 742) and the weaknesses and unfairness in the electoral system. The introduction of a largely free internet environment in Malaysia played an important role in shaping political discourse.

In 1996, then-Prime Minister Mahathir Mohamed decided not to censor the internet in order to grow Malaysia's economy, with the aim to see through "Vision 2020", his goal for Malaysia to achieve fully developed status by the year 2020. The ten-point Multimedia Bill of Guarantees was then introduced, one of which promised that there would be no censorship of the internet. The guarantees were made in attempts to lure foreign entities to invest in Malaysia's Multimedia Super Corridor—originally envisioned as the Asian Silicon Valley—set up in 1995 to attract IT and multimedia companies (Weiss 2012). This meant Malaysians were able to be more critical of Barisan Nasional online than they could via traditional media platforms. The award-winning *Malaysiakini*—founded in 1999—is one such example of an alternative online news site that had considerable success employing what George (2006) describes as "contentious journalism" in order to attempt to hold the government accountable.

Many individuals in Malaysia also took to the internet to document political life or to exercise their freedoms of expression. Blogs in particular were said to have played an important role: Sabri Zain's blog *Reformasi Diary* is considered one of the most significant documentations of the *Reformasi* (reformation) movement which followed the sacking of Deputy Prime Minister Anwar Ibrahim in 1998 by Mahathir. Scholars like Khoo (2016, p. 82) note that similar to *Malaysiakini*'s journalists, Sabri was one of the early activists to publicly—using his own name—provide "biting" online commentary about the events happening on the streets. Politicians also took to blogging to speak out against Barisan Nasional. In 2008, even retired Prime Minister Mahathir Mohamad started blogging because he felt the government-controlled media did not report his opinions during the term of his successor Abdullah Ahmad Badawi (Hounshell 2008).

Social media was introduced in the late 2000s and continued the role of "new" media in Malaysia to promote various social movements. During this time, the role of social media in Malaysia was being compared to the Middle East and North Africa during the so-called "Arab Spring", and the "Occupy Movement" in the United States. Postill (2014), for example, argues that social media platforms empowered and connected opposition voices and Malaysian activists to help movements such as HINDRAF (Hindu Rights Action Force) and *Bersih* to gather momentum.

Bersih is arguably the most successful social movement in Malaysia, bringing hundreds of thousands of Malaysians to the streets pushing for electoral reforms. The movement began in 2005 as a joint-action group consisting of opposition political parties, civil society groups and non-governmental organizations. By 2011, the organizers rebranded itself as a non-partisan movement and would organize another four political rallies over the decade, spreading its influence across the globe. Indeed, the movement's "embeddedness in social media" (Welsh 2011, p. 2) did not just mobilize the hundreds of thousands of citizens to rally on the streets in Malaysia but also Malaysians living in other countries around the world, dubbed as "Global *Bersih*". The coming together of Malaysians and other supporters of the movement around the world on the internet has led to what Lim (2017, p. 221) calls "a nation that is a crisscrossing of multiple solidarities online".

Bersih's success in energizing citizens to stand-up against Barisan Nasional was a result of the organizers building on the pro-opposition sentiments that had been manifesting online for a decade. Political opponents of Barisan Nasional kept up their effective use of the internet to gain and mobilize supporters after having been locked out of the mainstream media landscape for decades. The "opposition playground" thus did not only include political parties, but flourished with contributions from the aforementioned alternative news outlets, non-governmental organizations as well as bloggers and other activists whose values and expressions were not consistent with Barisan Nasional's.

Among the social media campaigns included the more partisan *Asalkan Bukan UMNO* (Anyone But UMNO[4]) led by activist Hishamuddin Rais who was active in the *Reformasi* movement, and the non-partisan *PerlembagaanKu* (MyConstitution, or MyConsti) organized by the Bar Council, which regulates the profession of lawyers. While these are generally not affiliated to any political parties, the campaigns are consistent with some of the pro-democratic values seemingly espoused by the opposition parties. The MyConsti campaign in 2009, for example, aimed at simplifying the Federal Constitution for Malaysians. Then, there were also other efforts such as *UndiMsia!* (Vote Malaysia) in 2011, organized by Loyar Buruk, a group of lawyers seeking to build communities of young people mobilizing their peers to vote. Momentum was clearly building for a grand coalition of forces all around the country which allied themselves as "anti-Barisan Nasional" and generally promoted the goals of a more democratic Malaysia, thus threatening the ruling government's legitimacy.

OPPOSITION CAMPAIGNING AND ELECTION BATTLES

By the 2013 election, political discourse in Malaysia was increasingly mediated on social media, and became increasingly crucial to a national election campaign. Barisan Nasional still won the election in 2013, but they lost both their crucial two-thirds majority in parliament (as they had in 2008) and the popular vote, leaving them open to accusations of malapportionment in order to maintain power. Other factors identified by scholars include the deeply entrenched communal politics, the extent of BN's political machinery and wallet promoting vote buying, and the coalition's effective incentivization strategies targeting rural Malay areas (Chin 2013; Pepinsky 2013; Weiss 2013).

Thus, social media alone was not sufficient to defeat the incumbent, although it did help the opposition make in-roads, particularly in the more urban parts of Malaysia such as Penang, Selangor and Perak, where there are higher internet penetration rates. Some scholars caution giving too much value to the urban-rural "internet penetration" divide, however. Weiss (2013) argues that the findings in this area are inconsistent, as many voters who migrated to cities returned to their "rural" hometowns to vote, buoyed by campaigns such as *Balik Undi* (return home to vote) which found significant traction online.

When Barisan Nasional lost the popular vote at GE13, the electoral reform demands called for by *Bersih* in the preceding years (such as the cleaning up of the electoral roll, reforming the postal ballot process, use of indelible ink during elections, and a minimum of twenty-one days campaign period) took centre stage. The sacked former Deputy Prime Minister Anwar, by now leading the opposition Pakatan Rakyat (People's Alliance), used social media to mobilize support for the Blackout 505 rally to protest the election results within days of the results (Gomez 2013). During the election period, radio announcers from the Malaysian Chinese Association (MCA)-owned Chinese-language station 988 FM staged a silent protest on Facebook by updating their profile picture with black and white photographs in response to its owner's decision to run scathing political attacks on the opposition parties. That same year, *Bersih* held a People's Tribunal to collect testimonies from the public of election irregularities and its report widely condemned the Electoral Commission (Chan 2018).

Thus, the reform movement continued to gain momentum in the aftermath of the 2013 elections. In 2014, the government faced criticisms both in print and online—domestically and internationally—of its handling of the MH370 incident, where the Malaysian Airlines aeroplane disappeared (Mohd Azizuddin 2015). By the 2015 *Bersih* rally, again mobilized on social media, the organizers added an additional call for the resignation of Prime Minister Najib amid accusations that he was guilty of corruption related to the state-owned investment corporation 1Malaysia Development Berhad (1MDB). An image created by artist-activist Fahmi Redza depicting Najib's face as a clown was posted on social media and soon went viral (Lee 2017), leading to the artist later being sentenced to one-month's jail and fined RM30,000.

The anti-Najib sentiment in the online space would carry on until the 14th General Election. In 2016, *Bersih* again demanded his resignation and electoral reform, in anticipation of a general election being called, by way of a three-day rally leading up to Hari Merdeka (Independence Day) which was backed up by a strong digital campaign (Azlan 2018). At the rally, former Prime Minister Mahathir—who had taken to his blog to attack Najib—showed up unexpectedly on two different days, sending protestors and the media into a frenzy (Lee 2017). This show of solidarity with the perceived "opposition" pre-empted the Save Malaysia movement that was announced later that year, bringing together Mahathir and his former political rivals, some of whom had suffered under his previous use of draconian laws to detain them (Case 2017). Using the #SaveMalaysia and #SelamatkanMalaysia hashtags, the campaign called for the public to sign a "Citizens' Declaration" calling for Najib's resignation.

This campaign would set down the roots for the pact among opposition parties (including Mahathir's new party Parti Pribumi

Bersatu Malaysia, or Bersatu) to form Pakatan Harapan for the 2018 election. The use of social media featured heavily in the opposition's campaign in 2018, particularly taking advantage of Facebook's live streaming feature which allowed them to show the strength of support at rallies nationwide (Nadzri 2018). On the night before polling day, both Najib and Mahathir gave simultaneous speeches in their respective constituencies. As has always been the case, Najib could rely on the traditional media and his speech was broadcast live on state television. Mahathir, on the other hand, used Facebook Live to reach an impressive 15 million viewers—just shy of half of Malaysia's population.

This section has argued that social media has been central to activism in Malaysia, which has moved directly to the political realm and where a national election allows for the coalescence of anti-government forces to solidify their demands and rally for reforms. Facebook and Twitter in particular were used to organize mass protests, most notably the *Bersih* rallies, which led to hundreds of thousands of people protesting on the streets. Images of these masses dressed all in yellow were circulated widely on the internet. Barisan Nasional played down the numbers of protestors, but the pictures circulated widely on the internet proved otherwise, showing streets packed with people all dressed in yellow. Later, social media commentary, memes and other information shared on Facebook and WhatsApp were essential in exposing the corruption scandal surrounding Prime Minister Najib. As social media platforms grew, the opposition's cause became more accessible to a wider range of citizens, bridging the traditional urban-rural divide. Thus, new digital technologies have undoubtedly assisted the opposition forces and civil society. It is in this context that disinformation production became prominent and eventually normalized in the country.

BARISAN NASIONAL RESPONDS

Barisan Nasional realized that they had to engage more actively with social media platforms. Prime Minister Najib increasingly made social media platforms a key feature of his communication strategy, even in the 2013 elections. He created the *Ah Jib Gor* (big brother Najib) Fan Club, using Facebook to chat with staff and students of a Chinese vernacular school in efforts to appeal to the Chinese community (Hah 2016). He asked the public to pose questions to him on Facebook and

Twitter using #tanyanajib (ask Najib) before answering them via videos on YouTube (Mohd Azizuddin 2014). He organized "tea parties" to meet his supporters, borrowing from the tradition of a "tweetup"—gatherings mobilized via Twitter (Hopkins 2014). But as this chapter has shown, these attempts at engaging with online popular culture could not fend off the criticisms of ineffective governance and lack of confidence in the ruling party. Najib then turned to disinformation production, which was growing globally as a campaign tool.

Cybertroopers

Barisan Nasional clearly needed to take a more aggressive approach in their online strategy and became more proactive when it came to practices associated with social media campaigning and discourse. This included mobilizing pro-government agents on the internet known locally as "cybertroopers". Media reports of cybertroopers in Malaysian media date back to 2004—generally associated with UMNO—although there are indications that these agents have been involved in pro-BN activities on the internet as far back as the 1990s. George (2003, para. 260) notes that BN-linked activists were spreading pro-government messages on websites and bulletin boards in the mid-1990s, "to counter what they felt were unbalanced, ill-informed and irresponsible opinions circulating in cyberspace". Tun Faisal Ismail Aziz, who headed UMNO's New Media Unit in the late 2000s and was believed to be responsible for the mobilization of some pro-government cybertroopers, claims to have been involved in cyber warfare for the party in 1999, where he "fought our wars, put forth our thoughts" through chatrooms, mailing lists and online groups (Tan 2013).

While in the 1990s they did not refer to themselves as cybertroopers, the descriptions above are consistent with the 2004 news report calling them "cyber activists" whose role was to participate in a "cyber war" to correct alleged lies and slander posted online by "the Opposition" (*New Straits Times* 2004). Many of these activists operated as bloggers in the early to mid-2000s, leading up to GE12 in 2008. Tun Faisal confirmed in an interview on BFM Radio prior to the 2013 election that UMNO's cyber war shifted to websites and blogs in the noughties, in part, "to counter false allegations, slanders and lies by the opposition" (Tan 2013). Scholarship discussing the existence of cybertroopers indicates that these agents were initially mobilized in a more defensive role, countering pro-opposition messages—tracking blogs and monitoring online discourse as part of efforts to "to fend off attacks and respond to political attacks" (Mohamed et al. 2011, p. 19).

Social media's rise in the late 2000s coincided with Barisan Nasional's dismal results at GE12 in 2008; it was in this period that cybertroopers became more pro-active in their attempts to go beyond just defence in order to balance out online sentiment. This attempt to even out the social media playing field continued into the early part of the new decade, leading up to GE13 in 2013. Scholarship discussing cybertroopers during this period refers to units set up to manage Barisan Nasional's image in the online space (Ding, Koh and Surin 2013), and to balance "the temperature which has been favourable to the opposition" (Badrul Azmier, Mohammad Agus and Zaliha 2014, p. 110). However, all indications suggest that this practice overlapped with more aggressive behaviour from cybertroopers as the general elections period approached.[5] Between 2011—the year of the second *Bersih* rally—and GE13 in 2013, cybertroopers took on a more attacking stance, describing some of the practices in militaristic terms (Leong 2015; Zakaria 2014). Studies of GE13 indicate that cybertroopers were more actively slandering their opponents (Tapsell 2013), with Badrul Azmier, Mohammad Agus and Zaliha (2014, p. 109) noting that these agents adopted "provocative-style writing and communication which were in contrast to the friendly image of leaders".

My findings from an empirical study into cybertroopers, which included the analysis of hundreds of emails from a mailing list distributing pro-BN content and instructions between 2012 and 2014, confirmed the observations of the aforementioned literature (Cheong 2019). The tone of the emails in itself indicates the shift from defence to attack; early communication claims that the mailing list was simply an effort to "assist" the government to win the "coming" GE13 but eventually transformed into an instructional platform with regular "deployment strategies" communication. The content found in these instructional emails—clearly crafted for dissemination on both blogs and social media platforms such as Twitter—were a mix of pro-BN propaganda and negative messages against parties associated with Pakatan Rakyat. Instructions were also given for coordinated social media targeting and attacks on key opposition politicians such as then-opposition leader Anwar Ibrahim.

Concurrently, cybertroopers were deployed to maintain this "chilling effect" on social media users online. Among messages they posted during the *Bersih 3: Duduk Bantah* (Sit-in) in 2012 were calls for the authorities to arrest participants of the "illegal" rally, who they considered to be "traitors" (Johns and Cheong 2019). In her study on protests spaces in Malaysia, Azlan (2018, pp. 23–24) argues that Barisan Nasional's attempt at control of the "digital and material space" to be running parallel, noting that "cybertroopers were disrupting protest exchanges on Twitter". These activities jell most closely with manipulative practices associated with disinformation practices also conducted in other parts of the world, particularly in less liberal countries such as China, Azerbaijan, Russia and Hungary (Calingaert 2010; Gero and Kopper 2013; Hung 2010; Pearce 2015). Not all the content crafted for dissemination were false, but there was a clear use of negative spin as a tactic to attack and vilify Barisan Nasional's opponents.

In the years following GE13, the mobilization of cybertroopers became more hostile. In line with global trends of political regimes relying on automated accounts for online manipulation of information in recent years (Woolley and Howard 2019), bots were also found to be heavily used by Barisan Nasional during GE14. Within the first few days of the campaigning period, researchers found thousands of pro-government bots disrupting Twitter conversations in Malaysia (Azlan 2018). Some scholars have argued that efforts by cybertroopers were successful in moderating *Bersih*'s social media effectiveness and that the chilling effect had successfully made citizens more cautious about what they post online, at least in some cases (Johns and Cheong 2019; Tapsell 2018).

Draconian Laws

These disinformation practices engaged by cybertroopers were not used in isolation but were very much part of a larger Barisan Nasional strategy at controlling information in the country. Even before Najib's regime, former Malaysian leaders Mahathir and Abdullah Badawi clamped down on opposition and civil society leaders and journalists via a range of draconian laws. Not long after Najib became Prime Minister in 2009, the Malaysian Communication and Multimedia Commission requested *Malaysiakini* to remove clips that were "provocative and offensive" (Gomez and Chan 2010, p. 7). Staff at the news outlet were hauled in for a three-day investigation when they refused to remove the clip.

While Najib initially committed his government to the promise of a free internet (Chooi 2011), the reality could not be any more different. While in power, Najib took advantage of existing laws that had been introduced by his predecessors to control the broadcast media and the internet such as the Communications and Multimedia Act 1998. Even when he finally repealed the Internal Security Act, the archaic law was replaced with the Security Offenses (Special Measures) Act 2012 (SOSMA) which still allowed for detention without trial. As expected, criticism online and offline were rife, and the prime minister was forced to promise that the new SOSMA law—claimed to have been drafted to respond to terrorism threats—would not be used for political reasons (Varkkey 2017). Nonetheless, the law continued to be used by Barisan Nasional, including former *Bersih* chairperson Maria Chin Abdullah in 2016.

In the years following GE13, Najib would tighten his iron fist even more. This was likely due to pressures he was facing internally within UMNO—led by Mahathir—for him to be ousted due to the dismal results by Barisan Nasional at the elections in 2013, and externally as accusations of kleptocracy related to the siphoning of funds from 1MDB emerged in 2015.

Within the first eighteen months after the 13th General Election, over forty people were charged under the Sedition Act, while twenty-five students faced action under the Universities and University-Colleges Act for their participation in student activism (Hazis 2015). In 2015, whistleblowing website *The Sarawak Report* was blocked, and the Home Office suspended the licence of newspaper *The Edge* as a result of its reports on 1MDB. As a way of circumventing the ban, *The Sarawak Report* started posting its articles on online publishing platform *Medium*, which was subsequently blocked in 2016 for not removing an article critical of Najib (*Medium* 2016). That year, news portal *The Malaysian Insider* was also banned, showing how far Najib had shifted from his free-internet stance in just five years.

Threats of legal nature were now being used against individuals, hauled in for investigation and arrests over their comments and conversations on social media. One high profile case was cartoon satirist Zulkiflee Anwar Haque (or Zunar) who in 2015 was arrested and detained under the Sedition Act. Zunar had already previously been arrested for his drawings but the 2015 charges were related to postings he made on Twitter questioning the jailing of Anwar Ibrahim on sodomy charges (Blackstone 2015). These repressive laws had already resulted in social sanctioning to silence opposing views even among friends or colleagues on close-messaging applications. Johns and Cheong (2019) found that Malaysian youths were increasingly cautious about what they posted on social media even among networks of people they personally knew, while Tapsell (2018) cites one user who shocked members of his WhatsApp chat group by informing them that he was going to file a police report on materials shared in the group.

In Barisan Nasional's last act in its attempt to control the flow of information in Malaysia under its rule, Najib's government steamrolled through Parliament an Anti-Fake News Act just ahead of the 14th General Election of 2018. The law made spreading information deemed "fake" illegal both offline and online, and included specific mentions of Facebook and WhatsApp (Nadzri 2018). Within days of the election campaign period, Mahathir Mohamad—now competing against his old party—was investigated under the law (Fernandez 2019).

The rise of disinformation production in Malaysia is most exemplified in the case of Barisan Nasional's use of cybertroopers, which was conducted concurrently with crackdowns on the press and freedom of expression more broadly. The legal crackdowns were about silencing influential critics online, but stifling widespread anti-government discourse was more difficult and required new strategies that disinformation production provided. In this regard, from 2013 to 2018 Malaysia looked very much like other countries in Southeast Asia whereby a semi-authoritarian government hardened in the face of dissent, and utilized state funds to employ citizens to manipulate political discourse online. For a time, it seemed that social media disinformation might indeed be a benefit to Najib's increasingly heavy-handed rule, and was a factor in the regime's "resilience" (Welsh and Lopez 2018), given its ability to adapt to the shifting nature of social media production. But the fragility of the BN regime, and Najib's rule, was quickly exposed, as Malaysia's historic 2018 elections caused a spectacular result for opposition parties and their supporters.

MALAYSIA'S HISTORIC CHANGE OF GOVERNMENT

Despite all their efforts at neutralizing the "opposition playground", an increasingly desperate Barisan Nasional seemed one step behind their opponents on social media campaigning. By the general election of 2018, popular sentiment online had become fervently anti-Najib, due in large part to his 1MDB corruption scandal, and his Barisan Nasional coalition lost the election in a landslide. What does this tell us about BN's disinformation practices, if they ultimately lost the election? Why was social media campaigning by activists and the opposition so effective in Malaysia while elsewhere disinformation from the state was a useful tool in supporting authoritarian governments? In this section I answer these questions via two main arguments. The first is by understanding the nature of the Malaysian political regime, which is ultimately different to other regimes in Southeast Asia. The second is to highlight the role of new(er) technologies which entered Malaysia prior to the election; most notably encrypted messenger sites like WhatsApp which allowed for a shifting distribution of information and political discourse.

To understand the BN's fall in 2018, we must understand how Barisan Nasional—and by extension, Malaysia—has projected itself as a democratic country. Even in its most authoritarian years, the government of the day has operated under a veil of democracy as a form of legitimacy. In describing Malaysia as an authoritarian regime, Case (1993, p. 186) argues that Barisan Nasional has successfully brought together elements of soft dictatorship, with "the state's tolerating the formation of opposition parties and interest groups even as it closes off electoral routes and lobbying channels to state power" and hard democracy, which involves "the state's scrupulously calling elections while preventing opposition elements from organizing effectively to contest them". The use of legal mechanisms as threats generally works to maintain this notion of democracy in action. As an example, Anwar Ibrahim was twice jailed on sodomy charges, giving an excuse for two different prime ministers to put away their biggest political rivals at the time. Even the use of cybertroopers allowed Barisan Nasional to essentially get away with their disinformation practices by giving them plausible deniability from the mobilization of these agents of online manipulation.

Najib himself suggested that there was free reign for online discourse in Malaysia, pointing to cybertrooping from the opposition camp. In accusing his opponents, the then-prime minister wrote on his blog that "keyboard warriors, cyber troopers and even news portals have made the online world their 'playground', constructing their own version of 'reality' with click bait headlines that serve their own agendas" (Razak 2016, para. 3). A year later, when discussing his party's own cybertroopers, Najib was quoted as saying: "Members must be ready to defend the party in the cyber and digital world as cyber troopers" (Zakaria 2017, para. 9). Promoting this narrative allows Barisan Nasional to attempt to maintain that the election is free and fair, and both parties have access to the same set of resources, which of course is not the case in the mainstream media nor political party campaign funds among other discrepancies. This approach was similar to when Prime Minister Abdullah officially accredited online news sites such as *Malaysiakini*, giving them legitimacy for the first time. It gave the sense the media environment was open, when in reality *Malaysiakini* was an outlier, and most of the mainstream media was owned and controlled by the government.

The Barisan Nasional's encouragement of internet and social media use have allowed the pro-opposition voices to grow to an unprecedented scale. This impacted on social media campaigns that Najib had run. Once, when conducting a #tanyaNajib session to answer his supporters' questions, so many users had clicked on the thumbs down button on YouTube, and in response pro-BN cybertroopers were mobilized urgently to respond by clicking the thumbs up button instead (Cheong 2019). The sort of volume that Barisan Nasional was going up against—not just from opposition politicians but also from civil society and increasingly global media—also meant that its disinformation campaigns did not always get the traction it needed. Images and videos of police violence at the *Bersih* rallies, for example, outnumbered those posted by the police accusing protestors of disobedience. At the 2018 elections, news about how pro-Barisan Nasional social bots were found in large numbers by researchers quickly spread on social media and in the international media.

The people behind Barisan Nasional's online disinformation strategy were also facing numerous issues. Infighting among cybertroopers has previously been documented by scholars, with different factions within the party mobilizing their own teams. Hah (2016) found that in the mid-2000s, groups of pro-UMNO political bloggers had come together in what she refers to as the "band of brotherhood" with other bloggers from civil society and some opposition parties to pressure then-Prime Minister Abdullah to resign. These bloggers, Hah argues, were not pushing for a change of government but instead for a change of leadership within the party. Even among other parties in Barisan Nasional, cybertroopers have been accused of being used for factional attacks.[6]

The split in UMNO likely exacerbated this, especially if accusations linking the then-Chief Minister of Kedah Mukhriz Mahathir, who followed his father in quitting UMNO to set up Bersatu, to the disgraced Cambridge Analytica data analytics firm are anything to go by. Media organizations investigating Barisan Nasional's link to the company accused of harvesting Facebook user data to help political parties with their campaigns were told by the Prime Minister's Office that Mukhriz had previously been in contact with companies linked to Cambridge Analytica. At that time, Mukhriz denied the allegations; in early 2020, reports emerged into claims from leaked documents related to the firm's activities that other UMNO leaders—including then-Deputy Prime Minister Ahmad Zahid Hamidi—had been in discussions with the firm instead ahead of GE14.

Thus, Malaysia's politics became an increasingly competitive space, where unlike in Thailand or Singapore, a credible opposition was allowed to be formed, genuinely independent media companies were present and elite fractures were more prominent. This relatively competitive environment allowed for greater contestation than Najib wanted, but he still thought he had it under control. This was clearly not the case, as even Malaysia's seemingly robust electoral authoritarian regime was ultimately overthrown, as new parties were able to be formed and other parties joined in the opposition coalition, fanned by the flames of online discourse calling for the ousting of Najib as prime minister.

The second trend which contributed to the fall of the Barisan Nasional was the shift from open social media platforms to closed messaging groups or private accounts. Government surveillance on "open" platforms like Twitter and to a lesser extent Facebook were able to be monitored, but on closed messenger groups this was less possible.

It also meant that cybertroopers were excluded from conversation spaces, such as encrypted group chats on apps like WhatsApp and Telegram, which they previously could cause disruption (Johns 2020). In his assessment of social media use at GE14, Tapsell (2018) found that WhatsApp, among other social media platforms, was an important tool for resistance and a vessel through which details related to Najib's kleptocracy scandal were shared. This, he argues, was amplified by the increasing smartphone penetration beyond the urban population and into semi-rural communities that had for a long time remained elusive to the opposition parties.

Closed messenger groups allowed for the extensiveness of the 1MDB scandal to resonate, and Barisan Nasional's disinformation campaign was unable to counter it. In the years ahead of the elections, the ruling coalition tried to blame the criticisms on alleged opposition cybertroopers (Cheong 2019), but the scale of accusations coming from both local and international media meant that the excuse did not have much impact. In addition, investigations into the 1MDB case were opened in countries such as the United States, Singapore and Switzerland (Case 2017). While Najib used the sort of leverage Barisan Nasional leaders conventionally had access to domestically, such as by getting the Attorney General to dismiss the case against him, the global scale of the scandal meant that Barisan Nasional could not legitimately distract from the issue. These international reports were widely spread on closed messenger groups, and spread via social media platforms in the lead up and throughout the 2018 elections.

The corruption accusations against Najib—alongside the unpopularity of his wife Rosmah—affected the tone of online sentiment. The online space was no longer simply pro-opposition; it had morphed into an anti-Najib space. The "memefication" of satirical works by the likes of Fahmi Reza and Zunar, among others, were shared widely on social media platforms and closed WhatsApp groups. Barisan Nasional lost the narrative of social media discourse for a number of reasons, but this shift in platforms mattered greatly. The ruling coalition in general, and Najib Razak personally, were the subject of numerous jokes and memes, with details of the corruption spreading wide. No amount of disinformation, cybertrooping nor anti-fake news law were enough to stop the compelling narrative that Najib needed to be voted out of the Prime Minister's Office.

CONCLUSION

This chapter has argued that social media's presence has had significant consequences on the political discourse in Malaysia, and in this regard is consistent with global trends. Social media expanded the "opposition playground" via the Malaysian online political sphere at a scale never previously seen in the country. By helping social movements like *Bersih* grow both domestically and internationally, social media has also emboldened citizens to express themselves against a government that had long controlled the flow of information in the country. Collectively, these sentiments allowed the opposition parties to benefit from a trust deficit in Barisan Nasional, and later the Prime Minister Najib Razak himself, contributing to Pakatan Harapan's victory at the 2018 general election.

That unprecedented, and arguably unexpected, transition of power in 2018 makes Malaysia a central place for the discussion of the role of social media as a force for democracy. Social media undoubtedly contributed to a more democratic Malaysia. However, it would be unwise to assume that the battle against disinformation in the country has been won. As the various political parties flow in and out of power, they all engage in their own manipulative practices, including having their own teams of cybertroopers, a practice that has continued despite their inability to shape the 2018 election in the BN's favour.

It is also pertinent to note that Malaysia is not shielded from the global epidemic of post-truth politics and other emerging trends in disinformation. Najib's continued denial of his corruption in itself shows how disinformation—in the actual sense of the term—has already become part of mainstream politics. The former prime minister still uses social media to grow and retain his base of supporters, using hashtags among other features, to peddle the narrative that the accusations against him are politically driven. Even the discourse surrounding the existence of cybertroopers—the agents of disinformation in Malaysia—has shifted. As if to indicate the normalization of such practices, mentions of cybertroopers these days are greeted with a sense of resignation as just how things are in the current political climate.

In February 2020, Malaysian politics witnessed another shift of power with parties and factions from Pakatan Harapan controversially splitting with the coalition to form a new government with a few other parties including Barisan Nasional. With so many of BN's leaders in the Cabinet, led by Prime Minister Muhyiddin Yassin who was formerly with the BN, new forms of disinformation may emerge. For over a decade now, Malaysians have witnessed political parties, civil society groups and activists adapt their use of social media to alter the country's political landscape. However, while seemingly less effective, the previous Barisan Nasional's engagement in disinformation practices have also evolved alongside the advancement of new communication technologies—from forum and chat rooms to blogs, and from social media to chat apps. As technological advancement continues, political parties will turn to new campaign tools which become available to them, including disinformation. But hopeful Malaysians can at least count on history to remind them that social media adoption by political parties, civil society groups and individuals who share the same values have in the past managed to overcome disinformation practices.

NOTES

1. The Barisan Nasional Coalition consisted of three major parties: the United Malays National Organisation (UMNO), the Malaysian Chinese Association (MCA) and the Malaysian Indian Congress (MIC). It was founded in 1957 as the Alliance Party, which was renamed as Barisan Nasional in 1973 in the aftermath of the 1969 election.
2. The first was during the General Election in 1969, the results from which lead to the most significant racial riots the country has ever experienced.
3. *Bersih* means clean in Bahasa Melayu. The movement called for clean and fair elections in Malaysia.
4. UMNO is the largest party in the Barisan Nasional; until 2018, all of the past Malaysian prime ministers and their deputies were from that party.
5. Although GE13 was eventually held in May 2013, speculation that the Parliament would be dissolved to pave way for an early general election was a "constant theme in Malaysia for much of 2011" (O'Shannassy 2012, p. 165). Although he became prime minister in 2009, Najib Razak inherited the position when his predecessor resigned and as such, had not yet gone to the polls for his personal mandate.
6. According to media reports, former MCA leader Ong Tee Keat had claimed to being attacked online by teams of cybertroopers reporting to his successor Chua Soi Lek (Cheong 2019).

REFERENCES

Azlan, Nurul Azreen. 2018. "Seditious Spaces". In *A+BE: Architecture and the Built Environment*. Netherlands: Delft University of Technology. https://superheroscitech.tudelft.nl/index.php/abe/article/view/2661.

Badrul Azmier, Bakar, Mohammad Agus Yusoff and Hj Hussin Zaliha. 2014. "The Paradox of Social Media: The De-Democratization of Malaysia". *International Review of Basic and Applied Sciences* 2, no. 7: 104–12.

Blackstone, Helena. 2015. "Thrown in Prison for Drawing Cartoons". *The Independent*, 27 October 2015.

Calingaert, Daniel. 2010. "Authoritarianism vs. the Internet". *Policy Review* 160: 63–75.

Case, William. 1993. "Semi-Democracy in Malaysia: Withstanding the Pressures for Regime Change". *Pacific Affairs* 66, no. 2: 183–205. https://doi.org/10.2307/2759366.

———. 2017. "Stress Testing Leadership in Malaysia: The 1MDB Scandal and Najib Tun Razak". *The Pacific Review* 30, no. 5: 633–54. https://doi.org/10.1080/09512748.2017.1282538.

Chan, Tsu Chong. 2018. "Democratic Breakthrough in Malaysia – Political Opportunities and the Role of Bersih". *Journal of Current Southeast Asian Affairs* 37, no. 3: 109–37. https://journals.sub.uni-hamburg.de/giga/jsaa/article/view/1150/1157.

Cheong, Niki. 2019. "Cybertroopers and the Online Manipulation of Political Communication: The Barisan Nasional Years". PhD thesis, University of Nottingham.

Chin, James. 2013. "So Close and Yet So Far: Strategies in the 13th Malaysian Elections". *The Round Table* 102, no. 6: 533–40. https://doi.org/10.1080/00358533.2013.857145.

Chooi, Clara. 2011. "Najib Repeats Promise of No Internet Censorship". *The Malaysian Insider*, 24 April 2011. http://www.themalaysianinsider.com/malaysia/article/najib-repeats-promise-of-no-internet-censorship.

Ding, Jo-Ann, Lay Chin Koh and Jacqueline Ann Surin. 2013. *Mapping Digital Media: Malaysia*. London: Open Society Foundations.

Fernandez, Joseph. 2019. "Malaysia's Anti-Fake News Act". *Pacific Journalism Review* 25, nos. 1 & 2: 173–92.

George, Cherian. 2003. "The Internet and the Narrow Tailoring Dilemma for 'Asian' Democracies". *The Communication Review* 6, no. 3: 247–68. https://doi.org/10.1080/10714420390226270.002.

———. 2006. *Contentious Journalism and the Internet: Towards Democratic Discourse in Malaysia and Singapore*. Singapore: NUS Press and University of Washington Press.

Gerö, Márton and Ákos Kopper. 2013. "Fake and Dishonest: Pathologies of Differentiation of the Civil and the Political Sphere in Hungary". *Journal of Civil Society* 9, no. 4: 361–74. https://doi.org/10.1080/17448689.2013.844449.

Gomez, James. 2013. "Malaysia's 13th General Election: Social Media and its Political Impact". *MediaMalaysia.Net*. http://mediamalaysia.net/wp-content/uploads/2013/09/GE13_Social_Media_James_Gomez-090913.pdf.

Gomez, James and Han Leong Chang. 2010. "New Media and General Elections: Online Citizen Journalism in Malaysia and Singapore". Paper presented at the "Malaysia and Singapore Workshop: Media, Law, Social Commentary, Politics", Centre for Media and Communications Law and Asian Law Centre, Melbourne Law School, The University of Melbourne, Australia, 10–11 June 2010. https://www.academia.edu/242554/New_Media_and_General_Elections_Online_Citizen_Journalism_in_Malaysia_and_Singapore.

Hah, Foong Lian. 2012. *New Media and Old Politics: The Role of Blogging in the 2008 Malaysian General Election*. New Zealand: University of Canterbury.

———. 2016. *Power Games: Political Blogging in Malaysian National Elections*. Singapore: ISEAS – Yusof Ishak Institute.

Hazis, Faisal S. 2015. "Malaysia in 2014: A Year of Political and Social Ferment". In *Southeast Asian Affairs*, edited by Daljit Singh, pp. 189–204. Singapore: Institute of Southeast Asian Studies.

Hopkins, Julian. 2014. "Cybertroopers and Tea Parties: Government Use of the Internet in Malaysia". *Asian Journal of Communication* 24, no. 1: 5–24. https://doi.org/10.1080/01292986.2013.851721.

Hounshell, Blake. 2008. "Mahathir Mohamad has a Blog". *Foreign Policy*, 1 May 2008. https://foreignpolicy.com/2008/05/01/mahathir-mohamad-has-a-blog/.

Hung, Chin-fu. 2010. "China's Propaganda in the Information Age: Internet Commentators and the Weng'an Incident". *Issues & Studies* 46, no. 4: 149–80.

Johns, Amelia. 2020. "'This will be the WhatsApp Election': Crypto-Publics and Digital Citizenship in Malaysia's GE14 Election". *First Monday* 25 (12 SE-Articles). https://doi.org/10.5210/fm.v25i12.10381.

Johns, Amelia and Niki Cheong. 2019. "Feeling the Chill: *Bersih* 2.0, State Censorship, and 'Networked Affect' on Malaysian Social Media 2012–2018". *Social Media + Society* 5, no. 2: 1–12. https://doi.org/10.1177/2056305118821801.

Khoo, Boo Teik. 2016. "Networks in Pursuit of a 'Two-Coalition System' in Malaysia: Pakatan Rakyat's Mobilization of Dissent between Reformasi and the Tsunami". *Southeast Asian Studies* 5, no. 1: 73–91. https://doi.org/10.20495/seas.5.1_73.

Lee, Fiona. 2017. "Rites of Change: Artistic Responses to Recent Street Protests in Kuala Lumpur". *Southeast of Now: Directions in Contemporary and Modern Art in Asia* 1, no. 2: 65–90. https://doi.org/10.1353/sen.2017.0014.

Leong, Pauline Pooi Yin. 2015. "Political Communication in Malaysia: A Study on the Use of New Media in Politics". *JeDEM – EJournal of EDemocracy and Open Government* 7, no. 1: 46–71. https://doi.org/10.29379/jedem.v7i1.372.

———. 2019. *Malaysian Politics in the New Media Age: Implications on the Political Communication Process*. Singapore: Springer.

Lim, Joanne B.Y. 2017. "Engendering Civil Resistance: Social Media and Mob Tactics in Malaysia". *International Journal of Cultural Studies* 20, no. 2: 209–27. https://doi.org/10.1177/1367877916683828.

Medium. 2016. "The Post Stays Up", 26 January 2016. https://blog.medium.com/the-post-stays-up-d222e34cb7e7.

Mohamed, Badrul Azmier, Mujibu Abd Muis, Azni Syafena Andin Salamat, Nur Zafifa Kamarunzaman, Syazliyati Ibrahim, Robekhah Harun and Zetty Harisha Harun. 2011. "Control and Usage of the Virtual Space in Facing the Upcoming 13th General Election: A Critical Evaluation of Space and Opportunities for Barisan Nasional". *Asian Social Science* 7, no. 12: 14–21. https://doi.org/10.5539/ass.v7n12p14.

Mohd Azizuddin, Mohd Sani. 2014. "The Social Media Election in Malaysia: The 13th General Election in 2013". *Kajian Malaysia* 32, no. 1: 119–48.

———. 2015. "Political Marketing in Malaysia: Examining the Case of Political Campaigning in the 2014 Kajang By-Election". *Philippine Political Science Journal* 36, no. 2: 167–89. https://doi.org/10.1080/01154451.2015.1084745.

Muhamad, Rosyidah. 2015. "Online Opposition and Elections in Malaysia". *Asian Social Science* 11, no. 10: 281–91. https://doi.org/10.5539/ass.v11n10p281.

Nadzri, Muhamad M.N. 2018. "The 14th General Election, the Fall of Barisan Nasional, and Political Development in Malaysia, 1957–2018". *Journal of Current Southeast Asian Affairs* 37, no. 3: 139–71. https://doi.org/10.1177/186810341803700307.

Ndoma, Ibrahim and Makmor Tumin. 2011. "Virtual Civil Society: Malaysia's 2008 General Elections Revisited". *Global Journal of Human Social Science* 11, no. 8: 1–10.

New Straits Times. 2004. "Umno Youth goes on Cyber-War Footing". 25 February 2004. p. 4.

O'Shannassy, M. 2012. "The More Things Stay the Same, the More Things Change?" *Asian Survey* 52, no. 1: 165–75. https://doi.org/10.1525/as.2012.52.1.165.

Pearce, Katy E. 2015. "Democratizing *Kompromat*: The Affordances of Social Media for State-Sponsored Harassment". *Information, Communication & Society* 18, no. 10: 1158–74. https://doi.org/10.1080/1369118X.2015.1021705.

Pepinsky, Thomas B. 2013. "The New Media and Malaysian Politics in Historical Perspective". *Contemporary Southeast Asia* 35, no. 1: 83–103. https://doi.org/10.1355/cs35-1d.

Postill, John. 2014. "A Critical History of Internet Activism and Social Protest in Malaysia, 1998–2011". *Asiascape: Digital Asia* 1, nos. 1–2: 78–103. https://doi.org/10.1163/22142312-12340006.

Razak, Najib. 2016. "Netizens for the Greater Good". *NajibRazak.com*, 26 February 2016.

Saravanamuttu, Johan and Maznah Mohamad. 2019. "The Monetisation of Consent and its Limits: Explaining Political Dominance and Decline in Malaysia". *Journal of Contemporary Asia* 50, no. 1: 56–73. https://doi.org/10.1080/00472336.2019.1569710.

Tan, K. 2013. "Cybertroopers, Social Media and the State of Media in Malaysia". *BFM 89.9*, 13 January 2013. https://www.bfm.my/podcast/morning-run/current-affairs/current-affairs-190112-cybertroopers-tun-faisal-hishamudin-rais.

Tapsell, Ross. 2013. "Negotiating Media 'Balance' in Malaysia's 2013 General Election". *Journal of Current Southeast Asian Affairs* 32, no. 2: 39–60.

———. 2018. "The Smartphone as the 'Weapon of the Weak': Assessing the Role of Communication Technologies in Malaysia's Regime Change". *Journal of Current Southeast Asian Affairs* 37, no. 3: 9–29. https://journals.sub.uni-hamburg.de/giga/jsaa/article/view/1146/1153.

Varkkey, Helena. 2017. "Malaysia in 2016: Persistent Crises, Rapid Response, and Resilience". In *Southeast Asian Affairs 2017*, edited by Daljit Singh and Malcolm Cook, pp. 203–19. Singapore: Insitute of Southeast Asian Studies.

Weiss, Meredith L. 2009. "Edging Toward a New Politics in Malaysia: Civil Society at the Gate?" *Asian Survey* 49, no. 5: 741–58. https://doi.org/10.1525/as.2009.49.5.741.

———. 2012. *Politics in Cyberspace: New Media in Malaysia*. Berlin, Germany: fesmedia Asia, Friedrich-Ebert-Stiftung. http://library.fes.de/pdf-files/iez/09068.pdf.

———. 2013. "Malaysia's 13th General Elections: Same Result, Different Outcome". *Asian Survey* 53, no. 6: 1135–58. https://doi.org/10.1525/as.2013.53.6.1135.

Welsh, Bridget. 2011. "People Power in Malaysia: Bersih Rally and Its Aftermath". *Asia Pacific Bulletin* 128. Washington, D.C.: East-West Center.

Welsh, Bridget and Lopez Greg, eds. 2018. *Regime Resilience in Malaysia and Singapore*. Lanham, Maryland: Lexington Books.

Woolley, Samuel C. and Philip N. Howard. 2019. *Computational Propaganda: Political Parties, Politicians, and Political Manipulation on Social Media*. New York: Oxford University Press.

Zakaria, Nordin. 2014. "Modeling Political Belief and Its Propagation, with Malaysia as a Driving Context". *Open Journal of Political Science* 4, no. 2: 58–75. https://doi.org/10.4236/ojps.2014.42008.

Zakaria, Rosli. 2017. "Umno on War Footing to Face Mother of All Elections". *New Straits Times*, 7 December 2017. https://www.nst.com.my/news/politics/2017/12/311797/umno-war-footing-face-mother-all-elections.

5

SOCIAL MEDIA, HATE SPEECH AND FAKE NEWS DURING MYANMAR'S POLITICAL TRANSITION

Nyi Nyi Kyaw

Social media entered Myanmar during its most monumental political transition from decades-long and repressive military dictatorship to a burgeoning electoral democracy. During this seismic political shift, Myanmar has been plagued by optimism for a more open and wealthier society coupled with fear of uncertainties that naturally accompany any significant societal and political change. Social media has become the arena where such tension plays out in the most toxic way: it gives rise to nationalist right-wing activism, polarization and disinformation that accompanied offline communal violence with devastating results. Despite the initial high hopes that the expansion of internet and social media connectivity would positively contribute to the country's democratic transition, today Myanmar is the site of one of the world's worst humanitarian crises—dubbed the world's first "Facebook genocide"—as more than 700,000 Rohingya minorities have been displaced and thousands feared dead (Mozur 2018). Facebook was forced to admit it failed to stop the use of its platform to perpetuate hate speech and violence in Myanmar, particularly against the Rohingyas (Hatmaker 2018).

Yet there was initial hope among activists and opposition groups in the late 2000s that social media could be a force for progressive change. Many of the pro-democracy networks and civil society groups were established overseas, particularly in neighbouring Thailand, and had access to internet and social media long before it became widely available in Myanmar. They understood firsthand the power of digital media in facilitating social and political change—they had used these tools to help facilitate the "Saffron Revolution" in 2007. The "revolution" was sparked by a YouTube video of the former leader General Than Shwe's daughter's lavish wedding, among other factors.

As internet access expanded, social media became a space of toxicity rather than civility as the right-wing nationalist voices became influential, subverting much of the critical, more progressive voices. What makes Myanmar so vulnerable to online falsehoods and hate speech? Entrenched political polarization and systemic state violence against the Rohingya minorities may have provided structural conditions that facilitate communal violence. I argue in this chapter that social media has become a readily available tool for mobilization of radical voices in Myanmar partly because there was little state intervention to stymie such radicalization, and partly because the nascent activist groups that emerged online were deeply divided over the issue. Lacking neither the political will nor civil society forces to hamstring the rapidly radicalizing groups online, social media has become an important culprit in one of the world's most tragic ethnic cleaning in contemporary times. As Facebook woke up to its tragic legacy and geared into action, its removal of Buddhist extremist pages from its platform did little to stop the tides of violence against the Rohingyas.

Hate speech and fake news—which include misinformation, disinformation and online propaganda—have been the two biggest problems in the social media sphere in Myanmar, after internet and social media access became affordable and widely available in 2012. Social media activism in Myanmar was marked by polarization from inception—pitting supporters of the old regime against the reformists and the opposition. Entrenched political struggle between the "old" elites led by Thein Sein and the ruling Union Solidarity and Development Party

(USDP) administration and "new" democratic forces led by opposition leader Daw Aung San Suu Kyi and her National League for Democracy (NLD) party was brought online. This political battle set a stage for a deeply divided social media environment. The landslide victory of the NLD in the 2015 elections resulted in a divided government, as the NLD was forced to share power with the old guards given the 2008 constitution written specifically to guarantee the military's continuation of political power after the regime change. As an ethnic and religious minority that has historically suffered from systemic marginalization, the Rohingyas became an easy target for the growing nationalist and extremist voices online.

Accompanying this dramatic political change was also an unprecedented liberalization of Myanmar's media and telecommunications sectors. The telecommunications industry in the 1990s and 2000s was nascent, extremely limited and highly regulated. Mobile phones with SIM cards, whose market prices reached exorbitant prices in the 2000s, were only reachable for "high" government officials and military officers, who were "given" mobile phones with SIM cards either free or at a price much lower than the market rate. Businessmen and other people who wanted mobile phones had to buy on the market. All this extreme digital poverty of Myanmar was ameliorated from 2012 onwards, and internet access became widespread. The introduction of Facebook Free Basics in 2015, which provides access to a light version of Facebook without incurring data cost, has meant that the "internet" for most people in Myanmar is Facebook as the app comes pre-installed on mobile phones. Initial excitement of having one's "own" mobile phones and Facebooking for social purposes soon led to an increase in political discussions—especially one about the Rohingya minorities—whose place in Myanmar's society has long been at best ignored and at worst despised. Led by a few prominent monks, these influencers took centre stage in constructing hateful and often false discourses against the Rohingyas as early as 2012, a time when so few people in Myanmar had social media access. As the number of social media users rose sharply, these radical Buddhist leaders already established themselves as powerful Facebook influencers, and were able to continue to attract more attention both online and from traditional media. Neutral spaces for critical and unbiased discussions of the Rohingyas online were unable to compete with the appeal of more radical spaces.

This chapter will chronicle Myanmar's social media evolution from late 2000s until the present day. The initial phase of social media development was marked by limited progressive activism in a relative open cyberspace. The second phase—the turning point—was characterized by the rise of Buddhist nationalist groups and their growing influence on Facebook. These groups utilized both hate speech and misinformation to shore up their online popularity and mobilize offline actions at the expense of the Rohingyas and other Muslims. The third phase is from 2015 onwards, following the victory of pro-democracy movements, culminated in the election victory of the NLD. Despite this change in political regime, the fate of the Rohingyas has changed little. The ruling NLD—mostly ethnic Burmans—were more or less aligned with the military in the continued marginalization of the Rohingyas. Civil society groups were deeply divided on the issue of the Rohingya minorities—making it difficult to counter the continued stream of hate speech and fake news on social media. In the conclusion, I look ahead as to how might Facebook play a greater role in helping to stem the tides of hate and falsehoods against the Rohingyas on its platform.

THE INTERNET'S ARRIVAL AND EARLY DIGITAL ACTIVISM

Myanmar, like several other Southeast Asian states, was a latecomer to cyberspace. When it was introduced to Myanmar in the late 1990s, the internet was extremely limited to a few hundred high-ranking government officials and people with connections to them. Internet connectivity expanded very slowly throughout the 2000s with the opening of several internet cafes in major cities, but around only one per cent of Myanmar people had internet connectivity in the early 2000s. Facebook was largely unknown to Myanmar until the mid-2010s. Online chatting, web surfing, blogging, and emailing grew in the 2010s, but users often had to bypass internet restrictions and censorship and access blocked sites even to Gmail—the most popular email service in Myanmar. The biggest impediment to internet connectivity in Myanmar was the cost of owning a mobile phone. SIM cards were astronomically expensive with a price of 50 million kyats (about $4,500) in the 2000s. Privatization and liberalization of the telecommunications sector from 2012 onwards reduced prices of SIM cards to $1, prompting an immediate boom in mobile subscription. In 2012, mobile subscription accounted for only 2 per cent of the population and by 2018 it skyrocketed to 113 per cent (World Bank 2020a). Internet and social media penetration followed suit with penetration sharply increasing after 2014 (see Table 5.1).

TABLE 5.1
Internet Penetration in Myanmar (% of Population)

Year	Percentage of Population
2003	0.024
2004	0.024
2005	0.065
2006	0.182
2007	0.217
2008	0.22
2009	0.22
2010	0.25
2011	0.98
2012	4.00
2013	8.00
2014	11.52
2015	21.726
2016	25.073
2017	30.678

Source: The World Bank (2020b).

Much of Myanmar's digital activism in this early phase of internet expansion came from dissident groups abroad. Homegrown activism was severely repressed under military rule, which meant that even with the opening up of an alternative space online, civil society groups in Myanmar were either too weak or too afraid to break away from strict censorship. Exiled activist groups, based and funded largely from overseas, stepped into the void by using internet and social media before it became widely available in Myanmar. By engaging with known activists based in Myanmar, dissident groups abroad were able to help finance and facilitate anti-government activities on the ground and continue to raise awareness about the struggle for democracy and human rights in Myanmar with the international community (Banki 2013; Egreteau 2012; Zaw Oo 2006).

The early phase of digital activism thus remained extremely limited in both scope and activity as most people in the country were unconnected with the exception of a few politicians, activists, and journalists with access to exile communities. A number of Myanmar-based dissidents were in touch with their exile compatriots and the broader international democratic opposition against dictatorship through the 1990s and the 2000s (Beatty 2010). This form of hybrid activism, centred on the exile and diasporic communities, has been a hallmark of activism in Myanmar since the 1980s (Beatty 2010). Though politically repressed and with almost no access to free media at home, people of Myanmar received entirely free coverage about the politics of their country from exile media outlets such as the Irrawaddy (based in Thailand), Mizzima (based in India), and Democratic Voice of Burma (DVB) (based in Norway), and Burmese services of Radio Free Asia (RFA), British Broadcasting Corporation (BBC), and Voice of America (VOA). RFA, BBC, and VOA had regular radio service, while DVB had both radio and video services. Radio services such as BBC (Burmese) and All India Radio (Burmese) (Myanmar exile-founded or -run media such as the Irrawaddy and DVB were not in existence yet) were notably influential in spreading dissident news and ideas to people of Myanmar before and during the 1988 Uprising against one-party rule of the Burma Socialist Programme Party (Maung Maung 1999; Tin Maung Maung Than 2013; Lintner 1990). Irrawady, Mizzima and DVB became more influential as internet access became available.

The hallmark of a coordinated transnational activism was the 2007 "Saffron Revolution", named after the saffron-coloured robes widely associated with Buddhist monks, who were at the forefront of the demonstrations. The internet became front and centre in coordinating offline protests and popularizing it to the international media, even when the military junta sought to control information from leaking out (Chowdhury 2008; Egreteau 2012; Danitz and Strobel 1999, 2001; Green 2016; Troester 2001; Fitzgerald 2001; Humphries 2009). By this time, the number of pro-democracy bloggers and online news abroad expanded significantly, making it much harder for the military to quell dissident voices. Ko Htike, a Burmese dissident based in London, ran a blog, *ko-htike.blogspot.com*, which was heavily relied upon by Western journalists for information relating to the Saffron protests. Ko Htike had up to forty people in Myanmar sending him photos and information on the ground, which he then broadcasted to the world (Drash and Black 2007). As images of the brutal crackdowns during the protests began to emerge, a coordinated international campaign by a number of Myanmar's dissident and diasporic communities and their sympathizers abroad culminated in the Global Day of Action for Burma on 6 October 2007, which led to offline protests against the junta in over thirty countries around the world (Burma Campaign 2007). While Myanmar had received unprecedented international attention on the protests, thanks largely to digitally mediated transnational activism, the "revolution" ended in its usual fashion: brutal repression. The internet proved, however, to be a crucial tool for pro-democracy transnational networks (Danitz and Strobel 2001).

The Saffron Revolution prompted the military to seriously begin its internet censorship regime and disinformation campaigns online. Prior to Saffron Revolution, the military set up websites such as BurmaNet and Myanmar.com to promote state-sanctioned online news on Burma and counter the growing popularity of Irrawaddy and Mizzima (Chowdhury 2008). As the Saffron protests unfolded, a growing number of websites started to be blocked including a number of foreign news sites, followed by a complete internet shutdown on 28 September 2007 (Tran 2007). The Myanmar government then began to track down locally based dissidents, taking advantage of its total control of the country's internet service providers (ISPs). The OpenNet Institute conducted a sweeping investigation of censorship tactics used by the Myanmar government and found an increasing array of surveillance, internet filtering and intimidation being ramped up during the revolution (OpenNet Institute 2007). This pattern of limiting individual access to internet access, strict control over media, frequent internet filtering and surveillance as well as an iron fist approach to any individual found to be engaged in political activities continued on uninterrupted until the government privatized the communication sector in 2012, bringing in an onslaught of millions of new internet users and the sudden surge in adoption of social media.

That the military government had implemented pervasive internet controls long before most people even have internet access is an important example of internet and digital media development in Myanmar. Despite its initial rudimentary techniques to censor the internet, the Myanmar military recognized that information controls were critical to regime security. In the years following Saffron Revolution and during its political and media liberalization reforms, filtering of political content became more pervasive (OpenNet Institute 2012). Cyber attacks against websites and blogs of dissidents—both local and abroad—and intermittent blocking of foreign media websites were systemic. The UN Special Rapporteur on the human rights situations in Myanmar noted in 2009 that there were over 2,100 prisoners of conscience including journalists and bloggers arrested in the aftermath of the revolution (United Nations 2009). Such strict information controls continued following one of the country's most significant political changes. These included the 2010 general elections, the release from house arrest of opposition leader Aung San Suu Kyi, and the taking office of Thein Sein. Massive cyber-attacks that cut off internet connectivity three days before its 2010 elections was one of many examples of the length the military regime was willing to go to control information at its most sensitive time (Hindstrom 2016). According to Freedom House, military sources inside Myanmar revealed that military officers were dispatched to Singapore, Russia and North Korea for information technology training (Freedom House 2011).

THE RISE OF HATE SPEECH AND FAKE NEWS

The turning point in Myanmar's state-society relations online came when rising Buddhist nationalist sentiment grew alongside the growth of social media adoption. Against the backdrop of an evolving internet censorship regime, Myanmar began to liberalize its media and telecommunications industries, leading to a sharp rise in internet and social media penetration and a flurry of new actors in the online news sector. This unprecedented increase in freedom of speech and press, coupled with a rapid expansion of connectivity, became a doubled-edged sword. On the one hand, the relaxation over media regulations was most welcome not just among journalists and activists alike, but also for ordinary internet users. This period of the "Burmese Media Spring", as dubbed by Reporters Without Borders, followed electoral victories of the opposition party, the NLD, in the 2012 by-elections, and gave hope to progressive voices in Myanmar and abroad that perhaps genuine political change could indeed occur. Major protests—the largest since Saffron Revolution—broke out in Mandalay and Yangon in 2012, and were not met with a crackdown from the military (Al Jazeera 2012). The civil society sector grew rapidly, aided especially by an influx of international non-governmental organization (NGO) operations into the country and networked by the increasing availability of digital media (Asian Development Bank 2015). Demonstrations became legalized and foreign journalists were allowed even to interview high-ranking military officers. The changes were rapid, progressive and promising.

However, this new-found freedom to speak openly online became extremely toxic, and particularly deadly, when it came to discourse around the Rohingyas. Sparked by horrific images of the rape and murder of a young Rakhine Buddhist woman, Thida Htwe, by three Rohingya/non-Rohingya/mixed Muslim men in a village in Rakhine State in May 2012, the torrent of hate speech against the Muslim Rohingyas quickly turned violent. This incident was immediately followed by an angry Rakhine Buddhist mob that killed ten Muslim passengers from other parts of Myanmar on a bus from Thandwe in southern Rakhine to Yangon. The graphic pictures of those Muslims lynched spread online, angering the Rohingya communities concentrated in northern Rakhine State. In reporting two incidents, the state-owned newspapers of 5 June used the inflammatory racio-religious slur *Muslim kala* (Kyaw Zwa Moe 2012), which was found highly offensive by Muslims in other parts leading to a protest by them on the same day in Yangon (Aung Thet Wine 2012). Global freedom of information watchdog Reporters Without Borders (Ismaïl 2016), with its Myanmar partner Burma Media Association, expressed suspicion of the timing of the inflammatory reports by state newspapers. On 8 June, the numerical majority in Maungdaw in northern Rakhine, angry Rohingyas took revenge on Rakhine Buddhist neighbours, who were called "terrorists" by the state newspapers the next day (Kyaw Zwa Moe 2012). The gathering storm of online hate resulted in violence offline and soon spread to other places in Rakhine where Buddhists took revenge on Muslims. The June violence was followed by another episode in October 2012 and another in September 2013, resulting in at least 192 deaths and destruction of 8,614 houses and 120 businesses (Inquiry Commission on Sectarian Violence in Rakhine State 2013, p. 20).

Deep-seated discrimination against the Rohingyas, triggered by the June 2012 murder incident, culminated in the beginning of a series of social media hate and disinformation campaigns against Rohingyas and Muslims. The Western media coverage of the violence against the Rohingyas angered Myanmar Buddhist majority, leading to a surge in nationalist and Buddhist narratives online, creating a fertile ground for radical Buddhist nationalist groups to emerge (Nyi Nyi Kyaw 2015, 2019). In the immediate aftermath of the second round of violence in Rakhine State, the symbolic *969* Buy-Buddhist campaign emerged in October 2012, followed by the establishment of the *Ma Ba Tha* (the Organization for Protection of Race and Religion) in June 2013. A network of five young monks established *969* in Mawlamyine, and started preaching across Myanmar a "radically different dhamma" (Kyaw Zwa Moe 2013). They encouraged the use at Buddhist homes and shops of a colourful *969* emblem (Nyi Nyi Kyaw 2016)—9, 6, and 9 represent the nine qualities of Buddha, six qualities of Dhamma or his teachings, and nine qualities of Sangha or his monastic order, respectively. *969* leaders later joined *Ma Ba Tha*. During the three years of its hyperactivity (2012–15), both online and offline, *Ma Ba Tha* maintained a core group of monastics around prominent monastic and *Ma Ba Tha* chair Ywama Sayadaw based at the Ywama Pariyatti Teaching Monastery in Insein, Yangon. But it had a loose network of operatives across the country who were either *Ma Ba Tha* members or likeminded nationalist individuals and networks that joined in *Ma Ba Tha* activities.

Generally, *969* and *Ma Ba Tha* provide three reasons for their Islamophobia based on population and cultural dynamics. First, symbolically popularized by the *969* emblem ubiquitous in Myanmar in 2012–14, they claim that Muslims plot to increase the wealth of their own community by buying from Muslim-owned shops only, and lure and marry poor Buddhist women and convert them to Islam. Second, *969* and *Ma Ba Tha* assert that Muslim men are polygamous or at least allowed to be so by Islam, and they practise it by taking both Muslim and Buddhist women as wives, again intentionally to exponentially increase the size of the Myanmar Muslim community. Third, due to Muslim men's plan to convert their non-Buddhist wives, Buddhist women who marry Muslims have no option but to leave Buddhism and lose their religious freedom. By doing all these, the *969* and *Ma Ba Tha* master narrative argues, Muslims plot to outgrow Buddhists, who find themselves at the verge of a demographic apocalypse.

To prevent this Buddhist doomsday, *969* and *Ma Ba Tha* offer two solutions: one economic or market-based and the other legal. Economically, Muslims' financial lifeline must be cut by Buddhists stopping transacting with Muslims and buying from Buddhist-owned shops only—the symbolic message of the *969* emblem. Legally, religious conversion in and out of wedlock must be restricted, polygamy stopped, Buddhist women's interfaith marriage with non-Buddhist men restricted, and families' childbearing practices be checked. Hence, *969* propagated the symbolic Buy-Buddhist campaign. And *Ma Ba Tha* launched unprecedented monks-led legal mobilization by using a vast repertoire of movement, all offline: collecting millions of signatures, publishing weekly and bi-weekly journals, pamphlets, statements, and books, holding monks and lay people's protests, giving monks' sermons, holding lay people's talks, conferences, public consultative workshops, and press conferences, and photography shows, producing pictures, songs, and movies, and holding life story telling sessions. Facebook gave *Ma Ba Tha*'s ideologues and followers enormous connective, communicative, and spreading power of what they do offline, invoking the power of the internet for their social-movement style campaign (Van Laer and Van Aelst 2010; Rolfe 2005).

969/Ma Ba Tha monks preached a hate narrative that targets Islam and Muslims. This includes U Wirathu who made the cover of *Time* magazine in July 2013. U Wirathu made statements like "Muslims are like the African carp. They breed quickly and they are very violent and they eat their own kind … the Burmese people and the Buddhists are devoured every day" (Tin Aung Kyaw 2013). *969* leader Wimala Biwuntha agreed, "Muslim men try to win the love of poor Buddhist women for their reproductive tactics. They produce a lot of children, they are snowballing" (*The Diplomat* 2013). These words, apparently couched in both hate speech and fake news, that were said to journalists in private or recorded at the monks' public sermons, all in 2013, were only the beginning of the anti-Muslim hate speech and fake news. The speech soon spread like wildfire across Myanmar, when videos of the same sermons and many more in 2014 and 2015 together with *Ma Ba Tha*'s journals published from mid-2013 flooded the streets of cities and towns across Myanmar. So cheap were those video compact discs, which contained up to three or more sermons, and sold at 300–500 Myanmar kyats (roughly 30 cents) each disc. *Ma Ba Tha* also had a wide network of chapters and members across the country that further distributed the material, reportedly free in some places. All those offline hate speech materials were also spread online on Facebook and YouTube. U Wirathu and other *Ma Ba Tha* monks kept regular presence on Facebook, and hundreds of other accounts supposedly used by *Ma Ba Tha* followers or sympathizers were seen to spread hate speech in the form of messages, videos, pictures, and the like.

Anti-Muslim and anti-Rohingya rumours spread on Facebook with dangerous offline consequences. On 28 September 2012, a rumour spread that a twelve-year-old Rakhine Buddhist boy was hurt or killed by Rohingya Muslims, leading to an immediate gathering of angry monks and people in Sittwe, almost leading to a riot (Ma Su Mon 2012). Likewise, a rumour spread via social media that a riot was occurring in largely Muslim neighbourhood Mingalar Taung Nyunt in Yangon on 24 March 2013 led to the closure of shops at the nearby Yuzana Plaza, probably the largest wholesale and retail market in Yangon (Fuller 2013). Another false rumour that a Rakhine Buddhist woman in Thandwe, Rakhine State, was raped by two Muslim men in late June 2013 led to burning of houses and cars (Ko Moe Zaw 2013). False information on Facebook relating to a pro-Muslim documentary being produced by the Human Rights Film Institute in Myanmar in 2014 led to a number of threatening phone messages against a Muslim trainee at the Institute and a rumour that the screening location of the documentary would be burned (Mon Mon Myat 2014). The worst case of hateful fake news occurred on 1 July 2014 with a false allegation on Facebook that a female Buddhist staff at San Cafe in Mandalay was raped by two Muslim teashop owners Ne Win and San Maung. Shared by U Wirathu on his Facebook on 30 June (Justice Trust 2015, p. 21), riots broke out leading to deaths of a Buddhist man and a Muslim man. U Wirathu wrote on his Facebook page on 3 July, alleging Muslims of potential jihad and calling upon the government and the Buddhist people in and outside Myanmar for decisive action against Muslims (Justice Trust 2015, p. 21). U Wirathu's alarmism was convincing because Muslim fasting month Ramadan fell in July 2014 and thousands of Muslims were attending mosques in Mandalay.

CONCLUSION

This chapter has highlighted the interdependence between hate speech and fake news on social media in Myanmar in the three early years of its transition. The broader implication of this argument is that hate speech and fake news have a symbiotic relationship in creating effective and lasting disinformation narratives. As we have seen, fake news profusely produced in Myanmar in 2012–14 led to communal violence, which stems from hate speech against Muslims. Similarly, hate speech flavoured with fake news or rumour increased the impact and spread of disinformation.

Why was hate speech and misinformation against the Rohingyas and Muslim minorities allowed to run rampant to such an extent that communal violence occurred repeatedly in Myanmar? Part of the issue in Myanmar was that the military was complicit in such hateful narratives against the Rohingyas as they align with the military's political objectives (van Klinken and Aung 2017). Using the Rohingyas as scapegoats was convenient for the military and their political elites at a time of political transition because they would help maintain popular support for them post-transition, as many within the majority Buddhist populace supported an anti-Muslim stance (Chit Win and Kean 2017). Former President Thein Sein helped *Ma Ba Tha* by securing indoor stadiums to host rallies in 2015 (Fisher 2015), while in 2019 a Yangon military chief personally donated 30 million kyats (US$20,000) to the *Ma Ba Tha*, as nearly 1,000 monks gathered for an annual meeting in Insein (Htet Naing Zaw 2019). A military spokesperson explained at the meeting that the *Ma Ba Tha* is "a necessity to defend Buddhism". Even after the regime change following the 2015 elections, the NLD did not help to change the fate of the Rohingyas and other Muslims in Myanmar. Indeed, Aung San Suu Kyi has made so little comment regarding the atrocities committed against the minorities that she has received sustained critical condemnation by the international community, calling her a "pariah" (Paddock 2018). Yet, domestically, when she or any of the NLD legislators dared to defend the Muslims, they faced both personal and political attacks (Chit Win and Kean 2017).

The unexpected release from military dictatorship and repression, coupled with affordable mobile internet access, allowed for structural factors in Myanmar's society to promote hate speech and fake news. However, this does not exonerate the USDP regime's role in the violence.

The ruling government failed, intentionally or otherwise, to deal with and control the disinformation practices that flourished. Furthermore, the inability, or even complicity of the broader Myanmar civil society, were no better-equipped in terms of technical know-how to root out hate speech and fake news, despite some valiant efforts. Since 2017 the NLD government has largely neutralized *Ma Ba Tha*, and civil society seems more experienced and self-confident with the democratically elected and popular NLD in power, which is less likely to rely on hate speech and fake news for its political branding and marketing. Overall, the present and future of social media or internet activism as a force for positive reforms remains heavily reliant on the nature and trajectory of the "democratic" transition of the country.

While local political dynamics matters greatly, an important contributing factor to the social media-induced communal violence in Myanmar was the slow action on behalf of the Silicon Valley-based platforms themselves. Facebook has been widely criticized for enabling the genocide against the Rohingyas. Its CEO, Mark Zuckerberg, was questioned by the US Senate over its inaction in Myanmar, with one senator calling his platform "a breeding ground for hate speech" (Associated Press 2018). Repeated calls by Myanmar human rights groups to Facebook to stop viral and hateful content against the Rohingyas and Muslims went unanswered for many years, to the point that even Western media began to ask questions whether Facebook "could be tried for human rights abuses" (Burington 2017). Facebook has admitted its platform has been used to incite violence in Myanmar (Stevenson 2018). Since 2016, the tech giant implemented its new Myanmar strategy, beginning with its banning of ethnic armed Myanmar-based groups followed by the removal of 18 accounts and 52 pages associated with the military for inciting violence (Ellis-Petersen 2018). While these measures represent some progress in fighting against hate speech in Myanmar, Facebook continues to be criticized for not being more invested in rectifying the damage done in the country. The company has no physical presence in Myanmar, citing safety concerns for its staff, and employs 100 Burmese-speaking moderators to monitor content of over 20 million users (Thomas 2019). But overall the experience of the Rohingyas hate speech has belatedly meant Facebook is better prepared and acts more quickly in Myanmar when this material starts to spread.

However, it is important to emphasize the long-term, perhaps even generational, impact that social media's introduction will have in Myanmar. Anti-Muslim hate speech and fake news, which did not always distinguish between non-Rohingya Muslims and Rohingya Muslims in those years of *Ma Ba Tha*'s hyperactivity, is almost entirely anti-Rohingya today. While Myanmar people in general regard non-Rohingya Muslims as citizens, most Myanmar citizens still regard the Rohingyas as illegal migrants from Bangladesh. The brand of anti-Rohingya hate speech and fake news has been popularized, and continues to resonate. Once the disinformation and hate speech has been ingrained in the minds of many, it is hard to undo.

REFERENCES

"စစမျိုးဆက်တိုက်တွန်း" [88 Generation: Don't Engage in Preemptive Attack Due to Rumour], 28 March 2013. https://www.rfa.org/burmese/news/88-warm-rumour-03282013112455.html (accessed 12 April 2020).

Al Jazeera. 2012. "Power Outage Protests Hit Myanmar", 23 May 2012. https://www.aljazeera.com/news/asia-pacific/2012/05/20125235117172891.html (accessed 9 May 2020).

Asian Development Bank. 2015. "Civil Society Briefs: Myanmar", February 2015. https://www.adb.org/sites/default/files/publication/154554/csb-myanmar.pdf (accessed 9 May 2020).

Associated Press. 2018. "Zuckerberg Grilled Over Facebook Role in Myanmar", 10 April 2018. https://www.youtube.com/watch?v=drkVCgE7f9U (accessed 9 May 2020).

Aung Thet Wine. 2012. "State Media Comes under Fire for Stoking Sectarian Anger". Irrawaddy, 5 June 2012. https://www.irrawaddy.com/news/burma/state-media-comes-under-fire-for-stoking-sectarian-anger.html (accessed 30 April 2020).

Banki, Susan. 2013. "Paradoxical Power of Precarity: Refugees and Homeland Activism". *Refugee Review: Social Movement* 1, no. 1: 1–20.

Beatty, Linnea M. 2010. "Democracy Activism and Assistance in Burma: Sites of Resistance". *International Journal* 65, no. 3: 619–36.

Burington, Ingrid. 2017. "Could Facebook Be Tried for Human Rights Abuses?" *The Atlantic*, 20 December 2017. https://www.theatlantic.com/technology/archive/2017/12/could-facebook-be-tried-for-war-crimes/548639/ (accessed 9 May 2020).

Burma Campaign. 2007. "Global Day of Action", 6 October 2007. https://burmacampaign.org.uk/global-day-of-action-for-burma-saturday-october-6th-2007/ (accessed 9 May 2020).

Chit Win and Thomas Kean. 2017. "Communal Conflict in Myanmar: The Legislature's Response, 2012–2015". *Journal of Contemporary Asia* 47, no. 3: 413–39.

Chowdhury, Mridul. 2008. "The Role of the Internet in Burma's Saffron Revolution". Berkman Center Research Publication No. 2008-8, 1 September 2008. https://papers.ssrn.com/sol3/papers.cfm?abstract_id=1537703 (accessed 28 April 2020).

Danitz, Tiffany and Warren P. Strobel. 1999. "The Internet's Impact on Activism: The Case of Burma". *Studies in Conflict & Terrorism* 22, no. 3: 257–69.

———. 2001. "Networking Dissent: Cyber Activists Use the Internet to Promote Democracy in Burma". In *Networks and Netwars: The Future of Terror, Crime, and Militancy*, edited by John Arquilla and David Ronfeldt, pp. 129–69. Santa Monica, Calif.: RAND Corporation.

Drash, Wayne and Phil Black. 2007. "Blogs Helping Expose Myanmar Horrors". *CNN*, 27 September 2007. http://edition.cnn.com/2007/WORLD/asiapcf/09/27/myanmar.dissidents/index.html (accessed 9 May 2020).

Egreteau, Renaud. 2012. "Burma in Diaspora: A Preliminary Research Note on the Politics of Burmese Diasporic Communities in Asia". *Journal of Current Southeast Asian Affairs* 31, no. 2: 115–47.

Ellis-Petersen, Hannah. 2018. "Facebook Removes Accounts Associated with Myanmar's Military". *The Guardian*, 27 August 2018. https://www.theguardian.com/technology/2018/aug/27/facebook-removes-accounts-myanmar-military-un-report-genocide-rohingya (accessed 9 May 2020).

Fisher, Jonah. 2015. "Myanmar's Ma Ba Tha Monks Flex Their Political Muscle". *BBC News*, 8 October 2015. https://www.bbc.com/news/world-asia-34463455 (accessed 9 May 2020).

Fitzgerald, Peter L. 2001. "Massachusetts, Burma and the World Trade Organization: A Commentary on Blacklisting, Federalism, and Internet Advocacy in the Global Trading Era". *Cornell International Law Journal* 34, no. 1: 1–53.

Freedom House. 2011. "Freedom on the Net 2011: Burma". https://freedomhouse.org/sites/default/files/inline_images/Burma_FOTN2011.pdf (accessed 9 May 2020).

Fuller, Thomas. 2013. "Worries Over Violence Prompt Shutdown in Myanmar". *New York Times*, 25 March 2013. https://www.nytimes.com/2013/03/26/world/asia/worries-over-violence-prompt-shutdown-in-myanmar.html (accessed 28 April 2020).

Green, Geff. 2016. "From Bulletins to Bullets to Blogs and Beyond: The Ongoing Communication War of the Karen". In *The Digital Transformation of the Public Sphere: Conflict, Migration, Crisis and Culture in Digital Networks*, edited by Athina Karatzogianni, Dennis Nguyen, and Elisa Serafinelli, pp. 61–82. London: Palgrave Macmillan.

Hatmaker, Taylor. 2018. "In Senate Hearing, Zuckerberg Faces Blame over Violence in Myanmar". *Tech Crunch*, 11 April 2018. https://techcrunch.com/2018/04/10/myanmar-facebook-zuckerberg-senate-hearing-genocide/ (accessed 20 May 2020).

Hindstrom, Hanna. 2016. "Is Myanmar's Military behind Shadowy Cyber Attacks?" *The Diplomat*, 27 February 2016. https://thediplomat.com/2016/02/was-myanmars-military-behind-shadowy-cyber-attacks/ (accessed 9 May 2020).

Htet Naing Zaw. 2019. "Ma Ba Tha is a Necessity: Military". Irrawaddy, 19 June 2019. https://www.irrawaddy.com/news/burma/ma-ba-tha-necessity-military.html (accessed 9 May 2020).

Humphries, Richard. 2009. "Saffron-Robed Monks and Digital Flash Cards: The Development and Challenges of Burmese Exile Media". In *Development in Asia: Interdisciplinary, Post-Neoliberal, and Transnational Perspectives*, edited by Derrick M. Nault, pp. 237–58. Boca Raton, Florida: BrownWalker Press.

Inquiry Commission on Sectarian Violence in Rakhine State. 2013. *Final Report of Inquiry Commission on Sectarian Violence in Rakhine State.* Nay Pyi Taw: Inquiry Commission on Sectarian Violence in Rakhine State.

Ismaïl, Benjamin. 2016. "Crisis in Arakan State and New Threats to Freedom of News and Information". *Reporters Without Borders*, 20 January 2016. https://rsf.org/en/reports/crisis-arakan-state-and-new-threats-freedom-news-and-information (accessed 15 April 2020).

Justice Trust. 2015. *Hidden Hands Behind Communal Violence in Myanmar: Case Study of the Mandalay Riots.* New York: Justice Trust.

Ko Moe Zaw. 2013. " ညမထွက်ရအမိန့်ထုတ်ပြီး သံတွဲ အခြေအနေ ပြန်တည်ငြိမ် " [After Night Curfew Thandwe Becomes Stable]. Voice of America (Burmese), 1 July 2013. https://burmese.voanews.com/a/than-dwe-conflict-happened-again/1692567.html (accessed 15 April 2020).

Kyaw Zwa Moe. 2012. "Why is Western Burma Burning?" Irrawaddy, 15 June 2012. https://www.irrawaddy.com/opinion/why-is-western-burma-burning.html (accessed 16 April 2020).

———. 2013. "A Radically Different Dharma". Irrawaddy, 22 June 2013. https://www.irrawaddy.com/news/a-radically-different-dhamma.html (accessed 15 April 2020).

Lintner, Bertil. 1990. *Outrage: Burma's Struggle for Democracy.* Bangkok: White Lotus.

Ma Su Mon. 2012. " ကောလဟာလေကြောင့် စစ်တွေ မငြိမ်သက်မှုဖြစ် " [Sittwe Unstable Due to Rumour]. *VOA (Burmese)*, 28 September 2012. https://burmese.

voanews.com/a/rakhine-sittwe-erupted-/1516553.html (accessed 30 April 2020).

Maung Maung. 1999. *The 1988 Uprising in Burma*. New Haven: Yale University Press.

Mon Mon Myat. 2014. "'The Open Sky' လူ့အခွင့်အရေးရုပ်ရှင် ဘာကြောင့် မပြသလဲ" [Why 'The Open Sky' Human Rights Documentary Was Not Shown]. Irrawaddy, 27 June 2014. https://burma.irrawaddy.com/news/2014/06/27/61087.html (accessed 28 April 2020).

Mozur, Paul. 2018. "A Genocide Incited on Facebook, with Posts from Myanmar's Military". *The New York Times*, 15 October 2018. https://www.nytimes.com/2018/10/15/technology/myanmar-facebook-genocide.html (accessed 20 May 2020).

Nyi Nyi Kyaw. 2015. "Alienation, Discrimination, and Securitization: Legal Personhood and Cultural Personhood of Muslims in Myanmar". *Review of Faith & International Affairs* 13, no. 4: 50–59.

———. 2016. "Islamophobia in Buddhist Myanmar: The 969 Movement and Anti-Muslim Violence". In *Islam and the State in Myanmar: Muslim-Buddhist Relations and the Politics of Belonging*, edited by Melissa Crouch, pp. 183–210. Delhi: Oxford University Press.

———. 2019. "Adulteration of the Pure Native Race by Aliens? *Kapya* and their Socio-Legal Identity in Colonial Burma and Present-Day Myanmar". *Social Identities* 25, no. 3: 345–59.

OpenNet Institute. 2007. "Pulling the Plug: A Technical Review of the Internet Shutdown in Burma". https://opennet.net/research/bulletins/013 (accessed 9 May 2020).

———. 2012. "Research Profiles: Burma", 6 August 2012. https://opennet.net/research/profiles/burma (accessed 9 May 2020).

Paddock, Richard. 2018. "From Hero to Pariah: Aung San Suu Kyi Dashes Hopes About Myanmar". *The New York Times*, 29 September 2018. https://www.nytimes.com/2018/09/29/world/asia/myanmar-aung-san-suu-kyi-rohingya.html (accessed 9 May 2020).

Pidduck, Julianne. 2012. "Exile Media, Global News Flows and Democratization: The Role of the Democratic Voice of Burma in Burma's 2010 Elections". *Media, Culture & Society* 34, no. 5: 537–53.

Rolfe, Brett. 2005. "Building an Electronic Repertoire of Contention". *Social Movement Studies* 4, no. 1: 65–74.

Stevenson, Alexandra. 2018. "Facebook Admits It Was Being Used to Incite Violence in Myanmar". *The New York Times*, 6 November 2018. https://www.nytimes.com/2018/11/06/technology/myanmar-facebook.html (accessed 9 May 2020).

The Diplomat. 2013. "The Mad Monks of Myanmar", 9 July 2013. http://thediplomat.com/2013/07/the-mad-monks-of-myanmar (accessed 25 April 2020).

Thomas, Elise. 2019. "Facebook Keeps Failing in Myanmar". *Foreign Policy*, 21 June 2019. https://foreignpolicy.com/2019/06/21/facebook-keeps-failing-in-myanmar-zuckerberg-arakan-army-rakhine/ (accessed 9 May 2020).

Tin Aung Kyaw. 2013. "Buddhist Monk Wirathu Leads Violent National Campaign Against Myanmar's Muslims". *Global Post*, 21 June 2013. http://www.globalpost.com/dispatches/globalpost-blogs/groundtruth-burma/buddhist-monk-wirathu-969-muslims-myanmar (accessed 15 April 2020).

Tin Maung Maung Than. 2013. "The 1988 Uprising in Myanmar: Historical Conjuncture or Praetorian Redux?" In *Conjunctures and Continuities in Southeast Asian Politics*, edited by N. Ganesan, pp. 67–102. Singapore: Institute of Southeast Asian Studies.

Tran, Mark. 2007. "Internet Access Cut Off in Buma". *The Guardian*, 29 September 2007. https://www.theguardian.com/world/2007/sep/28/burma.marktran (accessed 9 May 2020).

Troester, Rod. 2001. "Using the Internet for Peace in Isolated Burma". *Peace Review* 13, no. 3: 389–94.

United Nations. 2009. "Report of the Special Rapporteur on the Situations of Human Rights in Myanmar", 11 March 2009. https://reliefweb.int/sites/reliefweb.int/files/resources/2E364AECDDB3CE3D4925757D001A85B1-Full_Report.pdf (accessed 9 May 2020).

van Klinken, Gerry and Su Mon Thazin Aung. 2017. "The Contentious Politics of Anti-Muslim Scapegoating in Myanmar". *Journal of Contemporary Asia* 47, no. 3: 353–75.

Van Laer, Jeroen and Peter Van Aelst. 2010. "Internet and Social Movement Action Repertoires". *Information, Communication & Society* 13, no. 8: 1146–71.

World Bank. 2020a. "Mobile Cellular Subscriptions (Per 100 People) – Myanmar". https://data.worldbank.org/indicator/IT.CEL.SETS.P2?locations=MM (accessed 22 February 2020).

———. 2020b. "Individuals Using the Internet (% of Population) – Myanmar". https://data.worldbank.org/indicator/IT.NET.USER.ZS?locations=MM (accessed 22 February 2020).

Zaw Oo. 2006. "Exit, Voice and Loyalty in Burma: The Role of Overseas Burmese in Democratizing Their Homeland". In *Myanmar's Long Road to National Reconciliation*, edited by Trevor Wilson, pp. 231–59. Singapore: Institute of Southeast Asian Studies.

6

SECURITIZING "FAKE NEWS": POLICY RESPONSES TO DISINFORMATION IN THAILAND

Janjira Sombatpoonsiri

In December 2019, two events related to disinformation received polar-opposite responses from the Thai government. The Constitutional Court announced it would rule on a sedition complaint that accused the Future Forward, the second biggest opposition party, of its linkage with the Illuminati who conspires to overthrow the monarchy. Drawn on online hearsay, the petitioner claimed that the Future Forward's upside down triangle-shaped logo was supposedly the evidence for this vile conspiracy (Sivasomboon 2019). In parallel, online disinformation regarding the government's 40 per cent tax hike for female tampons sparked nationwide outrage within hours. The government and its Anti-Fake News Centre immediately threatened to file a lawsuit against the purveyor of disinformation (*Bangkokbiznews* 2019). These two events illustrate the politics of handling disinformation in Thailand. Future Forward's connection with the Illuminati is virtually baseless and even absurd in view of some staunch conservatives (Weerawan 2019). But the politically-motivated Constitutional Court proceeded with the case that could have resulted in dissolving Future Forward (Macan-Markar 2020a).¹ In contrast, ruling elites swiftly dealt with what it viewed as false information to destabilize the government.

These events reflect a current development of internet-state-society relations that are shaped by protracted political conflicts. In the early stage of internet accessibility, Thailand's cyberspace was relatively open. But as Thai politics has become embroiled in protracted and divisive crises between the pro-establishment and anti-establishment forces, the internet became the site of mobilization for both camps. The establishment moved to curb growing cyber defiance, setting in motion the widespread of repressive policies that plunge Thailand deeper into autocracy. On the other hand, the anti-establishment sees the internet, and social media in particular, as a site of collective resistance to the establishment.

In this chapter, I examine how policies are framed and implemented to address what ruling elites consider the threat of disinformation. I argue that Thailand has taken on the securitization approach to disinformation. Securitization removes what is supposed to be a political matter from the normal political domain into the security sphere. Once an issue is labelled as a "security concern", the process of policy-making and implementation can evade political deliberations (Wæver 1995). Similar to some authoritarian countries, the Thai case shows that ruling elites and allies have relied on the two-pronged strategy to both control and manipulate online information. But the Thai case is distinct because of the predominant role of the military in shaping what is supposed to be civilian policies such as information management. Since 2006, the army has attributed the threat to political establishment to digital space enabling the promulgation of and access to the information alternative to the official truth. As we shall see, a string of cyber policies seek to address this threat to national pillars.

The chapter is organized into three sections. The first section explores the existing literature on the history of Thailand's information technology in the contexts of political struggle and authoritarian consolidation. In the second section, I highlight how Thailand's polarization shaped by the intractable conflict between anti- and pro-establishment blocs creates fertile ground for "divided disinformation". Policy responses to this predicament have been one-sided as they focus merely on blocking the information deemed opposing the "truth" the establishment espouse while propagating this truth at the expense of informational pluralism. The last section shows that despite efforts to control the information online, individuals and segments of civil society have made use of narrow digital space to defy ruling elites. Thailand's digital space is as controlled and manipulated as it is contested.

THE DEVELOPMENT OF THE INTERNET AND SOCIAL MEDIA

Thailand's early phase of digital space, from the late 1980s through to the 1990s, was marked with openness and freedom despite this period being under an autocratic rule and later fragile democracy. By the 1980s, the internet rapidly developed initially in an academic community led by the National Electronics and Computer Technology Centre (NECTEC), an orgnization overseen by the National Science and Technology Development Agency (NSTDA) at the Ministry of Science, Technology and Environment. Internet users grew, with the number jumped from 28 in 1992 to 23,000 in 1994 (Chaisukosol 2009, p. 96). By the end of 1994, internet access was, for the first time, commercialized through the collaboration between NECTEC and two state-owned enterprises, the Communications Authority of Thailand (CAT) and the Telephone Organisation of Thailand (TOT) (Chaisukosol 2009, p. 97). In the second half of the 1990s, the information and communication technologies sector grew rapidly, with eighteen commercial internet service providers (ISPs), four non-commercial internet hubs, two national internet exchanges, and one international internet gateway (Poetranto and Senft 2016, pp. 4–5). Although the CAT retained its monopoly of international access to ISPs, corporates such as the Vilailuck family, Samart Group, Telecom Asia as well as the Shinawatra Group seized this opportunity of IT commercialization and became "prominent telecommunications groups both in Thailand and the region" (Pathmanand 1998, p. 62).

Parallel with this increasing internet availability was the 1992 democratic transition, followed by economic transformations that empowered new elites, especially telecom tycoons, to compete with traditional powerholders. The palace network of royalists, the military, bureaucrats and Bangkok-based businesses have dominated the Thai state and economy. Challengers to this status quo sprung up in the mid-1970s and again in 1992 where popular uprising and altering geopolitics ended decades of military rule. This was followed by the 1997 passage of the constitution deemed by many as the most democratic for it strengthened majority-based parliamentary and checks and balances, while guaranteeing civil rights extensively. Together with the 1997 economic crisis conducive to "economic readjustments", including liberalizing the telecommunications sector (Poetranto and Senft 2016), the new constitution emboldened emerging capitalist elites whose profits were made "through monopolistic concessions on the domestic telecoms market" (Tejapira 2006, p. 24). Under these circumstances, Thaksin Shinawatra, who spent the 1990s building up this telecom empire and strengthening ties with political elites, rose to power by spearheading the Thai Rak Thai Party.

This period also saw the civil society's nascent cyber activism in the world wide webs. A pioneer was Sombat Boongnam-anong, a seasoned activist, who in 1995 founded the website "Bangkok.com" to communicate with the public about his organization's humanitarian missions and other related political concerns. In 1998, he created the website "Bannok.com" to publicize his organization's recruitment of teaching volunteers in remote areas. In his view, the internet could empower the marginalized (Wongkijrungreung 2009, p. 44). During this period, scholars also initiated a knowledge-based platform of "Midnightuniv.org", akin to present-day open sources, which made available academic research and contentious political insights (Chaisukosol 2009, pp. 141–42).

But it was the anti-Thaksin networks emerging in 2005 who effectively made use of news websites, webboards and weblogs for mass mobilization, setting the stage for politicizing social media. Online news outlets such as "Manager.co.th", "Thai-insider.com" and "Prachatai.com" were mouthpieces of anti-Thaksin protests although Prachatai would later shift to oppose anti-Thaksin networks. Meanwhile, critics increasingly penned their political opinion in weblogs. By 2006, the first generation of social networking sites such as Hi5, MySpace and MSN Messenger reportedly became a vehicle for fierce political debates. Parallel with fast growing numbers of internet users and cheaper smart phones, Facebook took over the social networking landscape from 2008 onward (Suriyawongkul 2012, pp. 30–35). As of 2018, the number of Thai Facebook users skyrocketed to 48 million, compared with 12 million Twitter users (Areepermporn 2018).

Turning Point for Digital Politics

The interplay between online surversion of the establishment and official efforts to suppress it marked a crucial point tipping Thailand's digital openness to surveillance. The first attempt to regulate digital space dated back to 2002, with the establishment of the Ministry of Information and Communication Technology (MICT) which introduced the first internet filtering policy (Ramasoota 2012, p. 83). Nevertheless, the MICT's impact on digital freedom had remained limited. This changed in 2006 when the conflict between Thaksin and his opponents came to a head, culminating in a military coup. Staunch supporters of Thaksin and anti-coup activists initially took to online platforms such as weblogs and comment sections of online press to express their frustration (Pongsawat 2002). The anti-establishment sentiment reached an unprecedented scale as the monarchy and its allies were subject to online criticisms. In 2007, the Computer-Related Crimes Act, otherwise known as the Computer Crime Act (hereafter CCA) was enforced, and bureaucratic bodies were set up to surveil online content. As Ramasoota (2012, p. 85) points out, the law was a response to the availability of online platforms which allowed public discussions on taboo subjects: "authorities ... zeroed in on Internet content as a target for censorship and surveillance in the post-2006 coup period". This purpose was despite the origin of CCA designed to cope with scams occurring through the computer system.

Between 2008 and 2010, the intractable political contest between pro- and anti-Thaksin camps deepened digital control in Thailand. Thaksin's political party and opponents engaged in another round of struggle that resulted in the former being ousted through a judicial intervention. Enraged supporters of Thaksin's party not only took to the streets, but vented their anger in Facebook. In 2009 and 2010, Facebook was key for mass mobilization against the establishment, with the number of users rising by 40 per cent in March 2010 alone (Montlake 2010). In addition, YouTube videos containing *lèse majesté* (monarchy offences) content were repeatedly uploaded and viewed.[2] In response, the Democrat Party-led government approved a new agency in June 2010 to handle violations of the CCA and to protect and take care of the royal institution (Ramasoota 2012, p. 86). Although the government representing anti-establishment voices returned to power in 2011, the curtailment of online defiance persisted. The Yingluck government created two more agencies responsible for cyber security and technological crime suppression (Sinpeng 2013, p. 430).

The military regime that resurged in 2014 would intensify the existing practice of digital control, toughen digital repression and set in motion the manipulation of social media content. Underlying these policies is the view that online dissent is a serious threat to national pillars and thereby national security. At the same time as containing subsersive information, the authorities have sought to consolidate the official "truth" in order to retain ruling elites' hegemony.

SECURITIZING DISINFORMATION THROUGH REGULATION AND POLICIES

Securitizing disinformation is about exercising discursive power through "speech acts" so as to affect policy trajectories. Securitizing actors such as the armed forces, government security council and security think tanks may frame the spread of the information different from the official version as a national security threat. As a result, addressing this threat should be relegated to experts who can authoritatively determine not only what it means by "true" and "false" information, but what we should do about the latter. By lifting responses to disinformation from the policy area of normal politics to security domain, these actors may pledge the public to authorize them the extensive power to urgently tackle the threat of disinformation (Köhler 2019; Cavelty 2008; Balzacq 2011). In autocracies, this process becomes a weapon ruling elites wield to undermine the opposition accused of propagating disinformation, thus getting an upper hand in an election (Neo 2019).

In Thailand, the process of securitizing disinformation relates to growing challenges of the political establishment, particularly the monarchy, whose hegemony has partly been upheld through an ideological engineering of what should be regarded as the truth and the opposite of it. As mentioned, the latest wave of contention stems from the digital space, propelling elites to wage the information warfare in defence of its hegemony (Lui 2014). The information alternative to the official truth is branded as a national threat so as to justifiably mobilize concerted efforts to suppress it. Achieving this necessitates securitizing actors such as the National Security Council (NSC), which through its 2014 policy document (NSC 2014), connects cyber dissent with cyber threat. Similarly, according to its policy plans of 2012–16 and 2017–21, the Internal Security Operations Command (ISOC) iterates that current conflicts are caused by "different opinions of people in the nation", and this disharmony results from distorted information which is destabilizing the nation. Most importantly, the policy blueprints identify social media as a dangerous site where "the information deemed offensive to the monarchy" gets shared (ISOC 2016, 2018). As the most authoritative security figure, the current army chief, General Apirat Kongsompong, reinforces the linkage between disinformation and security threat. He posits that:

> the threat now is fake news ... It's like cyber warfare. And when it combines with the (bombing) incident that happened last week ... it's like hybrid warfare ... Now it is not just an open enemy like the old time ... Some political parties, just born a couple of years ago ... had the platform of their propaganda directed to (people) when they were 16 and 17 ... They try to educate them with fake news (Johnson et al. 2019; see also BBC 2019).

When disinformation is securitized, elites galvanize resources and implement plans to avert threats. This pattern reflects in how state agencies overseeing cyber governance are organized and their policy trajectories largely influenced by the logic of securitization.

Policy Implementing Bodies

As cyberspace has become a new domain of military rule following the 2006 coup, state-society relations online has shifted evident in the military dominance in state agencies responsible for a civilian policy area such as cyber governance. Out of eight agencies overseeing cyber matters, four are military organizations, while the police and the NSC are currently under the army influence. The predominance of the military in contemporary Thai politics, in addition, propels civilian agencies such as the National Broadcasting and Telecommunications Commission (NBTC) and the Digital Economy and Society (DE) to follow the framework of securitization. For instance, although the DE's Anti-Fake News Centre, founded in 2019, seeks to combat all sorts of disinformation, its focal point remains the content relevant to national security and the government, with twenty-two allegations classified in these categories one month after its launch (Ruiz and Kamolvattanavith 2019). In some cases, opposition party figures have been charged with disseminating "fake news" about the government, not the other way round (Kaewjinda 2019). In parallel, the army has its own Cyber Centre, and the ISOC the Centre of Digital Security. The former was set up, among other things, to suppress the information ruling elites consider distorted facts about the monarchy and thus insulting it (Prachatai 2016). In comparison, the mission of the ISOC's Centre of Digital Security is less clear, but as of 2015, the ISOC has reportedly coordinated with then ICT to monitor and shut down 3,426 URLs (Pawakapan 2017, p. 5). As the Cybersecurity Bill was passed at the end of 2019, the National Cyber Security Committee (NCSC) was formed, comprising the prime minister, defence minister, DE minister, finance ministry's permanent secretary, justice ministry's permanent secretary, police chief and NSC secretariat. Despite some civilian functions, the NCSC is essentially mandated to prepare for cybersecurity incidents and warfare (*Bangkok Post* 2019a). Given Thailand's history of securitizing cyber laws—as examined further—exploiting the NCSC to undermine the opposition is not unthinkable. Figure 6.1 illustrates the ecosystem of state agencies relevant to securitizing disinformation.

FIGURE 6.1
Ecosystem of State Agencies Responsible for Disinformation

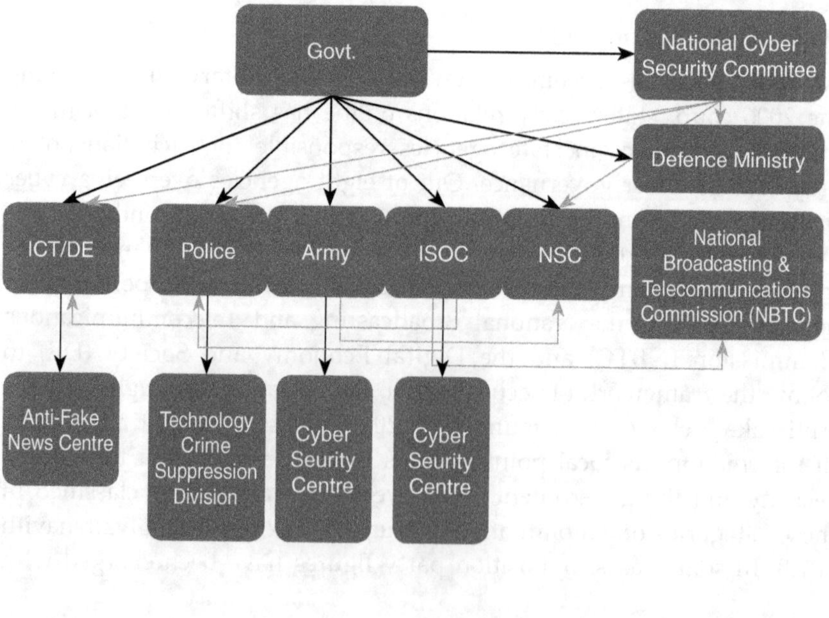

Policies: Control, Legal Repression and Manipulation

Three policy responses to "disinformation" are content block, legal sentences and content manipulation, carried out through legal mechanisms and civil society's surveillance. First, as with Southeast Asian counterparts (Ong 2019), digital repression in Thailand relies on the cocktail of draconian laws related to cyber crimes, and those concerning national security and defamation. These laws are namely:

- Computer-Related Crime Act (enacted in 2007)
- Amended Computer Act (enacted in 2016)
- Article 112 (*lèse majesté*) (enacted in 1956)
- Orders of National Council for Peace and Order (implemented in 2014)
- Criminal Code, Sections 326 to 333 on defamation
- Article 116 of the Criminal Code on sedition
- Cybersecurity Act (enacted in 2019)

For the purpose of this chapter, let us pay attention to the security-oriented framing of cyber laws, and its consequences on the freedom of expression when these laws are applied together with other draconian laws. The CCA focuses on content offences committed on a computer, which are defined as the import into a computer system of forged or false computer data. The latter is identified as the information that "is likely to cause damage to a third party or the public ... to damage national security or cause public panic ...[and to create] an offence against national security..." Although the Act includes transferring pornographic data as a crime, this is stated marginally.[3] The centrality of cyber offence as a national security threat reflects in the use of CCA together with *lèse majesté* law (Ramasoota 2012, p. 88). In 2010 almost a third of computer crimes prosecutions were related to *lèse majesté* content (Suksri et al. 2010). And in 2012, the court orders effectively blocked more than 74,000 URLs (Poetranto and Senft 2016).

By the time the military staged another coup in 2014, efforts to control the official truth were paramount. These were clearly demonstrated in coup-makers' edicts upon their power seizure, which prohibited "distorted online news reports which could cause social division and unrest, ... disseminating messages aimed at inciting violence, disrespect and violation of the law as well as provoking resistance". The junta furthermore ordered internet providers to "monitor, inspect and suspend transmission of any distorted and provocative information which might cause turmoil in the Kingdom or affect national security or the good morals of the people". Lastly, the ruling military forbade mass media entrepreneurs and ISPs from publishing "news which might be threatening to the national security, information and news which might cause confusion ..."[4] Despite these orders, social media especially Facebook became the site for mobilizing anti-junta sentiment that at times translated into street activism. Fearing popular defiance of its rule, the regime moved to charge almost 400 online and offline violators between 2014 and 2018 (Human Rights Watch 2019). It allegedly shut down Facebook for thirty minutes right after staging the coup, but this backfired (Quartz 2014). At times, the regime threatened Facebook and YouTube with legal actions if they refuse to take down content considered to insult the monarchy and junta leaders (Reuters 2016).

The junta amended the 2007 CCA, claiming to boost Thailand's digital economy while using national security to justify this legal modification. Information security was reinterpreted as a key ingredient for economic advancement in the digital age. This rhetoric gave many citizens the impression that the law would limit crimes affecting the growing sector of digital economy, thereby drawing popular acceptance (Human Rights Watch 2019). Despite diluting the security framework, the amended CCA remains an instrument to punish those importing "distorted", "forged" and "false" information into a computer system. The way untrue information is defined in opposition to the official truth is unchanged.[5]

Since CCA 2007 and its amended version came into effect, cyber persecutions have gone up, so has self-censorship. While computer laws mainly lead to content block, its application in conjunction with other draconian laws has cost the accused harsh jail sentences, thereby generating a "chilling effect". According to the online news outlet Prachatai, from 2007 to September 2016, there are approximately 704 cases of *lèse majesté*, each facing jail sentences up to fifteen years or more. The number was highest in 2015 under the junta (Wongwat 2017), with several cases involved social media postings, sharing or liking *lèse majesté* content (Human Rights Watch 2019). Despite *lèse majesté* allegations having subsided since 2018, those accused of violating the sedition alongside computer crime laws have steadily increased, and some of those persecuted under these laws have undergone the legal process similar to that of *lèse majesté*. Between May 2017 and May 2019, 117 people were charged with sedition, most likely facing up to seven-year jail sentences (iLaw 2019b). A most prominent case was that of the outspoken journalist, Praiwit Rojanapruk, who in 2015 posted criticisms of the junta in his personal Facebook page. He later faced the lawsuits of sedition and computer crime (Thai Lawyers for Human Rights 2017). The recent CCA case of the Twitter account owner, "Anonymous", was treated as if the accused violated *lèse majesté* (Thai Lawyers for Human Rights 2020). Moreover, the criminal defamation conducive to one-year imprisonment has been filed repeatedly against those addressing human rights violations by the military or pro-regime corporates (Haberkorn 2019). Prior to the 2016 amendment, the CCA was used together with criminal defamation to increase jail sentences (iLaw 2016).

The 2019 Cybersecurity Bill is another new institution created to further securitize information. The Bill addresses cyber threats to national infrastructure such as banking, energy and public transport, seeking to unify state agencies responsible for preventing and responding to cyber harms. In this sense, the law does not directly tackle disinformation. However, there remain clauses within the law open for a broad interpretation of what is considered "cyber threats that affect peace and order of the citizens, and destabilise the state". In line with the evolution of the CCA, critics argue that the Bill can be weaponized to silence the opposition alleged to implicate in "cyber terrorism". In times of crisis, the Bill furthermore licenses the authorities to intercept private online messages and intensify "real-time" surveillance (iLaw 2019a).

In conjunction with content block and legal repression, the security forces also rely on information manipulations as a strategy to shape public opinion. This scheme can be traced back to the 1970s and 1980s counter-communist insurgency when the ISOC launched the Information Operation (IO) and trained armed civilian groups as Village Scouts, Krating Daeng and Nawapol in grassroots surveillance. Despite its inactivity in the 1990s, the ISOC's surveillance networks and IO have resurged in the wake of the latest political conflicts (Pawakapan 2017). Concurrently, the Cyber Scouts programme was introduced in 2010 and has since 2014 been reactivated under then ICT. While the direct connection between the ISOC and the contemporary Cyber Scouts is difficult to establish, but as Schaffer observes, "it is not by chance that the Cyber Scouts were named after" the 1970s Village Scouts (Schaffer 2020). The Cyber Scouts' goal has been to police the internet, in search of "distorted information", while propagating among the younger generation royalist values. Their work includes befriending suspects on Facebook and starting conversations about sensitive issues. When violation of *lèse majesté* law occurs, the Scouts would report the alleged case to the authorities (Blum-Dumontet 2016). As of 2017, there were 388 schools committed to the programme. More than 120,000 students have been recruited as Cyber Scouts, and the number may double in the near future (*CIO World and Business* 2017).

While Cyber Scouts focuses on monitoring, other cyber units produce social media content favourable to the regime and hostile to the opposition. The ISOC allegedly hosts around forty IO units, comprising over 1,000 rank-and-file army personnel and possibly high school students in the reserve officer training corps (ROTC or in the Thai acronym *ror dor*).[6] According to a student's memoir, "[military] trainers guided us [students] how to respond and craft social media messages. Later, ... [we were told] to post comments displaying loyalty toward the nation and the monarchy" (Lebnak 2019; Macan-Markar 2020b). The cyber unit has reportedly received basic training workshops about social media usage and a lump sum of 100 to 300 Thai Baht (US$3–9) per person per month (Isranews Agency 2020). Through numerous weblogs and fake Facebook as well as Twitter accounts, cyber troops have effectively created online content containing disinformation and doctored images which portray pro-democracy politicians and dissidents as traitors. The disinformation then gets repeatedly shared in state-funded social media sites. Other assignments include clicking "like" on pro-government posts on Facebook and Twitter, generating pro-government and anti-opposition hashtags on Twitter, and trolling social media commenters who appear to support the opposition.[7]

Organized groups aside, ad-hoc civil society groups—from both pro- and anti-establishment camps—have discredited their respective opponents in social media platforms. Anti-establishment forces have created several Facebook pages that share disinformation regarding government policies, economic recession and its failure to handle health crises. The end game is to incite national panic possibly culminating in anti-government protests. But it is disinformation architected by the conservative segment of civil society that sometimes gets the greenlight from regime authorities who benefit from weakening the opposition. A storyline profoundly effective in achieving this objective is labelling dissidents as a foreign agent. Rightwing online media, including the Thai-language T-News, The Mettad, Chaopraya News and Deeps News, and the English-language Alt Thai News Network (ATNN) and New Eastern Outlook (NEO), ignited the propagation of this point by repeatedly denouncing pro-democracy movements and parties as "foreign lackeys" who receive funding from the West to overthrow the country's traditional pillars. Drawn on a conspiracy theory linking a series of coloured revolution in former Soviet spaces with Western powers, these online outlets insist that foreign support for Thailand's opposition movements is a Central Intelligence Agency (CIA) scheme for regime change in order to revive Western hegemony in Southeast Asia. Some of these media outlets have recently been taken down by Facebook due to reports of disinformation. It is also accused of linking with the Russian government.

Pro-regime traditional media outlets have also played a key role in the securitization process, largely by re-inforcing narratives on social media. For instance, in August 2016 *The Nation*—a mainstream, English-language newspaper—published the "Soros Leaks". Citing a New Atlas article, it claimed that the Fund for Open Society and the National Endowment for Democracy had sponsored a number of dissidents in Thailand. In early 2018 this alleged scandal resurged on the prominent Thansetthakit news website, reaffirming the narrative of Western transgression of Thailand's sovereignty. This sparked heated debates on social media. Many social media influencers with tens of thousands of followers actively reposted it and expressed their agreement with the story. In the comments section linked to the news article, Thai organizations receiving international support have been disparaged as "parasites" and "traitors". Some comments are extremely hostile, wishing the "wipe out" of "families of these traitors". In 2017, a columnist for *Thai Rath*, a national tabloid, proposed that the junta should enact a law that circumvents the international funding of non-governmental organizations (NGOs)—as happened in India, Russia and Hungary (Sombatpoonsiri 2018).

The tactics of legal repression and content manipulation mostly work in tadem in the securitization process. While anti-establishment protesters would be charged with CCA and related laws for allegedly spreading security-sensitive information, the IO troops would craft online messages discrediting protesters as traitors and foreign puppets. According to an official document, the authorities anticipate that multiple lawsuits would undercut the movement's morale and resources and thereby hinder effective mobilization. In making these lawsuits acceptable for the public, IO helps taints the image of protesters as a security threat. When this securitization process is complete, "the government [is seen to] pursue necessary measures to keep the peace and order ..."[8]

RECLAIMING CYBERSPACES BY CIVIL SOCIETY?

If securitizing disinformation shifts the status of a political matter to a security urgency, thus conveniently morphed into a political weapon that strangles contentious civil society, one way to resist this is to pursue a tactic of de-securitizing disinformation. That is to say, disinformation should be regarded as a highly contested political issue whose definitions are contingent on power relations between the accused of creating and spreading disinformation, and its accuser.[9] In the case of Thailand, the problem of disinformation does exist, but policy responses to it are shaped by the autocratic regime determined to preserve its status quo against forces of change. Accordingly, ruling elites have easy access to legal and bureaucratic tools, thus exploiting them to juxtapose the notion of "false", "fake" and "distorted" information with a national security threat defined as a challenge to the official truth.

So far concerted efforts to dismantle this juxtaposition is only nascent. For instance, in parallel with the DE's Anti-Fake News Centre, the Agence France-Presse (AFP) together with Facebook Thailand have recently initiated the "fact-check" bureau. It has cross-examined and filtered dozens of online news that are either misleading or false, including disinformation equally about the government and the opposition (*Bangkok Post* 2019b). A similar proposal is implemented by Line, the most used chat application in Thailand, and the Associated Press (AP) (*Naewna* 2020). Other media outlets, academics and civil society groups have carried out a host of projects and studies to increase media literacy and cope with online hate speech.

Despite the merits, these efforts remain separate from campaigns that address the process of securitization conducive to political abuse of existing cyber laws. Although the effect of these campaigns was limited partly due to narrow civic spaces under the previous military rule, one campaign stood out: anti-Single Gateway proposal. In 2015, the junta-appointed cabinet issued an order for relevant state agencies to unify the internet gateways, known as Single Gateway or the Firewall, claiming that it would help cope with cyber threats. The policy attracted widespread criticisms, from civil society groups emphasizing the impact on freedom of expression to entrepreneurs worried about data exposure that would discourage foreign investment to ordinary citizens dependent on speedy internet for entertainment, transport and communication. Campaigners harvested this public scepticism by launching online petition and alternative discussion forums. Meanwhile, affected business groups submitted their own petition to then ICT minister. These initiatives generated nationwide debates about this matter and effectively replaced the security language underpinning the proposal with the frame of everyday life inconvenience and economic recession potentially caused by "slow internet". Eventually, this policy became extremely unpopular and the junta decided to drop it (Sompatpoonsiri 2017).

What civil society can learn from this campaign is the way a cyber policy was lifted from the security domain through discursive reconfiguration. The notion of disinformation may be alarming for many, but that does not warrant it a matter of security urgency that bypasses democratic deliberation.

CONCLUSION

Autocratization and polarization continue to characterize Thailand's politics of disinformation. The country has been largely divided along the ideological lines of pro- and anti-establishment, with the former determined to defend traditional institutions and values at all cost and the latter resolved to achieve liberal democracy, pluralism and cosmopolitanism. The fault line seems to be between the past and the future; neither side is willing to compromise. But Thailand's polarization is infused with autocracy as ruling elites take the side of pro-establishment ideology. Under these circumstances, the notion of true information is contingent on whether or not it helps ruling elites to retain their status quo in political, economic and cultural domains. In this sense, the opposition's rhetoric that challenges elites' truth claims to potentially threaten this status quo; one way to curtail this threat is to associate the information deviating from the official version with a security threat. Despite disinformation stemming from different sectors in Thai society, measures such as online surveillance, legal sentences and content manipulation mostly target the opposition. Ultimately, ruling elites have sought to achieve the monopoly of online information by attributing it to safeguarding national security. Nonetheless, in the age of social media conducive to decentralizing digital spaces, securitizing disinformation can be met with resistance. Many Thais have risked legal penalities to expose political abuses of cyber laws and the illegitimacy of authorities' cyber trolling. Most importantly, they have used social media platforms to mobilize collective defiance against securitizing the pluralistic nature of online information.

NOTES

1. The Constitutional Court dissolved the Future Forward Party on 21 February 2020 on the ground of violating an electoral regulation.
2. *Lèse Majesté* or Article 112 is the legal code which subjects those accused of defaming royal family members to jail sentences up to fifteen years. The Article is vague and thus easily used as a political weapon. Between 2014 and 2018, 108 people were charged with *lèse majesté*.
3. Computer-Related Crimes Act, B.E. 2550 (2007), *Royal Gazette* no. 124, sect. 27 *kor*, 18 June 2007, p. 4.
4. National Council for Peace Order, Announcement 12/2014 and 17/2014, *Royal Gazette* no. 131, special sect. 84 *ngor*, 26 May 2014, p. 11; National Council for Peace Order, Announcement 18/2014, no. 131, special sect. 87 *gnor*, 28 May 2014, p. 5; and National Council for Peace Order, Announcement 26/2014, no. 131, special sect. 89 *gnor*, 29 May 2014, p. 3.
5. "(Amended) Computer-Related Crimes Act B.E. 2560 (2016)", *Royal Gazette* no. 134, sect. 10 *kor*, 24 January 2016, p. 24.
6. The Territorial Defence Department of the Defence Ministry offers a military training course for high school students. Students would serve in a reserve officer training corps (ROTC). Upon three to five years completion, graduating students are exempted from annual military constriptions.
7. This string of information about the ISOC's IO has been disclosed in detail by an opposition MP in the February 2020 confidence vote motion. For more details, see Thai PBS (2020). Civil society has long suspected the role

of the ISOC in manipulating social media content, but without detailed information. See Pawakapan (2017), p. 5.
8. Criminal Court Prosecutor, "Notes on Anti-NCPO Protests at Victory Monument on 10 February 2017", Chor 14 Aor 1197/2017.
9. For the concept of de-securitization, see Huysmans (1998).

REFERENCES

AFP Face Check. https://factcheck.afp.com/afp-thailand.
Areepermporn, Panchai. 2018. "Summary of Social Media Usage". *The Standard*, 2 March 2018. https://thestandard.co/thailand-social-media-statistics-2017/ (accessed 4 March 2020).
Balzacq, Thierry. 2011. "A Theory of Securitization: Origins, Core Assumptions, and Variants". In *Securitization Theory: How Security Problems Emerge and Dissolve*, edited by Thierry Balzacq. London: Routledge.
Bangkokbiznews. 2019. "Cabinet to Charge Source of Rumour on Tampon Tax", 17 December 2019. https://www.bangkokbiznews.com/news/detail/858601 (accessed 23 January 2020).
Bangkok Post. 2019a. "Political Stalemate Hits Cybersecurity Bill", 26 April 2019. https://www.bangkokpost.com/business/1667208/political-stalemate-hits-cybersecurity-bill (accessed 23 January 2020).
———. 2019b. "AFP to Assist Face-Check Programme", 18 October 2019. https://www.bangkokpost.com/business/1774454/afp-to-assist-fact-check-programme (accessed 23 January 2020).
BBC. 2019. "Apirat Kongsomphong: Communist Business Men, Politicians and Academics are a National Security Threat", 11 October 2019. https://www.bbc.com/thai/thailand-50009884 (accessed 23 January 2020).
Blum-Dumontet, Eva. 2016. "Friends, Followers, Police Officers, and Enemies: Social Surveillance in Thailand". *Privacy International*, 20 September 2016. https://www.privacyinternational.org/node/935 (accessed 5 November 2019).
Cavelty, Myriam D. 2008. *Cyber-Security and Threat Politics: US Efforts to Secure the Information Age*. London: Routledge.
Chaiching, Nattapoll. 2010. "Monarchy and the Royalist Movement in Modern Thai Politics, 1932–1957". In *Saying the Unsayable: Monarchy and Democracy in Thailand*, edited by Soren Ivarsson and Lotte Isager, pp. 146–78. Copenhagen: NIAS.
Chaisukosol, Charnchai. 2009. "Technology and Nonviolent Political Struggle: The Internet in Thailand". PhD dissertation, Chulalongkorn University.
Chaloemtiarana, Thak. 2007. *Thailand: The Politics of Despotic Paternalism*. Ithaca, NY: Cornell Southeast Asia Program.

CIO World and Business. 2017. "Cyber Scout as Social Protection Network", 15 February 2017. http://www.cioworldmagazine.com/supon-phrommaphan-cyber-scout/ (accessed 23 January 2020).

Haberkorn, Tyrell. 2019. "Defamation Case against Ngamsuk Ruttanasatian, Mahidol Lecturer and Human Rights Defender". Prachatai, 9 August 2019. https://prachatai.com/english/node/8170 (accessed 4 February 2020).

Hassine, Wafa Ben. 2016. "The Crime of Speech: How Arab Governments Use the Law to Silence Expression Online". *Electronic Frontier*. https://www.eff.org/pages/crime-speech-how-arab-governments-use-law-silence-expression-online (accessed 4 March 2020).

Human Rights Watch. 2016. "Thailand: Cyber Crime Act Tightens Internet-Control", 21 December 2016. https://www.hrw.org/news/2016/12/21/thailand-cyber-crime-act-tightens-internet-control (accessed 23 January 2020).

———. 2019. "To Speak Out is Dangerous: Criminalization of Peaceful Expression in Thailand", 24 October 2019. https://www.hrw.org/report/2019/10/24/speak-out-dangerous/criminalization-peaceful-expression-thailand (accessed 23 January 2020).

Huysmans, Jef. 1998. "The Question of the Limit: Desecuritisation and the Aesthetics of Horror in Political Realism". *Millennium – Journal of International Studies* 27, no. 3: 569–89.

iLaw. 2016. "Criminal Defamation Law as Strategic Lawsuit Against Public Participation", 2 August 2016. https://freedom.ilaw.or.th/blog/BasicDefamation (accessed 23 January 2020).

———. 2019a. "Cybersecurity Law 62: Possibility of State Surveillance of Dissidents", 25 February 2019a. https://ilaw.or.th/node/5173 (accessed 23 January 2020).

———. 2019b. "Latest Statistics", 21 May 2019b. https://freedom.ilaw.or.th/en/content/latest-statistic (accessed 23 January 2020).

Internal Security Operations Command (ISOC). 2016. "ISOC Strategy, B.E. 2555-2559 (A.D. 2012-2016)". http://www.isocthai.go.th/GorPorRor/4YearsPlan(2555-2558)Completed.pdf (accessed 23 January 2020).

———. 2018. "ISOC Strategy, B.E. 2560-2564 (A.D. 2017-2021)". https://www.isoc.go.th/wp-content/uploads/2018/01/strategy2560-2564.pdf (accessed 23 January 2020).

Isranews Agency. 2020. "Future Forward MP Claims Army-ISOC's IO Units Get 100-300 Baht Per Month", 25 February 2020. https://www.isranews.org/isranews-news/85973-isranews-85973.html (accessed 10 March 2020).

Johnson, Kay, Panu Wongcha-um and Panarat Thepgumpanat. 2019. "The Threat Now is Fake News: Thai Army Chief Describes Hybrid War". Reuters, 9 August 2019. https://www.reuters.com/article/us-thailand-military/the-threat-now-is-fake-news-thai-army-chief-describes-hybrid-war-idUSKCN1UZ1L3 (accessed 23 January 2020).

Kaewjinda, Kaweewit. 2019. "Thai Political Party Slammed with 'Fake News' Charge". *AP*, 5 March 2019. https://apnews.com/67480565c3054ed787b35e4f55816570.

Köhler, Imke. 2019. *Framing the Threat: How Politicians Justify Their Policies*. Berlin: Walter de Druyter.

Lebnak, Supachat. 2019. "Fake News and Social Media Government and Military Struggle to Control". *The Matter*, 14 August 2019. https://thematter.co/thinkers/fake-news-ghost-of-the-state/82654 (accessed 23 January 2020).

Lui Yangyue. 2014. "Transgressiveness, Civil Society and Internet Control in Southeast Asia". *The Pacific Review* 27, no. 3: 383–407.

Macan-Markar, Marwaan. 2020a. "Thai Judiciary on Trial as It Weighs Scrapping Pro-democracy Party". *Asian Review*, 19 January 2020a. https://asia.nikkei.com/Politics/Thai-judiciary-on-trial-as-it-weighs-scrapping-pro-democracy-party?fbclid=IwAR3Gaxb4MMncGJYtPx-15IHtAjPF7-uOgLjHLrYk0AGdEnujTzbitNrL7QQ (accessed 23 January 2020).

———. 2020b. "Thailand's Fearless Youth Stands Up to the Military and Monarchy". *Nikkei Asian Review*, 12 February 2020b. https://asia.nikkei.com/Spotlight/Cover-Story/Thailand-s-fearless-youth-stands-up-to-the-military-and-monarchy?fbclid=IwAR 36EsYWOgaFrIw6qTy4K_TaC1pHjVx0-2zXkS-A4wbXt3OI3ZK2_ddjrdY (accessed 13 February 2020).

Montlake, Simon. 2010. "Thailand's Red Shirts and Yellow Shirts Battle It Out on Facebook". *The Christian Science Monitor*, 24 May 2010. https://www.csmonitor.com/World/Asia-Pacific/2010/0524/Thailand-s-red-shirts-and-yellow-shirts-battle-it-out-on-Facebook (accessed 23 January 2020).

Naewna. 2020. "Thailand's Line Holds Workshop 'Stop Fake News'", 23 January 2020. https://www.naewna.com/lady/444926 (accessed 23 January 2020).

National Security Council. 2014. "National Security Policy, 2015-2021". http://www.nsc.go.th/Download1/policy58.pdf (accessed 23 January 2020).

Neo, Ric. 2019. "The Securitisation of Fake News in Singapore". *International Politics* 57: 724–40. 10.1057/s41311-019-00198-4.

Ong, Elvin. 2019. "Online Repression and Self-Censorship: Evidence from Southeast Asia". *Government and Opposition*: 1–22. https://doi-org.ezproxy.tulibs.net/10.1017/gov.2019.18.

Pathmanand, Ukrist. 1998. "The Thaksin Shinawatra Group: A Study of the Relationship between Money and Politics in Thailand". *Copenhagen Journal of Asian Studies* 13.

Pawakapan, Puangthong R. 2017. *The Central Role of Thailand's Internal Security Operations*. Trends in Southeast Asia, no. 17/2017. Singapore: ISEAS – Yusof Ishak Institute.

Poetranto, Irene and Adam Senft. 2016. "Internet Governance During Crisis: The Changing Landscape of Thailand". *GigaNet: Global Internet Governance Academic Network, Annual Symposium 2016*. http://dx.doi.org/10.2139/ssrn.2909377 (accessed 4 March 2020).

Pongsawat, Pitch. 2002. "Virtual Democracy in Thailand: Information Technology, Internet Political Message Board, and the Politics of Representation in Thailand after 1992". *Social Sciences Journal* 33, no. 1: 141–66.

Prachatai. 2016. "Army Cyber Centre Tasked with Lese Majeste Hunt", 1 November 2016. https://prachatai.com/english/node/6685 (accessed 23 January 2020).

Quartz. 2014. "The Thai Junta Briefly Blocked Facebook in a Dry Run for a Social Media Blackout", 28 May 2014. https://qz.com/214173/the-thai-junta-briefly-blocked-facebook-in-a-dry-run-for-a-social-media-blackout/ (accessed 23 January 2020).

Ramasoota, Pirongrong. 2012. "Internet Politics in Thailand after the 2006 Coup: Regulation by Code and a Contested Ideological Terrain". In *Access Contested: Security, Identity and Resistance in Asian Cyberspace*, edited by Ronald Deibert, John Palfrey, Rafal Rohozinski and Jonathan Zittrain. Massachusetts: MIT Press.

Reuters. 2016. "Thai Junta Pressures Facebook, Line to Censor Online Post", 31 January 2016. https://www.reuters.com/article/us-thailand-internet/thai-junta-pressures-facebook-line-to-censor-online-posts-idUSKCN0V90LW (accessed 23 January 2020).

Riggs, Fred W. 1966. *Thailand: The Modernization of a Bureaucratic Polity*. Honolulu: East-West Center Press.

Ruiz, Todd and Teirra Kamolvattanavith. 2019. "With the Anti Fake News Center, Thailand Gets Its 'Ministry of Truth'". *Cononuts Bangkok*, 12 December 2019. https://coconuts.co/bangkok/news/with-the-anti-fake-news-center-thailand-gets-its-ministry-of-truth/ (accessed 23 January 2020).

Schaffer, Wolfram. 2020. "The Social Media". In *Routledge Handbook of Contemporary Thailand*, edited by Pavin Chachavalpongpun, pp. 83–114. London: Routledge.

Schneider, Florian. 2018. *China's Digital Nationalism*. Oxford: Oxford University Press.

Shahbaz, Adrian. 2018. *The Rise of Digital Authoritarianism: Fake News, Data Collection, and the Challenge to Democracy*. Washington, D.C.: Freedom House. https://freedomhouse.org/article/rise-digital-authoritarianism-fake-news-data-collection-and-challenge-democracy (accessed 4 March 2020).

Sinpeng, Aim. 2013. "State Repression in Cyberspace: The Case of Thailand". *Asian Politics & Policy* 5, no. 3.

Sivasomboon, Busaba. 2019. "Thai Court to Rule on Case Linking Opposition to Illuminati". *AP News*, 23 December 2019. https://apnews.com/b4aba7ab43b84c64d12224022c5125c9 (accessed 23 January 2020).

Sombatpoonsiri, Janjira. 2017. "Growing Cyber Activism in Thailand". *Carnegie Endowment for International Peace*, 14 August 2017. https://carnegieendowment.org/2017/08/14/growing-cyber-activism-in-thailand-pub-72804/ (accessed 23 January 2020).

———. 2018. "Manipulating Civic Spaces: Cyber Trolling in Thailand and the Philippines". *GIGA Focus Asia* 3 (June). https://www.giga-hamburg.de/en/publication/cyber-trolling-in-thailand-and-the-philippines (accessed 23 January 2020).

Suksri, Sawatree, Siriphon Kusonsinwut and Orapin Yingyongpathana. 2010. "Situational Report on Control and Censorship of Online Media, through the Use of Laws and the Imposition of Thai State Policies". Heinrich Böll Stiftung Southeast Asia, 8 December 2010. https://th.boell.org/en/2013/11/12/situational-report-control-and-censorship-online-media-through-use-laws-and-imposition (accessed 23 January 2020).

Suriyawongkul, Arthit. 2012. "Facebook Politics: Culture-Politics on Thai Online Social Network (2010–2012)". Master's thesis, Thammasat Univesity, 2012, pp. 30–35.

Tejapira, Kasian. 2006. "Toppling Thaksin". *New Left Review* 39 (May–June).

Thai Lawyers for Human Rights. 2017. "Pravit Rojjanapruk Charged with 116-Computer Law", 18 August 2017. https://www.tlhr2014.com/?p=4921 (accessed 23 January 2020).

———. 2020. "Memoir of 'Niranam' Before Bail", 24 February 2020. https://www.tlhr2014.com/?p =16191 (accessed 10 March 2020).

Thai PBS. 2020. "Opposition Alleges Army Behind Cyber Attacks on Critics, Holds PM Responsible", 26 February 2020. https://www.thaipbsworld.com/opposition-alleges-army-behind-cyber-attacks-on-critics-holds-pm-responsible/ (accessed 10 March 2020).

Wæver, Ole. 1995. "Securitization and Desecuritization". In *On Security*, edited by Ronnie D. Lipschutz, pp. 46–86. New York: Columbia University Press.

Weerawan, Suwij. 2019. "Illuminati and Future Forward". *Manager Online*, 26 December 2019. https://mgronline.com/daily/detail/9620000123125 (accessed 23 January 2020).

Wongkijrungreung, Thatchai. 2009. "Mirror.or.th: Reflecting on Volunteering Work on the Internet". *Sarakadee* 25, no. 296.

Wongwat, Mettha. 2017. "One Decade of 112 Case". Prachatai, 14 November 2017. https://prachatai.com/journal/2017/11/74108 (accessed 23 January 2020).

7

CAMBODIA: FROM DEMOCRATIZATION OF INFORMATION TO DISINFORMATION

Mun Vong and Aim Sinpeng

This chapter chronicles the evolution of social media in Cambodia from its inception as a relatively unfettered platform for social interaction, to becoming an emergent venue for political participation, and finally to its role in the suppression of political opposition. In so doing, it is argued that social media enables simultaneously bottom-up, expressive civic activism and top-down, proactive exercise of political domination by the ruling party, the Cambodian People's Party (CPP).

Cambodians had reasons to be optimistic when the internet and social media arrived in the late 2000s. Despite a long history of restrictions on traditional media, there was no indication early on that the Cambodian government would seek to curtail freedom in cyberspace. Indeed, up until 2014, internet censorship did not go beyond restricting sexually explicit materials online and blocking of only a few anti-government websites (Freedom House 2009). Entrepreneurs, activists and journalists alike were excited by the economic, social and political transformations these information and communication technologies (ICT) could bring. Social media and the internet were seen to have provided a relatively free space for ordinary Cambodians to exchange information, interact and share viewpoints—all of which could strengthen social capital and increase political efficacy. The level of freedom found online was so unprecedented in comparison to other media outlets that some activists placed high hopes it could usher in the era of "digital democracy" in Cambodia (Chak 2009). The early optimism of the democratizing power of the internet lived on for several years, thanks to a slow expansion of internet connectivity and a low ICT adoption rate, which had kept the cyberspace relatively free of government interventions. Internet enthusiasts were so optimistic about the digital future that the first "internet party"—the Chatter Party—was founded as early as in 2006 through networks of bloggers and web service provider associations (Bun 2006). A small Cambodian blogosphere was emerging with some bloggers even sharing critical views of the government freely online. With half of its population under the age of twenty-five and a high rate of mobile subscriptions, Cambodia was poised for the digital disruptions that could spawn social and political change.

Yet Cambodia's cyberspace today quickly became more repressive (Freedom House 2019). The consecutive decline in internet freedom is a recent development, but one that is in line with existing patterns of traditional media controls. What explains Cambodia's autocratizing turn when it comes to digital media? We argue that cyber controls by the Cambodian government are motivated by concerns over regime security: the ability for Hun Sen and the ruling CPP to maintain political dominance. The key turning point for Cambodia's road to digital authoritarianism was the 2013 general elections where the CPP nearly lost to the opposition party, Cambodia National Rescue Party (CNRP). For Hun Sen, who has been the country's leader for over three decades, this near electoral defeat signalled to him the need to take social media seriously. Social media was not just an expansive and influential place for political opposition, but also a critical space for the ruling party to reconnect with its people, with whom they had been out of touch. From 2014 onwards, Hun Sen rebranded himself as the "man of the people"—offline and online—reconstructing his identity around his digital popularity.

As in some other parts of Southeast Asia, Cambodia's information landscape is dominated by Facebook, the dominant social media platform in the country. That the platform is transnational and does not operate at the whims of the Cambodian government serves to weaken the CPP and Hun Sen's ability to control information at will. Unlike in Russia and China, whose social media platforms are indigenous and within arm's length of the state, the CPP will have to contend with a much more contentious situation when it comes to manipulating social media for its own gain. Ultimately, it is the lack of the Cambodian state's ability to exert greater control over what happens on the platform that provides an opportunity for civil society expression.

This chapter contains three parts. First, it discusses the period of more open internet and social media in Cambodia. The second section examines Cambodia's autocratizing turn in its internet regime, following the CPP's electoral debacle in 2013. It elaborates on the rise of expressive political participation and the incorporation of social media into the CPP's political strategy in light of the 2013 election result. Third, we discuss the role of social media in the dissolution of the CNRP and the political and social ramifications of disinformation. In the conclusion, we discuss the future of social media and state-society relations in Cambodia as internet and social media adoption reaches a critical mass.

THE EMERGENCE OF DIGITAL PLATFORMS

Digital transformations in Cambodia came slowly and gradually. Lagging behind almost all other Southeast Asian neighbours, Cambodia's internet penetration did not take off until 2015 (see Figure 7.1). The slow internet and social media growth had meant that traditional media delayed its digital conversion and most Cambodians continued to consume radio and television, leaving the cyberspace unregulated and open. Up until 2016, television and radio had been the most important news sources in Cambodia. These mass media, however, are primarily owned and run by friends and relatives of the government leader (Holman 2015). In broadcasting government-friendly news, critical voices are censored and can hardly be heard. Without fair access to the media by the political opposition, the electoral playing field had been skewed in favour of the incumbent. With the CPP controlling many broadcasting and radio channels and increasing crackdown of print media in the late 2010s, the internet and social media became the only safe space for dissenting and critical voices in Cambodia, be they from civil society, journalists or ordinary citizens.

FIGURE 7.1
Internet Penetration in Southeast Asia, 2011-19 (% POP)

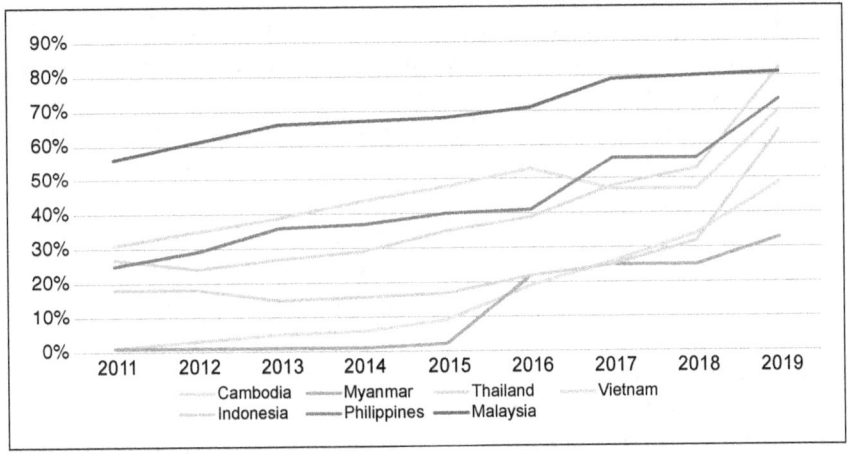

Sources: World Bank, Internet World States.

The arrival of the internet and social media was a positive development in Cambodia: it provided new space for information exchange, generated public discussions on important issues and contributed to the expansion of the civil society. Facebook is where Cambodia's largest LGBT organizations—the Rainbow Community Kampuchea and Cambodia Pride—originated. New space for information exchange gave rise to the democratization of information. Facebook pages set up by government supporters and opposition activists alike mushroomed vying to articulate their own versions of the stories. Some Facebook personalities from both government and opposition camps, such as Pheng Vannak and Thy Sovantha, have a large number of followers who in turn make possible the rapid transmission of information. These social media influencers spread sensitive stories and news that can easily speak to the emotion of their followers and the wider audience. Some of these "information blasts" have become topics of popular gossip and newsworthy stories for mainstream media (Vong and Hok 2018).

Social media enables broader critical reporting from foreign outlets, such as the US-funded Voice of America and Radio Free Asia that is not subject to government control. These foreign broadcasters have become hugely popular on Facebook pages in Cambodia. Their popularity is a reflection of decreasing appetite for CPP-centric narratives promoted on state and state-linked media. *The Cambodia Daily*, a highly regarded English-language newspaper, which was forced to shut down in 2017 over an unsettled tax dispute with the government, remains active on Facebook by producing original contents in the form of interviews with political commentators. Mobile phones and other electronic devices allow activists to capture human rights violations and other instances of state misconduct. Social media enables them to spread these documented incidents more rapidly and to a wider domestic and international audience. For example, monk Luon Sovath has engaged in human rights advocacy through the circulation of videos of land evictions that he recorded with his digital devices earning him the nickname of "multimedia monk" (Radio Free Asia 2012).

Social media has also been particularly useful for small civil society organizations. Some have relied on Facebook to engage people in "national conversation", spread educational messages, and raise funds to sustain their activities (Gill 2017). It also enables them to have an alternative to street protests that are subject to growing suppression. For example, the arrest of human rights defenders implicated in Kem Sokha's sex scandal triggered a vigorous online campaign. The #FREETHE5KH (Free the Khmer Five) campaign was launched in August 2016 to advocate for their release. It was followed by the "I am the Five" photo campaign which encouraged social media users to post photos of themselves with faces of the five, and the "Black Monday" campaign when supporters of the five wore black on Mondays to "mourn" the country's declining human rights situation (Freedom House 2017).

By contrast, the ruling CCP was slow to react to the potential threat an expansive and open cyberspace could bring to regime stability. Its initial focus in the mid to late 2000s was to curb the use of text messaging by political opposition. The CPP was so threatened by the surge in the use of SMS messaging by opposition parties and civil society organizations alike that it banned its use for two days before the 2007 commune elections (*Sydney Morning Herald* 2007). At the same time, the CPP also deployed widely the use of mobile phones to activate and mobilize its support base, which contributed to its victory in the election (Kierans 2010). With growing repression on the use of mobile texts to campaign against the government, activists, regime critics and opposition parties resorted to using the internet and social media instead. The CNRP, more than any other opposition parties, took advantage of the largely uncensored cyberspace, especially on Facebook, to mobilize support both online and offline in the lead-up to the 2013 general elections (Meyn 2013a). It was not until the CPP nearly lost these elections that both Hun Sen and the key party officials took social media seriously.

What did the surge of alternative sources of information do to Cambodia? In the beginning, political activists took advantage of the less restricted online space to mobilize anti-government sentiment and support for opposition parties. The CNRP was most adept at harnessing the power of social media for political gain. Cambodia reached its turning point in the state-society relations online in the lead up to the 2013 national elections.

SOCIAL MEDIA AND POLITICAL ACTIVISM

Social media political activism in Cambodia was truly born in the run-up to the 2013 general elections. The elections turned out to be the moment the dominance of the ruling CPP was most closely threatened. The opposition CNRP—a merger between Sam Rainsy's self-named Sam Rainsy Party and Kem Sokha's Human Rights Party—surprisingly captured 44 per cent of the popular votes and 55 of the 123 parliamentary seats. Meanwhile, the CPP saw its popular vote share reduced to 49 per cent from 58 per cent in 2008 and its parliamentary seats to 68 from 90. The CPP's electoral disappointment coincided with growing significance of youth votes. In the 2013 elections, young people between the age of 18 and 30 constituted more than one third of the eligible voters. The CPP's emphasis on political stability failed to appeal to them as much as the CNRP's slogan of "change" represented by their welfare-oriented electoral pledge. Born in the more peaceful post Khmer Rouge period, the younger generation began to take political stability for granted and exhibited the aspiration for substantive reforms that translate into concrete developmental outcomes. Such preference provides the foundation for the attraction of the CNRP's populist policies.

The CNRP had taken advantage of social media with striking effect leading observers to attribute the party's electoral gain to its youth-driven online electoral campaigns. Both Sam Rainsy (then president) and Kem Sokha (then vice president) recruited young people with smart phones and laptops to capture their campaign trails and inundated their pages with updates. Facebook pages of grassroots activists too played a role. Updates on these "satellite" pages were credited for drawing supporters to the CNRP's campaign rallies, which drew some of the biggest and most youthful crowds in recent memory (Meyn 2013b). Commenting on the success of their communication strategy, a key member of the CNRP leadership Mu Sochua said: "The whole thing was social media. I would say 85 to 90 per cent of our youth in the city areas were able to mobilize everyday, and they were all organizing on Facebook" (Willemyns 2013).

The CNRP's electoral surge shocked Cambodia's ruling elites and its success on social media had not gone unnoticed by the CPP government. But instead of going down the path of access blocking and complete censorship, it has leveraged social media to complement its existing electoral strategy, which was found wanting in light of the election outcome. The once sophisticated system of deploying local authorities and clientelist systems to coerce and co-opt voters has been less effective in relation to rural youth who are less likely to own land and those who migrate to cities to seek employments. Their livelihoods are more dependent on market forces than party-sponsored development projects and handouts. Their political preferences are more likely to be shaped by their urban associates and social media than by "listening" to local authorities. Relative to their parents, their upbringing and mobility make them more insulated from local politics and electioneering. These forces combined to make the task of local leaders in rendering the younger population legible and "getting the vote out" very challenging. Hughes (2015) argues that the trend "has been building for years". Since at least 2003, local authorities have been uncertain about the youth's party preference as a village chief commented: "the father might be CPP, but the children not. It's difficult to tell" (Hughes and Sedara 2004). But this trend has slipped through the ruling party's attention.

Having realized the political significance of relating to youth, government officials, most notably Prime Minister Hun Sen became increasingly visible on social media. "Youth" often appears as a separate referent alongside "citizens" in his Facebook messages suggesting a targeted appeal to young people. The prime minister's foray into social media was formalized in September 2015 by an official announcement from his cabinet. It also triggered a more direct online political rivalry between the prime minister and Sam Rainsy, whose Facebook page was then the most liked among Cambodian politicians. The prime minister's fandom spiked rapidly from around one million to nearly three million in early 2016 amid accusations of "artificial likes" sourced from "click-farms" (Nass and Turton 2016).

Following the near defeat in the 2013 elections, Hun Sen took social media seriously and was determined to be the country's most popular person on social media. Today, with close to thirteen million followers, the prime minister's Facebook page is the most popular page in Cambodia and indeed in the world, behind only India's Prime Minister Narendra Modi and US President Donald Trump, two countries with much larger populations compared to Cambodia's fifteen million overall population. In his own words, the page is designed to "learn about citizens' livelihood", "give opportunities to citizens to get closer to me", "address social issues" and "improve efficiency of [public] services" (Fresh News 2016a). Without Facebook, he said in a public speech in 2016, problems would not be solved quickly. "Shouldn't such rapid way of solving problems be encouraged?" he asked. The prime minster would use Whatsapp to communicate with the concerned officials after he receives a complaint (Fresh News 2016c). In a move that further popularized social media uptake, the prime minister issued a guideline in February 2016 to ministers and provincial governors instructing them to set up working groups to "monitor and track daily news and requests from citizens that have been sent to the prime minister's page, and then respond and address [them] in a timely manner" (Fresh News 2016b).

It is not clear how the prime minister would navigate the myriad of complaints that eventually make their way to his attention. But in a rare interview, the prime minister's aid explained how his Facebook team would deal with critical comments on the prime minister's page. When they deem certain critical comments as "cross the line", they would reply directly to the users. Repeated offences would be handled by blocking the users, reporting to Facebook, and when this failed, reporting to the police (Rajagopalan 2018). It is then unsurprising that negative comments have largely been invisible on the prime minister's Facebook page.

From 2013 onwards, the government began to seriously increase information controls on the internet and social media platforms (see Figure 7.2). A new telecommunication law was passed in 2015 that gave the government greater control over the internet infrastructure. The bill can also hold telecom providers and ordinary users accountable to any breaches of proposed laws. Cyber-attacks against government critics and Facebook persecutions of dissenting voices have also increased, along with measures to increase surveillance on the internet and Facebook. Although the internet and social media continue to be the freest media in Cambodia, the country's internet freedom continues to be ranked as "partly free" with deterioration noted since 2018. A recent survey by local think tank Cambodia Development Resource Institute reveals that 55 per cent of Cambodian people are afraid of sharing or posting their political views online (Eng et al. 2019). A leaked draft of the cybercrime law suggested that content that would threaten the security, moral and cultural values of society and integrity of government agencies would not be permitted (Cybercrime Law Formulation Working Group of Council of Ministers 2019). As of July 2019 the draft law is still under ministerial review.

FIGURE 7.2
Cambodia's Net Freedom

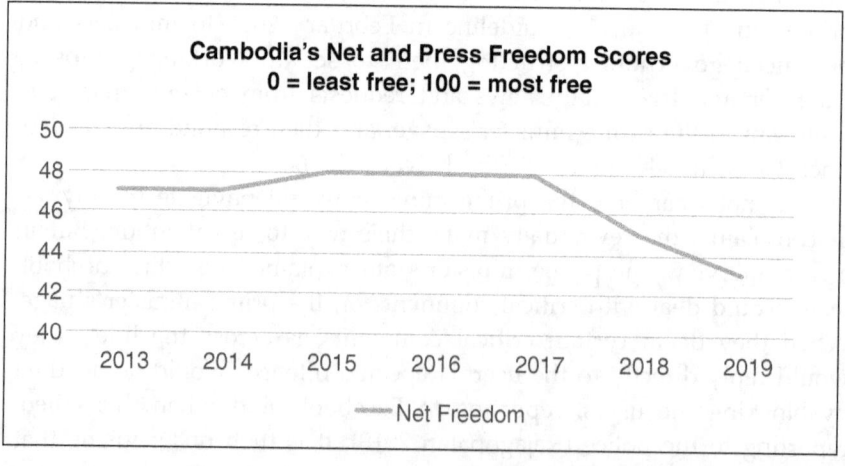

Source: Freedom House.

The social media landscape in Cambodia then is increasingly under the domain of Hun Sen's government. The twin programmes include: (a) a government eager to use social media to collect societal signals having been reeled from its poor performance in the 2013 elections, and (b) a tightening up of online expression to combat authority-challenging public criticism. Under such conditions, social media users who remain faithful to the efficacy of online engagement in producing government responsiveness have to thread the situation carefully. Some have become more mindful about information authenticity before sharing any content in order to avoid being accused of spreading misinformation or being politically biased towards the opposition. Some abstract the "correct meaning" of critical or sensitive political messages with creative pictorial or textual framing. For example, a young person posted a picture of the spring season likening blossoming flowers to promises made during electoral campaigns (Lee 2018).

The advent of social media activism and government officials' increasing footprints on the platform have drawn both approval and criticism. Proponents reason that social media enables people to engage in public affairs without requiring ample amount of time. It promotes public debates on social issues, naming and shaming abusers of state power, and government responsiveness. Critics, on the other hand, argue that government actions should be based on rules rather than on "popularity of a story", or "public outcry" (Men 2014). Government officials' foray into Facebook drew the ire of some observers who sarcastically name the Council of Ministers "the Facebook Council of Ministers". In response, the prime minister pointed out that the move has been welcomed by the general public and defended that this is a form of "digital government" to address problems more efficiently (Fresh News 2016d).

Weighing on this issue, Vong and Hok (2018) consider the manifestations of expressive political participation a form of everyday politics and argue that the resultant outcomes such as policy concessions and other government measures in response to online complaints and appeals should not be discredited. Instead, micro-activism and incremental change should be seen as progress amid longstanding political apathy and enduring gap between the government and the governed. Hierarchical political culture characterized by distance between the government and citizens, deference and obedience to the authority has been a hallmark of state-society relations in Cambodia (Mabbett and Chandler 2015; Ovesen, Trankell and Ojendal 1996). The view of the government as "parents" or "guardian" and citizens as "children" is still common especially among the older rural population. Yet after decades of donor-driven democratic reform, scholars have documented a "discursive paradigm shift" that reflects subtle change in how adults and youth alike perceive the role of state authorities (Öjendal and Sedara 2006). Three pathways have been attempted to narrow down the enduring gap between state and society. First, regular general elections have been held since 1993. The vast majority of voters have turned out to cast their ballots reflecting citizens' embrace of this democratic procedure. But these elections, except the UN-organized 1993 elections, have not passed the test of free and fair elections as approved by credible international observers casting doubts over their effectiveness in selecting the government. Second, the roll-out of decentralization in 2002 has offered more opportunities to citizens to voice their concerns and demands in commune council and village meetings. Yet the fear of speaking out, hardship-induced apathy, local authorities' agenda-setting power, partisanship, and so on remain the stumbling blocks for genuine participation. Third, civil society organizations have played a pivotal role in infusing democratic values and linking citizens with the government. But they still face the challenges of dependence on external funding and the lack of social embeddedness. Moreover, consistent participation in formal organizations is ill suited for the highly mobile segment of the society. The impact of social media on state-society relations can only be appreciated when these broader background conditions are taken into account.

At the same time, the superficial and manipulative nature of the change should not be understated either. Given re-election incentives, the CPP government is more willing to make selective, low-cost responses to meet public concerns as long as they do not pose a menace to the prevailing institutional arrangements. The most eye-catching example is the prime minister's elaborate act in 2016 to pay a traffic fine incurred during a field trip when he rode a motorbike helmetless during a Facebook live. He later wrote on his Facebook page that the fine shows the force of law is superior to his personal power (Vong and Hok 2018):

> Today, I have fulfilled the requirements of the land traffic law ... I will be fined or punished if I commit the same or other misdeeds.

> My parliamentary immunity or bodyguards cannot protect me from my misdeeds. I can't mobilise millions of my supporters to protect me from law enforcement by the authorities through petitioning or demonstration. Neither can I use my power as Prime Minister to prevent the law from being enforced upon myself ... The country can prosper only with equality before the law and respect for the law. Don't rely on power, money, impunity to escape the web of law ...

While Facebook activism made this possible, it would be naive to anticipate social media to facilitate the kind of radical change that can significantly improve Cambodia's ranking on the Rule of Law index. The performance actually contributes to promoting the prime minister's public image as a down-to-earth leader who exhibits friendly and unrestrained behaviours in public, a leadership attribute that often draws public appreciation.

SOCIAL MEDIA AND THE DECLINE OF POLITICAL OPPOSITION

Government adaptation to the surprising results of the 2013 elections established social media as an important tool for state-society interaction. It has provided an alternative means for political participation and proven effective in inducing bounded responses from the government. In the meantime, anonymous pro-government users have gained traction on social media by leaking sensitive information, fake or otherwise, targeting the opposition leadership. In an unexpected twist, Facebook leaks spiralled into allegations of attempted overthrow of the elected government that eventually culminated in the unprecedented dissolution of the main opposition party before the 2018 elections, a move that plunged Cambodia into hegemonic authoritarianism (Morgenbesser 2019).

The CNRP's trouble started out with its then Vice President Kem Sokha. In February 2016, a series of recordings purported to be telephone conversations between Kem Sokha and a woman alleged to be his mistress were posted on the Facebook page "Sei Ha". The scandal was widely reported and discussed on social media. The party spokesman denied that the man was Kem Sokha and said that the leaks were merely a smear campaign to discredit Sokha and to cause "trouble" for the party. Kem Sokha himself had ignored the allegation. But the incident did not ebb away because of the denial and silence. It spiralled into the prosecution of five current and former staff members of human rights organization ADHOC for bribing Sokha's alleged mistress to deny the scandal. The "ADHOC 5" were sentenced to five years in prison but their sentences were suspended after having spent fourteen months in pre-trial detention. Kem Sokha himself was sentenced to five months in prison after having refused to appear in court as witness in a lawsuit involving his alleged affairs. He subsequently confined himself in the party's headquarter to avoid arrest. After spending months in self-imposed exile, Kem Sokha was granted a royal pardon in December 2016 after he wrote to Prime Minister Hun Sen seeking his intervention.

The involvement of social media in the suppression of the CNRP reached its zenith in September 2017 that eventually culminated in Kem Sokha's arrest and "treason" charge and the CNRP's dissolution by a Supreme Court ruling. The presentation of "evidence" used for the persecution began with the government-linked online media Fresh News publishing a video clip taken from the Facebook page "Kon Khmer" in which Kem Sokha was seen making a speech "thanking the US for political support and detailing strategies for democratic change" (Nachemson 2019). The speech was subsequently interpreted as the CNRP's collusion with the United States to overthrow the government. The Fresh News report also backed up the claim of conspiracy with photos of Kem Sokha's daughter with an International Republic Institute (IRI) official alleged to be the CNRP's "political strategist"; photos of her taking part in election campaigns of the main Taiwanese opposition party in the 2016 presidential elections; and a diagram of the "U.S. Inference Network" illustrating the link between the Central Intelligence Agency (CIA), US-based non-government organizations (NGOs), and "color revolutions" in Eastern Europe and Central Asia (Fresh News 2017). The Fresh News reports were the precursor of a government-led effort to assemble evidence of the CNRP's attempts at forging colour revolutions and produce a video to educate the public about their dangers. *The Phnom Penh Post* reported that an inter-ministerial working group was created in October 2017 on the order of the prime minister to produce "anti-opposition propaganda" (Mech and Baliga 2017). This example indicates that while social media enables rapid circulation of information that feeds into greater political awareness and engagement, it also facilitates the dissemination of pro-government narratives in a way that bolsters state power (Oates 2013; Gunitsky 2015). Gunitsky (2015) argues that social media's "decentralized, interactive, and non-hierarchical" nature can give government-friendly discourse an easier route to circumvent "the appearance of artifice".

The CNRP reacted by calling the Facebook leaks and government-linked media coverage "smear campaign", "fake news", "false" or "fabricated" information churned out to discredit and split the party. Yet the opposition is not always at the receiving end of misinformation. For instance, an opposition senator was sentenced in 2016 to seven years in prison for presenting in a video clip posted on Facebook about a fake treaty between Vietnam and Cambodia to "dissolve" the border between the two countries (Niem and Turton 2016). Opposition sympathizers are also known to spread rumours of the prime minister's deteriorating health conditions and engaged in "hacktivism" notably during Sam Rainsy's public canvass on his return to Cambodia on 23 November 2019. Facebook pages of military generals, police departments, local governments and the like were hacked to show an identical post calling out the military to be nonpartisan and restrain from bloodshed (Fresh News 2019). The message echoed Rainsy's insistent plea to the military to defy the government to pave the way for his return and catalyze political change.

While both parties have claimed to be "victims" of fake news, what separates their fortunes is that the government has at its disposal the coercive and legal tools to suppress social media content that it considers disturbing. A recent inter-ministerial directive on website and social media control empowers the Ministry of Posts and Telecommunication to block or take down websites and social media pages that host content considered to undermine "national security, public interest and social order". The directive also stipulates the formation of a "task force" to monitor fake news on social media (Kaan 2018). Earlier, the ruling party's spokesman announced that the government was looking to follow the path of Malaysia which passed the anti-fake news law that carries a draconian punishment of up to six years in prison (Mech and Baliga 2018). The fake news ordinance was received poorly among civil society groups citing threat to "privacy rights and freedom of expression" (Licadho 2018). Civil society groups feared that its vague wordings would give the authorities outsize power to silence online dissent. The protest against social media regulation can be interpreted as a reflection of a problem that lies deeper than fake news itself: the underlying distrust of state institutions whose ability to enforce law and adjudicate impartially have long been questioned.

CONCLUSION

Social media helps to empower the voices of ordinary Cambodians and contributes to a more diverse media landscape, yet it will not spawn democratic change. The ruling CPP, having initially left the cyberspace relatively free and open, paid a high price for its inaction. Having nearly lost power after the 2013 general elections, the government enacted a series of institutional and legal mechanisms to exert greater control over information and stymie dissent. At the same time, the ruling party also sees social media as a crucial platform to enhance its legitimacy and lengthen its rule as this new media can reveal what citizens want in addition to what election results can do. As the CPP tightens its grip following the banning of and purging of members of the only viable opposition party, social media would play a less pivotal role in mobilizing electoral and grassroots support for anti-government activities. Despite the rise of state-sponsored social media discourse, Cambodians remain keen to source news from Facebook (Millar 2017). Social media will remain a significant channel of political participation especially for young people and at the same time be an important tool for the CPP to shape public opinion to help lengthen its rule. Facebook will continue to be the main avenue for rapid information production and misinformation. But the lack of digital literacy programmes means that Cambodians are vulnerable to all sorts of manipulations designed to serve specific political interests. At the same time, dishonest politicians can protect their interests by brushing off real news as fake news, as is the trend globally. In the absence of credible investigative journalism and fact-checking in the country, it will be difficult for citizens to find reliable and independent sources of information, reassess their political preferences, and make voting decisions.

REFERENCES

Bun, Tharum 2006. "The First Internet Party Ever Held in Cambodia". *Global Voices*, 22 May 2006. https://globalvoices.org/2006/05/22/the-first-internet-party-ever-held-in-cambodia/ (accessed 8 January 2020).

Chak, Sopheap 2009. "Digital Democracy Emerging in Cambodia". *Sopheap Focus*, 11 November 2009. https://sopheapfocus.com/digital-democracy-emerging-in-cambodia (accessed 8 January 2020).

Cybercrime Law Formulation Working Group of Council of Ministers. 2019. "Cybercrime Law", Draft 1, unofficial English translation. Article19.org. https://www.article19.org/data/files/medialibrary/37516/Draft-Law-On-CyberCrime_Englishv1.pdf (accessed 19 December 2019).

Eng, Netra, Ang Len, So Hengvotey, Hav Gechhong and Chhom Theavy. 2019. "Cambodia's Young and Older Generation: Views on Generational Relations and Key Social and Political Issues". Working Paper Series No. 116. Phnom Penh: Cambodia Development Resource Institute.

Fresh News. 2016a. "ស្តាបទឹក Facebook របស់សម្តេចតេជោ ហ៊ុន សែន ជានរណា?", 2 February 2016a. http://www.freshnewsasia.com/index.php/en/localnews/17242-2016-02-02-05-26-48.html (accessed 12 November 2019).

———. 2016b. " សម្តេចតេជោ ហ៊ុន សែន បញ្ជាឱ្យស្តាប់ថែ ក្រសួង និងអាជ្ញាធរ ដោះស្រាយបញ្ហារបស់ពលរដ្ឋ ដែលរាយការណ៍នៅលើទំព័រ Facebook នាយករដ្ឋមន្ត្រី", 2 February 2016b. http://www.freshnewsasia.com/index.php/en/localnews/17633-2016-02-08-06-11-52.html (accessed 12 November 2019).

———. 2016c. " សម្តេចតេជោ ហ៊ុន សែន៖ Facebook ខ្ញុំ មិនមែនប្រាំងនរណាទេ តែដើម្បីពន្លឿន នការងារដ្ឋនប្រជាពលរដ្ឋ", 11 February 2016c. http://www.freshnewsasia.com/index.php/en/localnews/17758-2016-02-11-04-37-39.html (accessed 12 November 2019).

———. 2016d. "សម្តេចតេជោ ហ៊ុន សែន ប្រតិកម្មនឹងអ្នករិះគន់ថា « គណរដ្ឋមន្ត្រី Facebook»", 11 February 2016d. http://www.freshnewsasia.com/index.php/en/localnews/17785-2016-02-11-08-53-48.html (accessed 12 November 2019).

———. 2017. "Facebook បន្ទុកឃ្លាំយវីដេអូ៖ សូមស្តាប់លោក គឹម សុខា សារភាពថា ផ្តើមបញ្ហារបស់អាមេរិក ក្នុងការផ្តួលរំលំរាជរដ្ឋាភិបាលកម្ពុជា ដូចគ្នានឹងប្រទេស ", 2 September 2017. http://freshnewsasia.com/index.php/en/64419-facebook-video-inside-2.html (accessed 11 November 2019).

———. 2019. "TOP NEWS: ដំណឹងបន្ទាន់! Facebook តាមក្រសួងស្តាប់នរដ្ឋ និងថ្នាក់ដឹកនាំកងកម្លាំងប្រដាប់អាវុធមួយចំនួន ត្រូវបានក្រុមឧក្រិដ្ឋជននាយ ប្រហារ (Hack) ជាបន្តបន្ទាប់នៅថ្ងៃទី០៨ វិធីការនេះ ជាមួយខ្លឹមសារពាក់ព័ន្ធនឹងកងទ័ព", 9 November 2019. http://www.freshnewsasia.com/index.php/en/localnews/139221-2019-11-09-07-34-50.html (accessed 12 November 2019).

Freedom House. 2009. *Freedom in the World 2009*, pp. 134–38. New York: Rowman and Littlefield.

———. 2017. "Freedom on the Net 2017: Cambodia". https://www.freedomonthenet.org/country/cambodia/freedom-on-the-net/2017 (accessed 8 January 2020).

———. 2019. "Freedom on the Net 2019: Cambodia". https://www.freedomonthenet.org/country/cambodia/freedom-on-the-net/2019 (accessed 8 January 2020).

Gill, Jamie. 2017. "Facebook Explore – a Radical Test That Spells Bad News for Cambodia's NGOs and Media". *The Phnom Penh Post*, 30 October 2017. https://www.phnompenhpost.com/opinion/facebook-explore-radical-test-spells-bad-news-cambodias-ngos-and-media (accessed 16 November 2019).

Gunitsky, Seva. 2015. "Corrupting the Cyber-Commons: Social Media as a Tool of Autocratic Stability". *Perspectives on Politics* 13, no. 1: 42–54.

Heng Seiha, Vong Mun and Chheat Sreang. 2014. "The Enduring Gap: Decentralisation Reform and Youth Participation in Local Rural Governance". Working Paper Series No. 94. Phnom Penh: Cambodia Development Resource Institute.

Holman, Zoe. 2015. "Watchdog Finds Political Influence in the Media". *The Phnom Penh Post*, 3 December 2015. https://www.phnompenhpost.com/national/watchdog-finds-political-influence-media-sector (accessed 12 November 2019).

Hughes, Caroline. 2015. "Understanding the Elections in Cambodia 2013". *AGLOS: Journal of Area Based Global Studies* 1, no. 1: 10–14.

Hughes, Caroline and Kim Sedara. 2004. "The Evolution of Democratic Process and Conflict Management in Cambodia: A Comparative Study of Three Cambodian Elections". Working Paper Series No. 30. Phnom Penh: Cambodia Development Resource Institute.

Kierans, Kim. 2010. "Cambodia – A Land of Opportunity". In *Asia's Media Innovators Vol 2.0*, by Stephen Quinn and Kim Kierans. Singapore: Konrad-Adenauer-Stiftung. https://cambodia.mom-rsf.org/uploads/tx_lfrogmom/documents/12-400_import.pdf (accessed 12 December 2019).

Lee, Ashley. 2018. "Invisible Networked Publics and Hidden Contention: Youth Activism and Social Media Tactics under Repression". *New Media & Society* 20, no. 11: 4095–115.

LICADHO. 2018. "Civil Society Rejects Government Attack on Freedom of Expression". Statement, 8 June 2018. http://www.licadho-cambodia.org/pressrelease.php?perm=434 (accessed 20 May 2020).

Mabbett, Ian and David Chandler. 2015. *The Khmers*. Bangkok: Silkworm Books.

Mech, Dara and Ananth Baliga. 2017. "'Agitprop' Work of New Government Team". *The Phnom Penh Post*, 10 November 2017. https://www.phnompenhpost.com/national/agitprop-work-new-government-team (accessed 28 November 2019).

———. 2018. "Hun Sen 'Mulling Fake News Bill'". *The Phnom Penh Post*, 6 April 2018. https://www.phnompenhpost.com/national/hun-sen-mulling-fake-news-bill (accessed 28 November 2019).

Men, Kimseng. 2014. "Social Media a Potential New Tool for Good Governance, Expert Says". *Voice of America*, 3 December 2014. https://www.voacambodia.com/a/social-media-a-potential-new-tool-for-good-governance-expert-says/2544265.html (accessed 11 November 2019).

Meyn, Colin. 2013a. "Social Media in Cambodia Alters Politics". *Southeast Asia Globe*, 11 November 2013a. https://southeastasiaglobe.com/virtual-democracy-social-media-elections-cambodia-cpp-cnrp (accessed 11 November 2019).

———. 2013b. "Virtual Democracy". *Southeast Asia Globe*, 11 November 2013b. https://southeastasiaglobe.com/virtual-democracy-social-media-elections-cambodia-cpp-cnrp/ (accessed 8 January 2020).

Millar, Paul. 2017. "The Tangled Web: How Leaks, Lies and Fake News Took Over Cambodian Politics". *Southeast Asia Globe*, 7 March 2017. https://southeastasiaglobe.com/the-tangled-web-how-leaks-lies-and-fake-news-took-over-cambodian-politics (accessed 28 November 2019).

Morgenbesser, Lee. 2019. "Cambodia's Transition to Hegemonic Authoritarianism". *Journal of Democracy* 30, no. 1: 158–71.

Nachemson, Andrew. 2019. "Fresh News and the Future of the Fourth Estate in Cambodia". *Coda Story*, 22 February 2019. https://codastory.com/authoritarian-tech/fresh-news-and-the-future-of-the-fourth-estate-in-cambodia (accessed 24 October 2019).

Nass, Daniel and Shaun Turton. 2016. "Only 20 per Cent of PM's Recent Facebook 'Likes' from Cambodia". *The Phnom Penh Post*, 9 March 2016. https://www.phnompenhpost.com/national/only-20-cent-pms-recent-facebook-likes-cambodia (accessed 11 November 2019).

Niem, Chheng and Shaun Turton. 2016. "Senator Sok Hour Given Seven Years for Forgery and Incitement". *The Phnom Penh Post*, 8 November 2016. https://www.phnompenhpost.com/national/senator-sok-hour-given-seven-years-forgery-and-incitement (accessed 20 February 2020).

Oates, Sarah. 2013. *Revolution Stalled: The Political Limits of the Internet in the Post-Soviet Sphere*. Oxford: Oxford University Press.

Öjendal, Joakim and Kim Sedara. 2006. "Korob, Kaud, Klach: In Search of Agency in Rural Cambodia". *Journal of Southeast Asian Studies* 37, no. 3: 507–26.

Ovesen, Jan, Ing Trankell and Joakim Ojendal. 1996. "When Every Household is an Island: Social Organization and Power Structures in Rural Cambodia". Uppsala Research Reports in Cultural Anthropology No. 15. Uppsala: Uppsala University.

Radio Free Asia. 2012. "New Information and Communication Technologies' Influence on Activism in Cambodia", 8 November 2012. https://www.rfa.org/english/news/cambodia/footsteps-11082012174914.html (accessed 16 April 2020).

Rajagopalan, Megha. 2018. "This Country's Leader Shut Down Democracy – With a Little Help from Facebook". *BuzzFeed News*, 21 January 2018. https://www.buzzfeednews.com/article/meghara/facebook-cambodia-democracy (accessed 11 November 2019).

Sydney Morning Herald, The. 2007. "Cambodia Bans SMS Messaging Ahead of Sunday's Elections", 31 March 2007. https://www.smh.com.au/national/cambodia-bans-sms-messaging-ahead-of-sundays-elections-20070331-gdpt50.html (accessed 12 December 2019).

Tiquet, Nina. 2016. "Facebook and Politics in Cambodia: Not All 'Likes' are the Same". *The Asia Foundation* (blog), 5 October 2016. https://asiafoundation.org/2016/10/05/facebook-politics-cambodia-not-likes (accessed 25 November 2019).

Vicheika, Kaan. 2018. "Cambodia Forms Task Force to Monitor 'Fake News' on Social Media". Voice of America, 6 June 2018. https://www.voacambodia.com/a/cambodia-forms-task-force-to-monitor-fake-news-on-social-media/4425534.html (accessed 28 November 2019).

Vong, Mun and Kimhean Hok. 2018. "Facebooking: Youth's Everyday Politics in Cambodia". *South East Asia Research* 26, no. 3: 219–34.

Willemyns, Alex. 2013. "CNRP Wins with Local and Social Communications Strategy". *The Cambodia Daily*, 31 July 2013. https://english.cambodiadaily.com/news/cnrp-wins-with-local-and-social-communications-strategy-37682 (accessed 25 November 2019).

8

SOCIAL MEDIA'S CHALLENGE TO STATE INFORMATION CONTROLS IN VIETNAM

Dien Luong

Commentators often equate Vietnam's internet freedom as similar to China. Indeed, the West regularly includes Vietnam on its "state enemies of the internet" list, as it does for China, Iran, or Syria (Deutsche Welle 2013). There is some truth to the concerns of Vietnam looking towards China as a model, given how ideologically, politically and economically aligned Hanoi is with Beijing. Vietnam is embracing Chinese hardware and packages of security software to increase its technical and infrastructural capabilities for information controls (Sherman 2019). A prominent example to justify this observation is Vietnam's passage and enforcement of the 2018 Cyber-Security Law, which bears striking resemblances to a similar Chinese law (Trinh Huu Long 2017) which gives the government *carte blanche* to strictly police the internet, scrutinize personal information, censor online discussion, and punish or even jail dissidents.

While Vietnam sees China as a potential example to follow, I argue in this chapter that due to political, economic and technical reasons, Vietnam has only selectively taken a page out of the Chinese playbook in online censorship. Even in an authoritarian state like Vietnam, some measure of popular support is crucial to a regime's longevity, forcing the authorities to occasionally appear responsive, not just repressive, to public sentiment online. Vietnamese internet users, well aware of this grey area, have capitalized on the power of social media to successfully sway the political decision-making process for the public's sake. The 2014–15 period marked the beginning of digital activism in Vietnam that resulted in rare victories for the environment in a country where natural conservation is often dwarfed by economic development. This momentum has enabled social media users to continue testing the waters of what is allowed and not allowed within Vietnam's online sphere.

Unlike China, Vietnam's popular social media platforms are foreign-owned, making it more difficult for the state to exert the kind of controls and restrictions its Chinese counterpart could on their homegrown social media. In an unlikely move, Vietnamese authorities have also shown signs of tolerating, embracing or even co-opting social media, chiefly Facebook, to deploy their disinformation campaigns. The willingness of Facebook and Google to "cooperate" with Vietnamese authorities has raised major questions as to whether there is still any elbow room for online activism in Vietnam and what activists could do to sustain or reclaim their digital space. Censorship methods appear to have been emboldened by the acquiescence of American tech giants, chief among them Google and Facebook, as Vietnam has also demanded these two tech giants remove what it calls "toxic content" from their platforms (Vu 2019). Vietnam's history is rooted in global hegemonic power dynamics, and this current era is no different. At the heart of the digital revolution in Vietnam is power dynamics between China's state censorship approach and Silicon Valley's capitalist programmes which allow for greater freedom of expression.

This chapter examines the growth of social media and the blogosphere in Vietnam and explains why Facebook has become increasingly crucial to the growing online communities of critical voices. The chapter also describes the evolution of government-Facebook relations, from one of animosity to cooperation. Because of this rather convoluted relation, Vietnam's Facebook today is both home to growing digital activism and state-sponsored disinformation campaigns. The chapter concludes by offering some projections of what lies ahead as both the civil society online and the authorities in Vietnam seek to make the most of their unlikely alliance with Facebook.

VIETNAM'S BLOGOSPHERE AND ACTIVISM

The internet first arrived in Vietnam in 1997, but its usage remained exclusive to state agencies, which accounts for a small percentage of the population, and more or less off-limits to businesses and educational institutions (Le, Vaughn and Dandass 2007, p. 16). By 2000, a mere 0.2 per cent of the population in Vietnam were online (*Tuoi Tre News* 2017). The reasons were obvious: the authorities were still vigilant against opening up the internet market to the private sector out of fear they would lose control over it. They thought the internet would unleash the floodgates of anti-government propaganda and facilitate a freer flow of information, which would end up posing major threats to the legitimacy of the ruling Communist party (Hiep 2019, pp. 1–7). Given that mindset, the legal onus was on government-owned companies to manage the internet, whose infrastructure was chiefly to "accommodate e-mail and Web services over dial-up and leased lines" (Le, Vaughn and Dandass 2007, p. 16). But the business community and consumers soon clamoured for cheaper, faster and better internet access (Surborg 2008). Such legitimate demands, coupled with the need to boost e-commerce became key reasons for growing the online sphere, as Vietnam joined the international playground (Kelly and Minges 2002), compelling the authorities to slacken the state monopoly on internet controls and pave the way for more competition from the private sector. This move saw Vietnam's internet users jump from 3.1 million in 2003 to 10.7 million in 2005 (Vietnam Internet Network Information Centre 2012, p. 3). In 2004 and 2005, Google and Yahoo launched their Vietnamese-language versions, aggregating news from Vietnam's then two major print dailies—*Tuoi Tre* and *Thanh Nien*—and enabling an increasing number of Vietnamese to read news online (Abuza 2015, p. 9).

As Bui (2016, p. 93) points out: the surge in internet users during this period played a crucial role in virtual association in Vietnam, enabling social media, then chiefly the blogosphere, to challenge the mainstream state-owned media. Meanwhile, Vietnam's unrelenting prohibitions and crackdowns on traditional media outlets were continuing unabated. It is in this context that droves of disenchanted readers flocked to the blossoming blogosphere in search of alternative information. Seizing this opportunity, informal groups of intellectuals, retired government officials, professors, students, writers and independent activists took great strides in mustering up the power of the blogosphere to rail against government's thinking and policy (Bui 2016, p. 93). The exact number of bloggers was unknown, but few would dispute their continued growth and increased audacity to air grievances against the authorities and their policies (Abuza 2015, p. 10). The blogosphere also targeted and scrutinized media coverage that was dismissed as state propaganda. This dynamic meant Vietnam's blogosphere received increased exposure to foreign media (Abuza 2015, p. 10).

The blogosphere served as a much-needed vehicle for the otherwise nascent online discourse in Vietnam at that time. Popular blogs pulled in millions of readers and thousands of followers on a daily basis in the face of myriad state-sanctioned efforts to restrict access to them (Bui 2016). For instance, Anh Ba Sam, whose real name is Nguyen Huu Vinh, set up the namesake blog in 2007, aiming to keep Vietnamese netizens abreast of Vietnam's political, social, economic, and cultural issues from what the blogger saw as a different perspective. Besides functioning as a news aggregator, the blog content varied from translated versions of English- and French-language articles to excerpts from books (Bui 2016, p. 98). The rise of the internet has also propelled social media into playing an increasingly crucial role in shaping Vietnam's online discourses: it empowered public opinion and emboldened digital activism. It also enabled elite politics to become more visible and exposed to the public.

This is the context in which how the authorities respond to public sentiment online on controversial issues became a yardstick to gauge the impact of social media in Vietnam (Bui 2016, p. 90). Facebook arrived in Vietnam around 2007 at the very moment when online activism was yearning for an alternative to the now-defunct Yahoo!360 social network, which once dominated the Vietnamese social media landscape, boasting tens of millions of members across the country in 2009 (Do 2012). Vietnamese activists also flocked to Facebook to deal with increasing crackdowns on the blogosphere as the former was harder to block (Abuza 2015, p. 11). Just like the blogosphere, activists used Facebook to offer a counter-narrative to what they perceive as state propaganda on mainstream media. But it was the connectivity and intimacy on Facebook that was a significant and perhaps decisive pull factor, helping the activists to rally their peers behind a major cause (Nguyen 2012).

TRADITIONAL MEDIA CRACKDOWNS AND FACEBOOK'S ARRIVAL

The surge in online blogging continued its upward trend and appeared to hit its crescendo in 2008, a watershed year for Vietnam's political and socio-economic landscape. Nguyen Cong Khe, the founding editor of *Thanh Nien*, was one of the longest serving editors-in-chief in Vietnam. During his editorship spanning two decades, Khe ruffled the feathers of a slew of powerful and influential people by exposing corruption and social inequality. Although that was considered a risky move in a country where the press is strictly controlled and censored, there was some hope that the Vietnamese media would play a more crucial role in fighting rampant graft and corruption in government (Davies 2015).

But for those who remained hopeful, 12 May 2008 was a black day. After forcing a minister of transport to step down and exposing graft that sent scores of high-ranking officials to jail, two prominent Vietnamese journalists, Nguyen Van Hai and Nguyen Viet Chien, were arrested on that day and later jailed (Overlan 2008). In response to what it perceived as the persecution of its journalists, their newspapers ran extensive coverage that denounced the arrests. In its article titled "Top Vietnamese Journalists Arrested", *Time* observed that *Thanh Nien* used an "unusually confrontational tone" to bristle against the arrest in an editorial bluntly headlined "Free These Honest Journalists". In December of the same year, Khe—the editor-in-chief of *Thanh Nien*—and his counterpart from *Tuoi Tre* were fired. The authorities have never made public their rationale for their dismissal, but it was not difficult to fathom: they got the ax due to such "confrontational" coverage. The concurrent dismissal of the top editors of Vietnam's two largest selling and most influential dailies at that time was an unprecedented move in the history of the country's journalism. This crackdown on the press has also since upended the country's media landscape.

That was, however, not the only development that rocked Vietnam's political landscape in 2008, when soaring inflation left the economy sputtering (Hookway 2008). Feeling punished by the economic meltdown and rampant corruption, people flocked to the blogosphere to air their grievances online. The government started to take notice and became wary of online activism, leading to the enactment of Decree 97 on the Management, Supply, and Use of Internet Services and Electronic Information on the Internet in August 2008 (OpenNet Initiative 2012). To improve clarity of this decree, subsequent circulars were issued so that blogs would be restricted to only personal content and blogging platforms were mandated to maintain records of their users to provide to the authorities. These laws were designed to criminalize those who use the internet to "oppose the government; undermine the state and state unity, or threaten national security, public order, or social security; or incite violence or crime" (Abuza 2015, p. 10).

Against the backdrop of growing online activism and public resentment, Yahoo!360, the then default social network choice of the Vietnamese blogosphere, officially closed (Gray 2015, p. 4). This came at a very time when Facebook started to gain increasing popularity globally. It was in that context that the social media giant entered Vietnam, luring droves of internet users to what would become the country's most beloved social media platform for grassroots advocacy.

Facebook took over as a platform of choice for activists as blogging activism dissipated. Vo Nguyen Giap is a legendary and charismatic Vietnamese General who became a prominent critic of the government online (Gregory 2013). In 2009 Giap wrote letters to the Vietnamese government warning that two bauxite-mining developments in the offing would be detrimental to the environment, displace ethnic minority populations and threaten national security (Ruwitch 2009). The letters struck at the very heart of one of the most contentious issues in modern Vietnam: anti-China sentiment. Under the deal, the government awarded a Chinese firm the right to mine bauxite in the Central Highlands, a strategically important and sensitive region in Vietnam. Giap's letters compelled the Vietnamese government to swing into action, responding that the country would not consider exploiting the mineral at "any cost" and would recalibrate the project to minimize the environmental damage it might cause. The letters also paved the way for further debates at the National Assembly, Vietnam's legislature. More importantly, they opened the floodgates of criticism levelled against the government's policy on China that had already been brewing on social media, which included the launch of the Bauxite Vietnam blog (https://boxitvn.blogspot.com/), the year before. Carl Thayer, an Australia-based veteran Vietnam analyst, pointed out that 2009 saw organization of disparate groups—Catholics, anti-China factions, environmentalists and democracy activists—"using Facebook as a rallying area for their shared opposition" to the bauxite mining agreement and Vietnam's handling of China-related matters in general (Clark 2013).

Another case to Facebook's early capacity for activism in Vietnam occurred in 2011. After Chinese patrol boats attacked a Vietnamese oil survey off the coast of Vietnam, anti-Chinese protests broke out every Sunday in Hanoi and Saigon for two months, before being suppressed by the authorities (Hoang 2019). Activists attributed the fact that those protests were prolonged because of Facebook as activists were able to coalesce networks that only kept growing in the face of crackdowns (Nguyen 2012). In a country that prizes political stability above all else and that always treads carefully on its relations with China, the activists' ability to organize protests through a social media platform was a big headache for the authorities. Thus, what Vietnamese people began to witness was a crackdown of traditional media, and at the same time a rise in social media discourse that became the prominent space for criticism of the government. Rather than standing idle to endure government-sanctioned suppression, those critical voices morphed and evolved to Facebook.

FACEBOOK CRACKDOWNS FAIL

Vietnamese authorities were growing increasingly wary of their inability to rein in the influence of social media, forcing them into bringing about tougher controls. Efforts to block access to the blogosphere had been underway earlier, to little success, as Vietnamese netizens easily found workarounds like virtual private networks (VPNs). In July 2009, China blocked Facebook altogether in the wake of the Ürümqi riots in which Xinjiang activists used Facebook to communicate and spread out their messages (Blanchard 2009). Just a month later, a draft regulation requiring Vietnamese Internet Service Providers to block Facebook was leaked (Clark 2013). Its authenticity remains in question, but access to Facebook, which boasted around one million users at that time, indeed became intermittent later that year. Asked about this move, the spokeswoman of Vietnam's Ministry of Foreign Affairs neither confirmed nor denied whether the country blocked the social networking site. She instead offered a non-committal response: "A number of social websites have been misused to convey information with contents (sic) that oppose the Democratic Socialist Republic of Vietnam … threatening information security" (Toan 2009).

With such approach, Vietnam did not single out Facebook. But the burgeoning social networking site was increasingly becoming a major source of concern. Vietnamese authorities were watching the dramatic events unfolding in Egypt and Tunisia in 2010. Vietnamese leaders reportedly "conceded to foreign diplomats that they are worried about an Arab spring-type rising breaking out" (Bland 2011), according to *Financial Times*. It was unclear whether such concerns were genuine, given a number of differences in the geopolitical dynamics between the Middle East and Southeast Asia. But this was a good pretext for the Vietnamese authorities to rationalize tightening their screws on the internet and social media. In a scathing 2013 OpEd in the Communist Magazine, a Vietnamese military official pointed out the "unpredictable and pervasive effect social networks can have on demonstrations and political life". Using the standard argument of the Communist party, the OpEd was forthright:

> What happened in the 'Arab Spring' not only led to a change of government in several countries in the Middle East and North Africa, but also revealed a role that cannot be underestimated that social networks play in international relations, in 'peaceful evolution' activities of hostile forces and in political riots, and armed conflicts now and in the future.

It therefore called for "measures to strictly manage these websites and communication media" (Quan 2013).

Vietnam's Prime Minister Nguyen Tan Dung served as leader of the country for ten years, between 2006 and 2016. It was during the start of his second term (2011–16) that the crackdown on social media hit a peak. Throughout this second term, Dung adopted a familiar response pattern: cranked up the arrests of what the West called prominent blogger (Agence-France Press 2013) and weaponized the laws. In Decree 72, or the Management, Provision, Use of Internet Services and Information

Content Online—a highly contested decree that was signed by Dung and enacted in July 2013—Vietnam, according to different interpretations, sought to ban the sharing of news stories on various social networks (Palatino 2013). The decree was decried by advocacy groups as "the harshest offensive against freedom of information" or "nonsensical and extremely dangerous". Dung instructed the Central Youth Union in 2013 to set up a homegrown social networking site that would envisage rivalling and replacing Facebook (Inside Asia 2013). Between 2007 and 2017, Vietnam issued over 300 licences for homegrown social networking sites, but few remain active, much less were able to rival Facebook (Onishi 2019). Despite the attempt to encourage Vietnamese citizens to turn to other social media sites and away from Facebook, the strategy largely has not worked. Facebook remains the most popular platform for Vietnamese citizens using social media.

Instead, Facebook continued to be a prominent space for activism for Vietnamese netizens. In March 2015, the public heard about a plan by the Hanoi municipal administration to fell 6,708 trees lining the capital city's historic streets (Clark 2015). Later that month, the city government official unveiled the plan under a project that looked to "renovate" and "replace city green trees for the 2014–2015 period". It was, however, the lack of transparency and accountability from the authorities that have started to raise widespread eyebrows (Quan 2015). Online discussion on the impact of the tree-cutting project was swirling around on Facebook, ranging from the loss of historic and environmental assets to the environmental and emotional toll it was going to exact on the capital city and its people (Clark 2015). Such public sentiment was forceful enough for public figures and prominent intellectuals to join the cause. Tran Dang Tuan, the retired deputy general director of the state-run Vietnam Television, and Ngo Bao Chau, the first Vietnamese mathematician to win the prestigious Field Medal, wrote open letters to the Hanoi authorities calling for a brake on the project (*Vietnam News* 2015). Their letters were widely shared and went viral on Facebook, leaving the city government having no option but to respond. But in its first written statement to the public backlash, an official from Hanoi's propaganda organ only added fuel to the fire by saying it was not necessary to poll people's opinions on the tree-cutting project (*Xinhua* 2015), further pitting the authorities against an increasingly angry public.

More and more people flocked to Facebook to vent their grievances against what they considered a cavalier administration that did not take public concerns into serious consideration. A Facebook page named "6,700 people for 6,700 trees" was launched, regularly updating what was going on and how both the authorities and people reacted to the situation (Clark 2015). Cashing in on Facebook to spread out their messages, a number of actors from the entire society—public intellectuals, lawyers, journalists, lecturers, students, architects, artists, singers, NGOs and even the mainstream media—joined forces in disparaging and dismantling the plan, exerting growing pressure on the authorities. Such momentum quickly morphed into real actions that manifested in the physical place. A plethora of movements like tree hugs or tree mapping, tree location identification and tree protection walks were organized by young people (Bui 2016, p. 103). A lakeside demonstration billed as a "picnic" also took place but was quickly dispersed by the authorities (Peel 2015). The public backlash was serious enough for the authorities to become wary of it spiralling out of control, prompting both the central and local governments to swing into action. The Hanoi municipal administration eventually scrapped the tree-cutting plan altogether, issued a public mea culpa and punished the officials held accountable for missteps in handling the case along the way (Son and Quan 2015). The Hanoi mayor also reassured the public that the authorities would draw lessons on heeding public concerns and grievances when carrying out such public projects, particularly when it came to transparency and accountability (*Vietnam News* 2015).

A year later, in May 2016, environmental cause again coalesced Vietnamese Facebookers around another protest against the toxic discharge from Taiwan's Formosa Plastics' steel plant on the central coast (Paddock 2016). The public saw red as the company's unscrupulous discharged killed large swaths of fish, the meal ticket of millions of Vietnamese in central Vietnam. They were also frustrated over what they perceived as the "sluggish response" of the Vietnamese government to what it later called the country's worst-ever environmental catastrophe in decades (Pham and Nguyen 2016). As Duong (2017) pointed out in a paper titled "The Beginning of Online Social Movements in Vietnam", the anti-Formosa movement adopted

> a similar trajectory to the Hanoi tree movement, with the formation of online discussion forums sharing and analyzing the Formosa information

sourced from the mainstream media, scientists, freelance journalists and even laymen, and the gathering of protestors to demand the government to react officially against Formosa.

But the real-world impacts of the anti-Formosa movement was even bigger with demonstrations breaking out in different cities across Vietnam. A newly installed government led by Prime Minister Nguyen Xuan Phuc felt even more urgent to appear accommodating to public demands, forcing Formosa to accept its responsibility and ordering the Taiwanese group to pay US$500 million in damages to the affected fishermen (Nguyen 2016). The tree-cutting movement has been hailed and cited numerous times as a prominent example of how online activism capitalized on the power of social media to sway a political decision-making process for the public's sake. The tree-cutting plan in Hanoi paved the way for a wave of online activism that resulted in rare victories for the environment in a country where natural conservation is often dwarfed by economic development.

Having tried for nearly a decade to exert greater control over information online and to silence dissenting voices on social media, the Vietnamese authorities have recognized they could not act like China and ban Facebook altogether (Luong 2017b). Prime Minister Dung was a realistic and pragmatic leader. In January 2015, in a widely quoted statement he admitted to officials in his office: "You are all on social media, checking Facebook for information. What should be done to have correct information? It's impossible for us to ban it" (Associated Press 2015). Prime Minister Dung and the Vietnamese government needed a new approach which involved accepting that Facebook would continue to be a central platform for Vietnamese online discourse. Rather than crackdown on Facebook, or try to ban it or beat it with other home-growth competitors, the Vietnamese government looked to co-opt it and utilize it. As we shall see, this new approach has been largely successful.

CO-OPTING FACEBOOK

This section argues that Facebook has become a "partner in crime" for Vietnamese authorities. After a series of failed efforts to control content on Facebook, the Vietnamese authorities realized they would be better off exploiting the platform for their own gains than to try, in vain, to exert greater control. The government conceded to Facebook's popularity and began setting up its own page to keep the public in the loop on its policies. It began to live-stream press conferences that take place after its monthly cabinet meetings (Luong 2017a). Even the police, the subject of widespread criticism and lampoon, embraced Facebook by using the platform as a venue for the public to report traffic-related information or crimes (Luong 2017a). The authorities have also tried to appear increasingly responsive to public complaints on social media about corruption or official misconduct at the local level. These were perhaps a sign that social media was promoting a more transparent and inclusive Vietnamese government. However, there was a dark side to this policy shift, and it included a rising trend of state-sponsored disinformation production.

Public opinion manipulations through social media became a strategy of choice for the Vietnamese authorities—in line with a growing number of other governments around the world. In early 2013, the government admittedly deployed groups known as "public opinion shapers" to spread its own views and defend the state against detractors, or what it calls "hostile forces" (Pham 2013). In December 2017 the country officially unveiled its 10,000-strong military cyber unit, named Force 47. The task force, backed by the Ministry of National Defense and comprising mostly of "professional defense officers" (DFAT 2019), is charged with policing the internet, maintaining a healthy cyberspace, countering any "wrongful opinions" about the regime and protecting it from "toxic information" (Hookway 2017). These "well qualified and loyal" cyber-warriors work "every hour, every minute, every second" to scour and collect information on social media, participate in online debates to combat "negative, wrongful" views and "toxic content", and report sites or social media accounts deemed spreading fake news or unsavoury information (Hoa 2017). Critics, however, characterize the force's main objective as spreading "smear campaigns aimed at opponents of the government" (Freedom House 2018). But again, the Vietnamese authorities appear to deliberately muddy the waters by leaving the definition of different terms such as "fake news", "trash information", "toxic content", "wrongful views" and "hostile voices" to various interpretations. As Giang Nguyen-Thu (2018, p. 903) points out, the rationale is obvious: Vietnamese censors simply equate "these terms with any content that violates the censorship taboos traditionally applied to the mass media".

The modus operandi of Force 47 was also corroborated in a report by researchers at Oxford University (Alba and Satariano 2019). According to the report, Vietnam, along with other six Southeast Asian countries (Thailand, Cambodia, Indonesia, the Philippines, Myanmar and Malaysia), are among at least seventy countries that have deployed disinformation campaigns. This is part of a global pattern in which governments have capitalized on internet platforms like Facebook to spread disinformation, seeking to discredit political opponents, silence dissenting views or even meddle in foreign affairs. The report confirmed that Vietnam, making the most of the social media platform, encouraged "cyber troops to use their real accounts to spread pro-government propaganda, troll political dissidents, or mass-report content". The report also pointed out that Vietnam employed an army of people to actively shape public opinions and police speech through online channels (Bradshaw and Howard 2019, pp. 13–19). Recently, Vietnam's leadership have repeatedly harped on the threat of "toxic information" as something that is detrimental to their own reputation and the survival of the regime (Luong 2018). This is the context in which "toxic information" has been exhausted as a pretext for Vietnam to force foreign tech giants, chiefly Facebook and Google, to toe its line. In the name of fighting fake news and curbing toxic information, since 2017 Vietnamese censors have frequently asked Facebook and Google to remove and block content said to have slandered and defamed Vietnamese leaders (Luong 2018). The government also looked to hit the tech giants where it hurts most—their pockets, urging all companies doing business in Vietnam to stop advertising on YouTube, Facebook and other social media until these platforms hammer out a solution to "toxic" anti-government information (Pham 2017).

Co-opting Facebook also involved pressuring them to take down content the Vietnamese government did not like, such as removing and flagging clips and posts at the behest of the Vietnamese government. Google too was more active in taking down content in Vietnam on its platform, YouTube (Facebook 2020; Google 2020). Notably, Facebook confirmed that it cranked up the amount of content the social media restricted access to in Vietnam by over 500 per cent in the last half of 2018 (Pearson 2019). Vietnamese politicians have also used such conformity of Facebook as a talking point to brag as their achievements and embellish their reports to the top echelons. Taking the parliamentary floor in August 2019, Minister of Information and Communications Nguyen Manh Hung said that Facebook was restricting access to "increasing amounts" of content in Vietnam, adding that the social media giant "meets 70 to 75% of the Vietnamese government's requests, compared to around 30% earlier" (Vu 2019).

It is always not easy to gauge if these tech giants are yanking off political content at the behest of the Vietnamese government which should otherwise not be taken down. This question becomes even more tricky against the backdrop of the global clamour for Facebook and Google to be more active in removing disinformation. A closer look at the number of videos Google took down and its rationale for doing so may capture some pattern, however: of more than 6,500 videos Vietnam asked Google to remove in 2017, mostly because they criticized the government, the tech giant executed "a majority of the requests" (Nguyen and Weber 2018). On the other hand, Facebook has been more adamant in dismissing accusations that its content removal stemmed from political pressure. The social media giant has instead clung to its "community standards" to justify such takedowns (Nguyen and Weber 2018). But in what appeared to be a surprise move in April 2018, an open letter, signed by sixteen activist groups and media organizations as well as thirty-four well-known Facebook users (Rajagopalan 2018), was directed to Mark Zuckerberg to accuse the social media giant of abetting Vietnam to crush dissenting voices. The letter singled out Force 47 and called the unit "state-sponsored trolls" that spread fake news about the activists (Nguyen 2018). Specifically, the letter pointed out that Force 47 cashed in on loopholes in Facebook's community policies that allow for automatically pulling content if enough people lodge complaints about certain Facebook accounts. In other words, the letter alleged that the government, by mustering up a large number of Force 47 members to report to Facebook, could have target accounts suspended and content belonging to activists removed. This move could "silence human rights activists and citizen journalists in Vietnam", the letter opined (Nguyen 2018). It cited another example in which high-profile citizen journalists were prevented from posting ahead of and during a high-profile trial of pro-democracy activists in April 2018 (Rajagopalan 2018).

Activists blamed the rising frequency of takedowns and Facebook's reluctance to assist them to restore accounts and content to a meeting between Facebook's Head of Global Policy Management Monika Bickert with Vietnam's then Information Minister Truong Minh Tuan in 2017. "It would appear that after this high profile agreement to coordinate with a government that is known for suppressing expression online and jailing activists, the problem of account suspension and content takedown has only grown more acute", the April 2018 open letter stated (Rajagopalan 2018). During the course of writing this chapter, I also interviewed a couple of activists who confirmed such pattern in which their accounts were inexplicably suspended after being informed by Facebook that they have violated its "community standards". On the one hand, these activists say they have no concrete and compelling proof to show that Force 47 played a role in reporting their accounts to Facebook. But, on the other hand, they admit that it would be difficult to think of someone else to blame.

Facing growing pressure from the Vietnamese authorities, coupled with the lure of this market—58 million users (Nguyen 2019), Facebook's transactional nature has manifested where size does matter and where money talks. In April 2020, Reuters reported that Facebook had complied with a government request to "restrict access to content which it deemed illegal", after Vietnam slowed its traffic in order to put pressure on the company (Pearson 2020). Given that Facebook has never given up its hope to re-enter the Chinese market (Abkowitz 2017), perhaps the social media giant also seeks to telegraph an important message to Beijing: it is willing and can toe the line of authoritarian governments. Which begs a major question: with Facebook apparently buckling under the pressure of authoritarian countries in order to survive as a business, will the platform soon become a tool for the powerful rather than those whose voices were suppressed?

CONCLUSION

The Vietnamese government had hoped that it could somehow emulate the Great Firewall of China. After all, the Vietnamese Communist state has a long history of keeping a tight grip on the traditional media and it initially thought it could take on social media. Once Facebook took off in Vietnam, it completely changed the landscape of social media in the country. While the previous blogging communities were effective in providing alternative voices, overall they remained small in number and limited in contributing an impact in society. When Facebook entered Vietnam, it propelled a rapid expansion of online communities. Facebook became the key arena of digital activism, and one the government recognized it could not exert much control. The massive scale of its popularity meant the government could not shut it down. In this chapter I outlined a few key examples where Facebook allowed for a flourishing of activism online, notably the "tree-cutting movement". Environmental activism online, rather than direct political activism, remains the most likely space for netizens to be able to press for reforms in the country.

This chapter has explained how the Vietnamese government has shifted in its approach to Silicon Valley's social media platforms, in particular Facebook. In doing so, the authorities have adopted different approaches ranging from tolerating to embracing to even co-opting social media, chiefly Facebook, to deploy their disinformation campaign. This provides a grey area for social media as a space for reform in Vietnam. What lies ahead is how activists will make the most of such grey area and their fickle alliance with Facebook to protect their digital space and tiptoe around Vietnam's increasingly perplexing political landscape.

REFERENCES

Abkowitz, Alyssa, Deepa Seetharaman and Eva Dou. 2017. "Facebook is Trying Everything to Re-Enter China—and It's Not Working". *Wall Street Journal*, 30 January 2017. https://www.wsj.com/articles/mark-zuckerbergs-beijing-blues-1485791106 (accessed 22 April 2020).

Abuza, Zachary. 2015. "Stifling the Public Sphere: Media and Civil Society in Vietnam". In *Stifling the Public Sphere: Media and Civil Society in Egypt, Russia and Vietnam*. National Endowment for Democracy, October 2015, p. 9. https://www.ned.org/wp-content/uploads/2015/10/Stifling-the-Public-Sphere-Media-Civil-Society-Egypt-Russia-Vietnam-Full-Report-Forum-NED.pdf (accessed 30 March 2020).

Agence-France Press. 2013. "Vietnam Arrests Well-known Blogger Truong Duy Nhat for Criticism". *South China Morning Post*, 27 May 2013. https://www.scmp.com/news/asia/article/1247215/vietnam-arrests-well-known-blogger-truong-duy-nhat-criticism (accessed 14 February 2020).

Alba, Davey and Adam Satariano. 2019. "At Least 70 Countries Have Had Disinformation Campaigns, Study Finds". *The New York Times*, 26 September 2019. https://www.nytimes.com/2019/09/26/technology/government-disinformation-cyber-troops.html (accessed 17 February 2020).

Associated Press. 2009. "Vietnam Internet Users Fear Facebook Blackout", 17 November 2009. https://phys.org/news/2009-11-vietnam-internet-users-facebook-blackout.html (accessed 13 February 2020).

———. 2015. "Vietnamese Leader Says Banning Social Media Sites Impossible", 16 January 2015. https://federalnewsnetwork.com/technology-main/2015/01/vietnamese-leader-says-banning-social-media-sites-impossible/ (accessed 15 February 2020).

Blanchard, Ben. 2009. "China Tightens Web Screws After Xinjiang Riot". Reuters, 6 July 2009. https://www.reuters.com/article/us-china-xinjiang-internet/china-tightens-web-screws-after-xinjiang-riot-idUSTRE5651K420090706 (accessed 14 February 2020).

Bland, Ben. 2011. "Vietnam: A Question of Balance". *Financial Times*, 24 November 2011. https://www.ft.com/content/0ae832b0-15e1-11e1-a691-00144feabdc0 (accessed 14 February 2020).

Bradshaw, Samantha and Philip Howard. 2019. "The Global Disinformation Order: 2019 Global Inventory of Organised Social Media Manipulation". Working Paper 2. Oxford, UK: Project on Computational Propaganda. https://comprop.oii.ox.ac.uk/wp-content/uploads/sites/93/2019/09/CyberTroop-Report19.pdf.

Bui, Thiem Hai. 2016. "The Influence of Social Media in Vietnam's Elite Politics". *Journal of Current Southeast Asian Affairs* 35, no. 2: 89–111.

Clark, Helen. 2013. "Vietnam's Dysfunctional Relationship with the Web". *XIndex*, 21 August 2013. https://www.indexoncensorship.org/2013/08/vietnams-dysfunctional-relationship-with-the-web/ (accessed 13 February 2020).

———. 2015. "Hanoi Citizens Protest Tree-Felling Plan". *The Diplomat*, 25 March 2015. https://thediplomat.com/2015/03/hanoi-citizens-protest-tree-felling-plan/ (accessed 16 February 2020).

Davies, Nick. 2015. "Vietnam 40 Years On: How a Communist Victory Gave Way to Capitalist Corruption". *The Guardian*, 22 April 2015. www.theguardian.com/news/2015/apr/22/vietnam-40-years-on-how-communist-victory-gave-way-to-capitalist-corruption (accessed 11 February 2020).

Department of Foreign Affairs and Trade (DFAT), Australian Government. 2019. *DFAT Country Information Report: Vietnam*, p. 29. https://www.dfat.gov.au/sites/default/files/country-information-report-vietnam.pdf (accessed 21 April 2020).

Deutsche Welle. 2013. "Online Surveillance Threatens Internet Freedom", 12 March 2013. https://www.dw.com/en/online-surveillance-threatens-internet-freedom/a-16655554 (accessed 21 April 2020).

Do, Anh-Minh. 2012. "Yahoo to Shut Down its Blogging Platform in Vietnam". *TechInAsia*, 7 December 2012. https://www.techinasia.com/yahoo-shut-blogging-platform-vietnam (accessed 21 April 2020).

Duong, Mai. 2017. "The Beginning of Online Social Movements in Vietnam". Paper presented at Australian and New Zealand Communication Association (ANZCA) 2017 Conference, p. 9. https://www.researchgate.net/publication/322559148_The_beginning_of_online_social_movements_in_Vietnam (accessed 29 March 2020).

Facebook. 2020. Facebook Transparency Report for Vietnam. https://transparency.facebook.com/government-data-requests/country/VN.

Freedom House. 2018. "Freedom on the Net 2018 – Vietnam", 1 November 2018. https://www.refworld.org/docid/5be16aeb3.html (accessed 21 April 2020).

Giang Nguyen-Thu. 2018. "Vietnamese Media Going Social: Connectivism, Collectivism, and Conservatism". *The Journal of Asian Studies* 77, no. 4: 895–908.

Goggle. 2020. Google Transparency Report. https://transparencyreport.google.com/government-removals/overview?hl=en&request_country=period:;authority:VN&lu=request_country (accessed 30 March 2020).

Gray, Michael L. 2015. *Control and Dissent in Vietnam's Online World*. Canada: The SecDev Foundation, Tia Sang Vietnam Research Report, p. 4. https://secdev-foundation.org/wp-content/uploads/2015/02/Vietnam.ControlandDissent.Feb15.pdf.

Gregory, Joseph R. 2013. "Gen. Vo Nguyen Giap, Who Ousted U.S. From Vietnam, is Dead". *The New York Times*, 4 October 2013. https://www.nytimes.com/2013/10/05/world/asia/gen-vo-nguyen-giap-dies.html (accessed 14 February 2020).

Hiep, Le Hong. 2019. "The Political Economy of Social Media in Vietnam". *ISEAS Perspective*, no. 2019/77, 27 September 2019, pp. 1–7.

Hoa, Mai. 2017. "Hơn 10.000 Người Trong 'Lực Lượng 47' Đấu Tranh Trên Mạng" [More than 10,000 Members of "Force 47" Fighting for Cybersecurity]. *Tuoi Tre*, 25 December 2017. https://tuoitre.vn/hon-10-000-nguoi-trong-luc-luong-47-dau-tranh-tren-mang-20171225150602912.htm (accessed 21 April 2020).

Hoang, Phuong. 2019. "Domestic Protests and Foreign Policy: An Examination of Anti-China Protests in Vietnam and Vietnamese Policy towards the South China Sea". *Journal of Asian Security and International Affairs* 6, no. 1: 1–29.

Hookway, James. 2008. "Vietnam Inflation Crisis is Feared". *The Wall Street Journal*, 30 May 2008. https://www.wsj.com/articles/SB121206638209529225 (accessed 9 February 2020).

———. 2017. "Introducing Force 47, Vietnam's New Weapon Against Online Dissent". *The Wall Street Journal*, 31 December 2017. https://www.wsj.com/articles/introducing-force-47-vietnams-new-weapon-against-online-dissent-1514721606 (accessed 17 February 2020).

Inside Asia. 2013. "Vietnamese Prime Minister Calls for Young People's Social Network", 14 May 2013. https://www.insideasiatours.com/southeast-asia/news/3140/vietnamese-prime-minister-calls-for-young-peoples-social-network/ (accessed 14 February 2020).

Kelly, Tim and Michael Minges. 2002. "Vietnam Internet Case Study". International Telecommunication Union. https://www.itu.int/ITU-D/ict/cs/vietnam/material/VNM%20CS.pdf (accessed 29 March 2020).

Le, Duy, Rayford B. Vaughn and Yoginder S. Dandass. 2007. "Challenges of Internet Development in Vietnam: A General Perspective". *The Journal of Defense Software Engineering* 2, no. 1: 16–19.

Luong, Dien. 2017a. "In Facebook, Young Vietnamese see an Ally". *VnExpress International*, 2 February 2017. https://e.vnexpress.net/news/news/in-facebook-young-vietnamese-see-an-ally-3535044.html (accessed 30 March 2020).

———. 2017b. "Vietnam Wants to Control Social Media? Too Late". *The New York Times*, 30 November 2017. https://www.nytimes.com/2017/11/30/opinion/vietnam-social-media-china.html (accessed 15 February 2020).

———. 2018. "Vietnam's Internet is in Trouble". *The Washington Post*, 20 February 2018. https://www.washingtonpost.com/news/theworldpost/wp/2018/02/19/vietnam-internet/ (accessed 17 February 2020).

Nguyen, Huong. 2012. "Internet Stirs Activism in Vietnam". *YaleGlobal Online*, 11 May 2012. https://yaleglobal.yale.edu/content/internet-stirs-activism-vietnam (accessed 30 March 2020).

Nguyen, Mai. 2016. "Formosa Unit Offers $500 Million for Causing Toxic Disaster in Vietnam". Reuters, 30 June 2016. https://www.reuters.com/article/us-vietnam-environment/formosa-unit-offers-500-million-for-causing-toxic-disaster-in-vietnam-idUSKCN0ZG1F5 (accessed 16 February 2020).

———. 2018. "Vietnam Activists Question Facebook on Suppressing Dissent". Reuters, 10 April 2018. https://www.reuters.com/article/us-facebook-privacy-vietnam/vietnam-activists-question-facebook-on-suppressing-dissent-idUSKBN1HH0DO (accessed 22 April 2020).

Nguyen, Mai and Jonathan Weber. 2018. "Vietnam Set to Tighten Clamps on Facebook and Google, Threatening Dissidents". Reuters, 18 May 2018. https://www.reuters.com/article/us-vietnam-socialmedia-insight/vietnam-set-to-tighten-clamps-on-facebook-and-google-threatening-dissidents-idUSKCN1IJ1CU (accessed 21 April 2020).

Nguyen, Phuong. 2019. "Vietnam's Social Media Crowd Swells with New Entrant to Take on Facebook, Google". Reuters, 17 September 2019. https://www.reuters.com/article/us-vietnam-cybersecurity/vietnams-social-media-crowd-swells-with-new-entrant-to-take-on-facebook-google-idUSKBN1W20NH (accessed 22 April 2020).

Onishi, Tomoya. 2019. "Vietnamese Social Media Networks Spring up to Challenge Facebook". *Nikkei Asian Review*, 14 August 2019. https://asia.nikkei.com/Business/Media-Entertainment/Vietnamese-social-media-networks-spring-up-to-challenge-Facebook (accessed 15 February 2020).

OpenNet Initiative. 2012. "Information Controls in Vietnam". *Citizen Lab*, 7 August 2012. https://opennet.net/research/profiles/vietnam (accessed 31 March 2020).

Overlan, Martha Ann. 2008. "Top Vietnamese Journalists Arrested". *TIME*, 16 May 2008. http://content.time.com/time/world/article/0,8599,1807113,00.html (accessed 9 February 2020).

Paddock, Richard C. 2016. "Taiwan-Owned Steel Factory Caused Toxic Spill, Vietnam Says". *The New York Times*, 30 June 2016. https://www.nytimes.com/2016/07/01/world/asia/vietnam-formosa-ha-tinh-steel.html (accessed 16 February 2020).

Palatino, Mong. 2013. "Decree 72: Vietnam's Confusing Internet Law". *The Diplomat*, 8 August 2013. https://thediplomat.com/2013/08/decree-72-vietnams-confusing-internet-law/ (accessed 14 February 2020).

Pearson, James. 2019. "Facebook Increased Vietnam Content Restrictions by 500% during 2018 – Report". Reuters, 24 May 2019. https://www.reuters.com/article/us-facebook-security-vietnam/facebook-increased-vietnam-content-restrictions-by-500-during-2018-report-idUSKCN1SU0YU (accessed 17 February 2020).

———. 2020. "Exclusive: Facebook Agreed to Censor Posts after Vietnam Slowed Traffic – Sources". Reuters, 22 April 2020. https://www.reuters.com/article/us-vietnam-facebook-exclusive/exclusive-facebook-agreed-to-censor-posts-after-vietnam-slowed-traffic-sources-idUSKCN2232JX.

Peel, Michael. 2015. "Hanoi Residents Mobilise to Save City's Cherished Trees". *Financial Times*, 27 March 2015. https://www.ft.com/content/54d07f2a-d462-11e4-8be8-00144feab7de (accessed 16 February 2020).

Pham, My. 2017. "Vietnam Urges Firms to Stop YouTube and Facebook Ads in Protest over 'Fake Content'". Reuters, 16 March 2017. https://www.reuters.com/article/us-vietnam-google/vietnam-urges-firms-to-stop-youtube-and-facebook-ads-in-protest-over-fake-content-idUSKBN16N110 (accessed 17 February 2020).

Pham, My and Mai Nguyen. 2016. "Vietnam Says Recovery From Formosa Industrial Disaster Could Take a Decade". Reuters, 24 December 2016. https://www.reuters.com/article/us-vietnam-environment-formosa-plastics/vietnam-says-recovery-from-formosa-industrial-disaster-could-take-a-decade-idUSKBN14C1F5 (accessed 16 February 2020).

Pham, Nga. 2013. "Vietnam Admits Deploying Bloggers to Support Government". BBC News, 12 January 2013. https://www.bbc.com/news/world-asia-20982985 (accessed 17 February 2020).

Quan, Le. 2015. "People See Red as Hanoi Starts Cutting Down 6,700 Trees". Thanh Nien News, 19 March 2015. http://www.thanhniennews.com/society/people-see-red-as-hanoi-starts-cutting-down-6700-trees-40014.html (accessed 16 February 2020).

Quan, Nguyen Hong. 2013. "'Arab Spring' Inspires Thoughts about Social Networks Management". Communist Review, 7 October 2013. http://english.tapchicongsan.org.vn/Home/Politics/2013/836/Arab-Spring-inspires-thoughts-about-social-networks-management.aspx (accessed 14 February 2020).

Rajagopalan, Megha. 2018. "Facebook Has Been Accused of Helping The Vietnamese Government Crack Down on Dissent". BuzzFeed News, 10 April 2018. https://www.buzzfeednews.com/article/meghara/facebook-vietnam-mark-zuckerberg (accessed 22 April 2020).

Ruwitch, John. 2009. "Vietnamese War Hero Urges Re-Think of Bauxite Plans". Reuters, 7 May 2009. https://www.reuters.com/article/idUSHAN466228 (accessed 14 February 2020).

Sherman, Justin. 2019. "Vietnam's Internet Controls: Following China's Footsteps". The Diplomat, 11 December 2019. https://thediplomat.com/2019/12/vietnams-internet-control-following-in-chinas-footsteps/ (accessed 31 March 2020).

Son, Thai and Le Quan. 2015. "Vietnam Capital Suspends Scores of Officials after Tree Felling Causes Public Uproar". Thanh Nien News, 22 March 2015. http://www.thanhniennews.com/society/vietnam-capital-suspends-scores-of-officials-after-tree-felling-causes-public-uproar-40119.html (accessed 16 February 2020).

Surborg, Bjorn. 2008. "On-line with the People in Line: Internet Development and Flexible Control of the Net in Vietnam". Geoforum 39, no. 1: 344–57.

Toan, Ta. 2009. "Áp dụng các biện pháp phù hợp theo pháp luật" [Applying Appropriate Measures in Accordance with the Law]. An Ninh Thu Do [Capital's Security], 5 December 2009. https://anninhthudo.vn/chinh-tri-xa-hoi/ap-dung-cac-bien-phap-phu-hop-theo-phap-luat/362801.antd (accessed 14 February 2020).

Trinh Huu Long. 2017. "Vietnam's Cybersecurity Draft Law: Made in China?" The Vietnamese, 8 November 2017. https://www.thevietnamese.org/2017/11/vietnams-cyber-security-draft-law-made-in-china/ (accessed 17 February 2020).

Tuoi Tre News. 2017. "The Internet Turns 20 in Vietnam: P6 – Wi-Fi and Household Internet", 12 November 2017. https://tuoitrenews.vn/news/features/20171112/the-internet-turns-20-in-vietnam-p6-wifi-and-household-internet/42600.html (accessed 29 March 2020).

Vietnam Internet Network Information Centre. 2012. *Report on Vietnam Internet Resources 2012*. Vietnam: Ministry of Information and Communications of Vietnam, p. 3. https://vnnic.vn/sites/default/files/tailieu/ReportOnVietNamInternetResources2012.pdf.

Viet Nam News. 2015. "Ha Noi Stops Felling Trees", 21 March 2015. https://vietnamnews.vn/society/267881/ha-noi-stops-felling-trees.html (accessed 16 February 2020).

Vu, Khanh. 2019. "Vietnam says Facebook Steps up Local Content Restrictions". Reuters, 16 August 2019. https://www.reuters.com/article/us-vietnam-security-facebook/vietnam-says-facebook-steps-uplocal-content-restrictions-idUSKCN1V523A (accessed 17 February 2020).

Xinhua. 2015. "Protests Halt Hanoi Plan to Chop Down 6700 Trees", 20 March 2015. https://archive.shine.cn/article/article_xinhua.aspx?id=273540 (accessed 16 February 2020).

9

SOCIAL MEDIA AND CHANGES IN POLITICAL ENGAGEMENT IN SINGAPORE

Natalie Pang

Singapore, an island city-state with a population of 5.6 million, reports some of the highest percentage of social media users in Southeast Asia. According to a report on digital users by We Are Social (Kemp 2020), 88 per cent of Singaporeans are online and 79 per cent are active on social media. With fast internet speeds, a highly educated population and a burgeoning digital economy, Singapore's socio-political landscape is really like no other in the Southeast Asian region. While other countries are characterized by highly diverse national versus regional dynamics, structures and institutions, Singapore's one-party led city-state allows for a far more controlled and top-down approach to shaping social media discourse. Singapore's place as a geopolitical powerhouse too is a factor; not just in the region and as a key member of ASEAN, but in terms of its strong relationship with larger powers like China and the United States. This international outlook is especially important for Singapore, which has significant and important diplomatic ties with other countries and a large English-speaking population. Big tech companies like Facebook and Google maintain their large and growing Southeast Asian offices in Singapore, and numerous international dignitaries, academic and business conferences and delegations flow through Singapore which debate the nature of social media discourse and disinformation. To give one example, in 2020 Reuters and Facebook announced an Asia-wide media verification programme and Third-Party Fact-Checking Program based in Singapore, focusing on English language content (Reuters 2020).

Nevertheless, the local context remains key to understanding how social media discourse has evolved in Singapore. This chapter will analyse how key events in Singapore's socio-political history shaped the use of social media for civic and political engagement. In the context of Singapore, events that have engaged citizens on a massive scale in terms of civic and political engagements have been elections. For this reason, the analysis undertaken in this chapter is through the lens of elections in shaping how social media has been used in the country. This chapter argues that the internet, largely through bloggers, was originally a burgeoning tool for alternative news and views in Singapore. It was in this context that social media was adopted. The 2011 election saw a vast range of online activism and alternative participatory media sites, but after that election the situation declined. By 2015, social media discourse had become "normalized" in that most sectors of government and business were using the main platforms, and citizens, fearing possible repercussions, did not find social media useful for pushing reformist causes. In the past five years, discourse has thus moved to closed groups on Facebook, WhatsApp and others, as citizens feel these avenues are more secure. The result has seen a growth in disinformation and state regulation around it.

SOCIAL MEDIA AND ACTIVISM

The internet was introduced to Singapore in the mid-1990s, most notably via the launch of internet service for the public, SingNet in 1994, a service by a telecommunications company SingTel. The growth and mass adoption of the internet can be attributed to two key developments: advances in internet infrastructure, and the liberalization of the PC/mobile industry (Pang and Schauder 2007). Up till the early 2000s, the use of the internet has largely been informational, although there were also social and entertainment uses documented. One example is the Internet Relay Chat (mIRC) that was popular in the 1990s for youths to meet new people, as well as multi-user dungeons (MUDs)—text-based multiplayer role-playing games modelled after the Dungeons & Dragons table top fantasy game. Even though the internet has always been used by political parties and activists since its growth here (for instance, creating websites to raise awareness and advocate for causes), it has been the growth of social media that has had the most impact on political discourse, activism and disinformation.

The development of internet services into more participatory forms, with the introduction of online podcasts, YouTube, blogs (e.g. Blogger, LiveJournal), social network sites (e.g. Friendster and much later, Facebook) has been important outlets for participation by activists and politicians in Singapore. This participatory turn of the internet has been described loosely as "Web 2.0" (Wesch 2007), providing the basis to describe various characteristics of social media, including perceived interactivity, mass personal communication, and user-generated value (Carr and Hayes 2015). In this section I outline some key trends from earlier elections in the country.

The 2006 General Election: Beginnings of Social Media for Activism and Discourse

The beginnings of social media discourse in Singapore is encapsulated by the emergence of Lee Kin Mun (mrbrown), widely known as the "blogfather" of Singapore. He is one of the earliest bloggers in Singapore with posts dating back to 1997, and well known for his ability to publish commentaries on socio-political issues through satire. Other than maintaining his blog at www.mrbrown.com, his podcast the mrbrown show remain popular. He went on to become a prominent adopter of social media, not just for the following he managed to gather, but also his ability to switch between multiple platforms to achieve different purposes.

Perhaps one of the most pivotal moments for the mrbrown show was its role in engaging the public during the 2006 General Election in Singapore, a time when few bloggers and activists were prominent on social media. Although opposition parties like the Singapore Democratic Party (SDP) were active in using the internet for their campaigns, the environment during this time was not one of considerable expression or participation from citizens. Crucially, in the weeks leading up to the General Election, all forms of "explicitly political" advertising involving new media (e.g. podcasts, vodcasts) were banned under the Elections Advertising Regulations (Au Yong 2011).

Lee Kin Mum's "mrbrown" rose to prominence with their satirical podcasts, titled as being "persistently non-political" in response to the ban on "explicitly political" content. One of the most popular podcast in the series was the *"tur kwa"* podcast by mrbrown (mrbrown.com 2006) involving an argument between a stall owner selling *bak chor mee* (a common dish found in food centres in Singapore) and a customer. This podcast was a parody that captured the tension between various members of the ruling party and then Workers' Party's candidate James Gomez. The podcast was evidently popular, with it being downloaded more than 100,000 times and incited reactions from citizens and politicians alike (Tang 2009). The "persistently non-political podcast" would be documented by scholars (Tang 2009; Khoo 2019) as the first example of citizens using the internet to introduce alternative political discourse using Singlish humour—both of which are associated with the "common Singaporean" (Khoo 2019).

Other than mrbrown, there were other prominent bloggers and forums which are important to highlight, not just for their popularity during the 2006 General Election, but also the manner by which social media was used to engage in discourse on civic and political issues. Benjamin Lee (Mr Miyagi) was one example, and another was Alex Au, an activist for LGBTQ rights then whose blog posts at *Yawning Bread* were often lauded for their analysis and insights (Tang 2009). *Yawning Bread* has also been credited with one of the most famous photographs during this time—a well-attended opposition rally which became widely circulated in forums and other blogs. It contributed to the development of public discourse by subverting the dominance of mainstream media in framing how opposition candidates, parties and election issues were viewed.

There were two other notable developments. Sammyboy.com, an online forum which is usually characterized by anonymous discussions of sexual topics, saw an increase in the number of discussions on election issues. These non-sexual topics were then moved to *Sammyboy's Coffee Shop,* but the same style that characterize Sammyboy forum dominated discussions of election issues as well. They were "crude, sexist, racist, xenophobic, homophobic, and profane" (Tang 2009, p. 19). Under the guise of anonymity and perhaps because of the character of the forum, many messages containing unverified rumours were also circulated in the forum. As a result, the credibility of the forum was questionable (Sim 2006).

While many observers and scholars observed that the internet has little impact on election outcomes in Singapore, these developments in the 2006 General Election provided much excitement on what may develop via online discourse, as younger citizens used the internet to advocate, mobilize and engage in discourse on important socio-political issues. Around six months later in December 2006, a community blog *The Online Citizen* was founded by activists Andrew Loh and Remy Choo Zheng Xi. The blog would later rise to prominence when it was gazetted as a political organization in the lead up to the 2011 General Election.

It is important to pay attention to the features of the platforms used during the 2006 General Election, which played a part in shaping both the development of discourse as well as the manner of engagement. As blogs and podcasts have to be fronted by identifiable individuals (in the case of *The Online Citizen*, a small group of individuals), they function like narrowcasting platforms where these individuals are primarily responsible for disseminating the content they have created to a following of people. These individuals bear primary responsibility for their content, unlike the forums where the quality of posts is often questionable especially in terms of credibility. But the anonymity in forums may also have their positives in terms of encouraging people to participate. Bloggers began to experience that their online writings can land them in trouble. Between 2007 and 2009, at least four bloggers were prosecuted either over insensitive comments about religion or comments construing contempt of the court (Ortmann 2009). Such conflicts between bloggers and the judiciary would continue until the general decline of blogs as a social media platform for activism and civic engagement.

The 2011 General Election: A Social Media Election?

By the time the 2011 General Election came around, there was much anticipation from many journalists, scholars and observers that it would be an "internet" or "social media" election (Hodal 2011). Such anticipation was not without basis, given a number of factors. The number of socio-political blogs has increased—in part due to the lifting of the Elections Advertising Regulation banning "explicitly political" content online for the 2011 General Election. *Temasek Review Emeritus* also joined *The Online Citizen* as another socio-political blog by this time. Unlike 2006 where there were only blogs and podcasts, there were more social media platforms that Singaporeans could go to for information, express opinions, and participate in online discussions on election issues. Facebook, YouTube, as well as Twitter had grown in popularity and were adopted quickly by Singaporeans. Opposition parties were also taking full advantage of social media; almost every opposition party which campaigned in this election used Facebook and Twitter to engage followers and potential voters. Additionally, all but one constituency (Tanjong Pagar) was being contested—implying that almost every Singapore will have to vote since voting is compulsory in Singapore. The General Election of 2011 was no longer an event that applied only to citizens living in certain areas, it was something that was the business of almost every citizen with voting rights.

Blogs continued to feature strongly in this election, even though newer social media platforms were emerging. In their analysis of blog posts written during this election, Pang and Goh (2016b) presented evidence that the blogs were most effective in surfacing agenda as well as present discourse that were not found on mainstream media platforms. While this contributed to the variety of perspectives that citizens could have access to, the perception that mainstream media favoured the ruling party and online media favoured the opposition would grow to become larger problems. An analysis by Pang and Goh (2016a) found early signs of polarization online: even as the number of blogs flourished, and blogs functioned as small publics facilitating exchanges between their followers, there was little tolerance for deviant opinions.

While blogs contributed to social interactions between their followers, it was Facebook that caught the attention of many with its social networking functions. Facebook was used most notably by opposition parties (Goh and Pang 2016) to keep their followers updated with photos, videos and at times, call for volunteers. Other than political parties, this was also an event which saw citizens using Facebook to share information, express opinions and connect to each other based on their interests in election issues or preferences for different parties. But such heightened usage was not always positive, as shown in the personal attacks on a PAP candidate Tin Pei Ling by social media users and *Temasek Review Emeritus* (George 2011). Although Twitter usage did not grow as quickly as Facebook for citizens and activists, political parties were active in using Twitter during the election. According to a report released by the Institute of Policy Studies (Soo 2011), the Workers' Party (WP) had the most number of followers on Twitter at the start of this election.

To conclude, the 2011 General Election was perhaps best poised as an election that would be a "social media election". First, perhaps riding on the momentum of the past election and the liberalization of online political campaigning, there were many more activists and participants who were willing to surface different agenda and develop different kinds of discourse. Second, there was now a plethora of social media platforms for them to choose from and use. Indeed, these conditions contributed to online debates which were highly critical of the ruling party. In the lead up to Polling Day, commentators and analysts thought that this election might be a turning point in Singapore's political history. The Workers' Party won a Group Representative Constituency (GRC) from the PAP in this election—a historic victory as no GRC had ever been lost by the PAP to an opposition party before since Singapore's independence. The PAP still won the majority of votes with 60.1 per cent of the popular vote share, but this was the lowest ever performance since independence in 1965.

Despite these results, analysts and scholars debated over whether the impact of social media on the election was limited (Lee and Tan 2011). To these scholars, social media remain limited in its effect. The PAP still remained in power, and lost only six seats out of eighty-nine in Parliament. A study by the Institute of Policy Studies also found in their survey that most did not consider what they read online as credible, or saw it as their main source of information during the election (Tan, Mahiznan and Ang 2015). With these findings, the conclusion that social media had a limited impact was reasonable.

A ritualistic view of communication would be much more telling in terms of analysing the impact of social media in Singapore. This view adopts the idea that the process of communication is significant in representing and shaping what people would come to understand as collective beliefs. While social media may not have impacted election outcomes as much, and still did not have much credibility, there was a cultural shift in civic and political engagement—both in terms of scale as well as engagement. This cultural shift was perhaps best described by Prime Minister Lee Hsien Loong in a post-election reflection, where he noted that the election had "heightened political consciousness and awareness" (Ibrahim 2011). This sentiment was also echoed by then Senior Minister Goh Chok Tong, who noted "a sea of change in the political landscape" (Chow 2011).

The Growth of Rallies Organized via Social Media

Facebook and Twitter continued to be used by activists after the 2011 General Election to organize rallies and events. The number of events increased steadily at Singapore's Speakers' Corner, the only venue for protests and rallies to be held in the city-state without permits. Eighty-five events were registered in 2011, followed by 98 in 2012, and reached a peak of 169 events in 2013. Of all the rallies and protests at Speakers' Corner, those that garnered the most number of attendees were based on issues that Singaporeans saw as salient to them (Pang and Goh 2016). One example was the White Paper Protest, which saw over 3,000 attendees protesting a population policy to import foreigners to the country, as it was believed that the population growth has been responsible for major infrastructural breakdowns and escalating living costs (Harjani 2014). Despite the large number of attendees at the White Paper Protest, Pang and Goh (2016) found mixed motivations in their survey of 220 participants who were interviewed in real-time. While some attended the protest because they believed in the cause for the protest, there were other personalized frames shared such as "Singapore for Singaporeans" which resonated with participants. Their findings reflect those of other scholars in other contexts, in that protests and collective action facilitated by social media take the form of connective action—where personalized action frames replace collective action frames (Bennett 2012).

With more citizens perhaps inspired by the awakening of "political consciousness" after the election, the years following the 2011 General Election saw a sharp increase in the number of blogs. A study by the Institute of Policy Studies in 2017 recorded around 240 blogs (by individuals) and socio-political sites. *Mothership.sg*, *Breakfast Network*, *Inconvenient Questions* and *Six-Six* joined *The Online Citizen*, *Temasek Review Emeritus* and *Yawning Bread* to offer content and style that resemble typical newsroom reporting, although the views were not necessarily similar. Sites like *Breakfast Network* and *Inconvenient Questions* aimed to provide more "centre-right or centre-left" discussions of issues (Mokhtar 2017). Other than new blogs and socio-political sites, more Facebook pages (e.g. Fabrications About the PAP) were also created with positions and views that opposed the anti-establishment voices online. In response, almost every Member of Parliament (MP) started a Facebook page—a development that would contribute to changes in the social media environment in the next election. Social media was clearly a new form of communication that was having significant impact in Singapore, and it was clear that certain policy changes were coming.

SOCIAL MEDIA REGULATION AND THE DECLINE OF BLOGS

Faced with this emerging landscape of bloggers and all sorts of online and social media commentary, the Singaporean government began to use legal and regulatory tools to shape political discourse. In 2013, Alex Au, the man behind the prominent socio-political blog *Yawning Bread*, was summoned by the court for contempt of court over his blog postings (Lum 2015). Other bloggers like Roy Ngerng and Leong Sze Hian were also taken to task for their postings—an approach that continued to-date (Lam 2018). These cases were seen by many as a signal to the general public that the Singaporean government believed content published online had to be held to the same standards as those published by mainstream media.

On 1 June 2013, the Broadcasting Act was expanded to include a law requiring online sites that "report regularly on Singapore and have a significant reach" (Gov.sg 2013) to apply for a media licence as individual entities. Under this law, licensees need to put up a $50,000 performance bond, and comply with taking down offensive content within twenty-four hours. Licensees are also prohibited from receiving foreign funding. In response to the new law, a movement began online titled "Free My Internet" (Wong 2013), comprising online and in-person protests. This included a one-day "blackout" where more than 150 bloggers and socio-political sites took part in shutting down their sites for twenty-four hours on 6 June 2013 as a sign of protest, although not all blogs were in agreement that this was the right response (Ong 2013). The Free My Internet movement also organized a rally at the Speaker's Corner on 8 June 2013 which attracted over 1,500 protesters (Soh 2013).

Other than websites operated by mainstream media such as *The New Paper*, *Today*, and *The Straits Times*, socio-political blogs like *The Independent Singapore* and *The Online Citizen* (Tham 2014) were soon asked to register under the new law. Months later, *Breakfast Network* (Yong 2013) was also approached to register under the new licensing scheme. This move prompted the closure of *Breakfast Network*, due to "onerous" requirements according to its founder Bertha Henson (Yong 2013), prompting the Media Development Authority (MDA) to respond with a public statement refuting the claims (Hicks 2013).

Scholars and observers debated whether the new law signalled the end of the "light touch" approach to internet content (George 2013; Ong 2013; Frater 2013). Those critical of the law cited concerns about the performance bond which would render sites with less resources untenable as well as what was felt to be a broad definition of prohibited content. On the other hand, others argued that the new law was reasonable on grounds that politics in Singapore should be defended against foreign influence, the need for online writings to be responsible, and the law was about regulations and not censorship (Othman 2013; Ong 2013).

The 2015 General Election

The developments post-2011 General Election as well as the new law in regulating the online sphere are important in order to understand the media environment (including social media) by the time the 2015 General Election came around. Soon, Tan and Nadzirah (2016, p. 7) described social media during the 2015 General Election as "the normalisation of political cyberspace ... more like the 'normal' offline world, where there is a wide range of views, with most opinions clustering around the centre". This "normalisation" meant that views on social media were no longer limited to the participation of opposition parties and voices that were critical of the establishment. This also implied that unlike the past two elections where the agenda and discourse on social media could be clearly juxtaposed against those of established media platforms, social media has become "mainstream". It was also this election that saw many political candidates, including those from the PAP, use Facebook and Twitter to engage voters.

The PAP won the overall majority with a 69.9 per cent popular vote share, almost a 10 per cent increase of the popular vote from the last election. Scholars and observers have attributed the good result of the PAP to many reasons (Sumiko Tan 2015; Chin 2016), such as the passing of senior statesman Mr Lee Kuan Yew around six months before the election, the policies implemented to address issues, as well as financial lapses discovered at the opposition-run Aljunied-Hougang Punggol East Town Council (AHPETC). Singh (2016) also argued that the results showed a rejection of most opposition parties by voters. Hence social media alone would not have been a singular factor.

However, there are a number of important arguments to be made about social media in this election. Comparing the effects of social media between the 2011 and 2015 general elections, Zhang (2016) observed that one of the main distinctions between the two elections was that there was greater mobilization by the PAP, both online and offline. Online mobilization, as Zhang (2016) argued, was effective for the opposition parties and the activists only when there was no other mobilization or engagement efforts by the ruling party, such as in 2011. This was not the case in 2015. In the same article, Zhang (2016) also argued that while younger citizens experienced the novelty of social media in providing alternative discourse in 2011, the novelty had worn off by 2015. Younger voters were also more likely to be swing voters who voted differently in 2015.

The use of social media to express opinions remained relatively low and much of the interactions were seen as relational and informational, according to a survey of 2,000 respondents on their media use and voting behaviours conducted by the Institute of Policy Studies (Samsudin 2015). For younger respondents in particular, social network sites like Facebook was the most popular social media source (69.6 per cent of respondents), followed by instant messaging platforms (62.7 per cent of respondents) reported as being used at least once a week for information and news on the election (Soon and Samsudin 2015). Only 56 per cent of respondents said that they used blogs or YouTube for information or news during the election. These findings point to how information exchange and postings during the election was growing more relational, in the sense that they were taking place in the context of one's social network. Such a context is different from using blogs as a source of information, where content was delivered from one blogger (or a group of bloggers) to a following of readers. This is an important turning point which would contribute to the impact of online misinformation and disinformation campaigns in the next section.

The Decline of Socio-Political Blogs

A study by the Institute of Policy Studies in 2017 showed that 35 per cent of around 240 socio-political blogs created in the run up to or after the 2015 General Election has been inactive (Mokhtar 2017). This may have been a result of the new law in regulating blogs or the number of legal cases involving bloggers. But given the rise of social media platforms, it was also quite likely that the number of followers of blogs was declining because they were finding it difficult to sustain their operations financially. This sentiment was shared by founders of *The Middle Ground* (previously known as *Breakfast Network*), as reported by Choo and Lee (2017). Bloggers were also switching over to other platforms, creating Facebook accounts or pages as well as YouTube channels.

This move from blogs to social media platforms tended to create a shift in political discourse. Scholars have observed and written about the phenomenon of "context collapse" in many parts of the world (Davis and Jurgenson 2014; Papacharissi 2012; Vitak 2012). This concept is built on Goffman's analysis that individuals tailor their performances and interactions with others based on distinct situations. With the growth of Facebook and the expansion of one's social network, individuals found themselves having to navigate multiple audiences in a single space. This has several implications, from privacy concerns (e.g. being tagged in family photos and having colleagues and acquaintances see them, according to Lang and Barton (2015)) to the blurring of boundaries between personal and professional networks (Davis and Jurgenson 2014).

"Context collapse" affects individuals with greater diversity in their networks, as they are more likely to encounter friends with very different backgrounds, experiences and opinions. The flattening of multiple audiences into a single social space that is Facebook or Twitter lead these individuals to adopt certain strategies when thinking about posting or responding to a post. In their study of Facebook users in 2010, Brandtzæg, Lüders and Skjetne (2010) found that because of the increased diversity in the social network (i.e. having friends, family members, colleagues, acquaintances all in one space), users exhibited greater social awareness and concerns about social surveillance. As a result, they adopt a strategy of conformity, where the sharing of content and opinions become less personal and private. Facebook's inability to be anonymous meant more open, direct and political content was lessened.

"Context collapse" can be used to explain a number of socio-psychological phenomenon on social media in recent years in Singapore. As Facebook users post content as guided by social conformity (Brandtzæg, Lüders and Skjetne 2010), citizens have turned to other online spaces with closer settings such as restricted Facebook pages, and smaller, personalized chat groups. These restricted pages, according to participants in Brandtzæg, Lüders and Skjetne's study (2010, p. 1023), are "more fun ... personal, because you know everyone very well". Likewise, in Pang and Woo's (2020) review of WhatsApp studies, one of the primary motivations for using WhatsApp especially for civic and political engagement is to avoid social surveillance and to have more authentic exchanges on topics of interest. However, within closed platforms and restricted pages, it is harder to have exposure to cross-cutting views as well and for falsehoods and rumours (if any) verified as quickly due to the nature of closed or restricted groups.

EMERGING DISINFORMATION

Scholars who have engaged in close studies of the internet and social media over the past decades have moved beyond a general optimism of the role of social media towards democracy. While there have been positive effects on civic and political engagement in Southeast Asia (Skoric, Zhu and Pang 2016), social media can also be used in ways that undermine democracy, the privacy and rights of individuals, and amplify social divides.

Numerous international studies outlined the manipulation of public opinions using methods like disinformation campaigns as well as micro-targeting by political groups, parties and foreign governments (Bradshaw and Howard 2019). In response to growing concerns about online disinformation and misinformation, governments around the world have responded in various ways. Fact-checking websites have been set up, driven by governments, civil society and commercial or news agencies. For instance, the International Fact Checking Network (IFCN) run by The Poynter Institute for Media Studies was set up in 2015 with the aim to set up a code of ethics for fact-checking organizations around the world. Other laws and regulations were being introduced in other developed countries. Germany, for instance, focused on the problem of hate speech and introduced the Network Enforcement Act on 1 January 2018. Under this Act, platforms like Facebook and Twitter are required to take down problematic content upon receiving a notification within twenty-four hours (Oltermann 2018). Critics of the Act pointed to self-censorship by social media companies, resulting in too much content being removed.

But there are also behavioural factors in contributing to the emergence of disinformation. Scholars have reported that news consumption on social media are incidental rather than purposeful especially for young people, in the sense that they encounter news rather than seeking them out (Newman et al. 2017). Associated with incidental type of news consumption behaviour, social media users are more likely to browse through headlines quickly rather than spend time reading each article deeply. As such, misleading headlines can result in wrong beliefs in people and contribute to the persistence of falsehoods. Even when corrections have been put up, the effects from headlines can be more lasting (Ecker et al. 2014). Van Dijck, Poell and de Waal (2018) describe the platform society, where platforms are the key means by which social and economic life are organized as well as produced. This implies that much of our online social life is fragmented even more than before. The idea of "common" or "public" goods or values are also fragmented and mediated through platforms, making it also harder for disinformation campaigns to be detected and disrupted. Much content as well as personal data that are generated and collected online rest in the hands of a few big US tech firms—Google, Facebook, Microsoft, just to name a few. More recently, Chinese-based platforms have also gained popularity: Alibaba is active in Singapore with Taobao and Alipay, and TikTok is also quickly gaining many users.

With the reliance on social media platforms for their news, young people may be unaware or are desensitized to political or social biases driving the information, failing to evaluate the credibility of information and detect falsehoods as a consequence. This was validated in a study by researchers at Stanford, who found that even digitally-savvy students focused more on the content rather than picking up cues that should tell them that the sources of the content were questionable (Wineburg et al. 2016). Such trends are worrying, as it shows that those who are digitally-savvy does not mean that they are able to perceive the credibility of information correctly. It can also mean that even digitally-savvy users can forward and/or share content without fact checking.

It is important to highlight these international findings because they relate to the Singaporean experience. Singapore government departments, academia and citizens are also keen consumers of international scholarship and often relate their situation to the Global North, given their developed world status, rather than situations which may be occurring in larger, neighbouring developing countries. The same observations made globally about incidental consumption of information via social media can also be observed in Singapore (Hao, Wen and George 2014), which implies that users here can also be prone to detecting and spreading misinformation in various scenarios. However, social media in Singapore is not a singular online sphere, but is fragmented according to platforms in which citizens predominantly use. This fragmentation adds to the complexity of detecting and understanding the effects of disinformation campaigns. The issue of disinformation campaigns documented elsewhere in the world has yet to be studied in Singapore and is an important gap to address. Without such a study it is hard to make conclusive judgements about the presence as well as effects of such campaigns.

One example of the challenges of social media in Singapore can be found in a (albeit rare) case of a riot in the suburb of Little India, an ethnic district in Singapore where many migrant workers from South

Asia often gather, in 2013. The riot was triggered by a fatal accident in which a thirty-three-year-old construction worker from India was run over and killed, angering onlookers nearby (*Today* 2013). The riot saw the participation of around 400 protestors and lasted for two hours before the situation was brought under control. In a study of misinformation circulated via Twitter during the riot, Pang and Ng (2017) found that deliberate falsehoods were circulated widely even though they were corrected quickly. While this alludes to the notion that sensational news can circulate much more than objective facts (Davis and McLeod 2003), the social context of the riot and responses on Twitter is important: those who participated in the riot were all migrant workers from India while those who tweeted about it were mostly Singaporeans—a phenomenon of "othering" (Pang and Ng 2016). Such "othering" is centred on social divides that can amplify the problems of misinformation, due to inherent biases and prejudices towards migrant workers, hindering people's ability to reason or check through information that are built on these biases.

The Little India case is important as it is perhaps one of the first cases that demonstrated the effects of misinformation escalated by social media in a crisis in Singapore—a city-state well known for its low crime rate and generally obedient citizenry. What is especially disconcerting are the moral panics that are built on misinformation. When misinformation escalates quickly, it becomes much harder to correct the falsehoods and more importantly, battle the stigmatization of individuals and groups that are targets of disinformation and resulting misinformation.

The concerns around the potential for spreading of misinformation and disinformation on social media continued to take root within the Singapore government. The Singapore government had already started their own fact-checking efforts by this time. "Factually" was set up in 2012 to clarify deliberate falsehoods and misinformation associated with government policies or issues of public interest. Furthermore, schools in Singapore have also started literacy campaigns and programmes to teach students how to spot falsehoods (Chia 2018).

But by 2018, the Singapore government felt it had to act more resolutely in reducing the potential for disinformation in the country. Singapore formed The Select Committee on Deliberate Online Falsehoods on 11 January 2018 and convened public hearings in March—and resulted in the Protection from Online Falsehoods and Manipulation Act (POFMA) on 2 October 2019. Unlike the Network Enforcement Act in Germany where problematic content had to be taken down completely, POFMA allows the original content to remain but had to be published together with the corrected information. The rationale is that this would allow users to compare and analyse the content for themselves. As in Germany, POFMA received many criticisms from civil society groups (Schetzer 2019) as well as academics (Zastrow 2019) for its potential in deterring scholarship and civil liberties. Since the introduction of POFMA, it had been used against opposition politicians and prominent activists, further leading to broader and international criticism that the use of the law would be politicized to suit the ruling government's agenda (Palma, Munshi and Reed 2020).

To be clear, POFMA is not the only solution that has been explored. Singapore has made use of a variety of tools—POFMA, Factually, Facebook and channels on instant messaging platforms such as WhatsApp and Telegram—to clarify falsehoods, including those associated with the Covid-19 pandemic. A broader socio-technical context of social media is important here in order to understand how the POFMA legislation and others have limitations. Singapore has seen increased popularity of instant messaging platforms such as WhatsApp. Unlike traditional SMS, it is possible to have up to 256 individuals in a group. Admins of each group can also remove or add contacts to the group, making each group on WhatsApp a micro social network—likely to be smaller than the size of one's social network on Facebook, but can still function like a social network. One can also have many group chats on WhatsApp compared to a single social network on Facebook (with multiple audiences flattened into one space), and messages in these group chats are protected with end-to-end encryption, which means that no one else other than those in the group would be able to see messages exchanges, unless they are forwarded. Taken together, these features of WhatsApp help to resolve the issues that users were experiencing with context collapse, but problems of disinformation and misinformation deepens. Because the groups are often organized around like-minded or strong networks, there are concerns about polarization that can result from manipulation through disinformation (Machado et al. 2019).

One other feature of WhatsApp which has been blamed for the spread of misinformation is the forwarding function. This feature allows one to forward a message—be it text, image or video—to other contacts (individuals and/or groups). While it used to be relatively unlimited, WhatsApp in its efforts to address the growth of misinformation, has been introducing limitations on the forwarding function over the years, including limiting the number of contacts one can forward a message to. In response, WhatsApp announced limits on "highly forwarded" messages, deemed as those that "had been forwarded more than five times, and did not originate from a close contact" (CNA 2020). This move should be understood in its context—Singapore's battle with the Covid-19 pandemic saw WhatsApp emerge as one of the most popular platforms used to circulate fake messages and rumours. Such messages have the potential to create unnecessary panic and trigger violence, a concern that many governments including Singapore share in common (Romm 2020). But while POFMA as a legislation also applies to instant messaging platforms, it is difficult to trace the source of disinformation via this platform (Choo and Koh 2020).

CONCLUSION

This chapter has provided an understanding of how social media has ebbed and flowed in Singapore since 2006. In the first five years especially, social media was used as a tool for activism, opinion, expression and mobilization largely by bloggers, civil and political activists and opposition parties. This changed in the 2015 General Election: social media became "mainstream" with the ruling party and established media also using it, and more blogs were set up with the aim of introducing centrist as well as pro-establishment perspectives. Accompanying this change was intensified "platformatisation" as well as the decline of socio-political blogs, contributing to the fragmentation of the online sphere.

The development of social media platforms began with much promise for democracy, but the fragmentation that comes with social media has evolved this online space as sites that can threaten democracy as well as institutions. To date, there has been no evidence documented about large scale disinformation in the country, but those with the means may explore opportunities to exploit social media platforms to pursue insidious intentions. Singapore is one of the first countries to introduce a legislation on disinformation, but may be limited in terms of its effectiveness as platforms continue to evolve.

What is clear is that legislations alone will not be sufficient and Singapore has reached a critical threshold for action. Individuals need to take ownership and verify information before sharing or forwarding it, but there is also room for all in recognizing that misinformation and disinformation campaigns can be an issue that threatens various sectors of society. Inherent biases against other groups can be difficult to recognize, and that is one of the main reasons why disinformation campaigns can take root. Independent fact-checking institutions which adhere to clear codes of non-partisanship, transparency and independence need to be supported by all, including research institutions and governments. More could also be done by engaging social media platforms in the ways content and personal data are analysed and used in pursuit of the goal to minimize the effects of disinformation and misinformation. For instance, algorithms driving newsfeeds could prioritize content from credible agencies and sites which have been endorsed by International Fact Checking Network. These algorithms can also be explored to provide more cross-cutting views in a social network. The burden is on every stakeholder, from the individual to civil society group to the tech platforms that collectively represent our digital public sphere, and not only just the government.

REFERENCES

Au Yong, Jeremy and Tessa Wong. 2011. "Green Light for New Media Use at GE". *The Straits Times*, 15 March 2011, p. 16. Retrieved from NewspaperSG (accessed 1 March 2020).

Bennett, W. Lance and Alexandra Segerberg. 2012. "The Logic of Connective Action". *Information, Communication and Society* 15, no. 5: 739–68. https://doi.org/10.1080/1369118X.2012.670661.

Bradshaw, Samantha and Philip N. Howard. 2019. "The Global Disinformation Order: 2019 Global Inventory of Organised Social Media Manipulation". Working Paper 2. Oxford, UK: Project on Computational Propaganda. https://comprop.oii.ox.ac.uk/wp-content/uploads/sites/93/2019/09/CyberTroop-Report19.pdf.

Brandtzæg, Petter Bae and Marika Lüders. 2018. "Time Collapse in Social Media: Extending the Context Collapse". *Social Media + Society* (January). https://doi.org/10.1177/2056305118763349.

Brandtzæg, Petter Bae, Marika Lüders and Jan Håvard Skjetne. 2010. "Too Many Facebook 'Friends'? Content Sharing and Sociability Versus the Need for Privacy in Social Network Sites". *International Journal of Human–*

Computer Interaction 26, nos. 11–12: 1006–30. https://doi.org/10.1080/10447318.2010.516719.

Carr, T. Caleb and Rebecca A. Hayes. 2015. "Social Media: Defining, Developing, and Divining". *Atlantic Journal of Communication* 23, no. 1: 46–65. https://doi.org/10.1080/15456870.2015.972282.

Chia, Lianne. 2018. "Thriving rather than Surviving: Teaching Students How to Spot Fake News". CNA, 25 February 2018. https://www.channelnewsasia.com/news/singapore/thriving-rather-than-surviving-teaching-students-how-to-spot-9960656 (accessed 25 April 2020).

Chin, James. 2016. "The 2015 Singapore Swing: Depoliticised Polity and the *Kiasi/Kiasu* Voter". *The Round Table* 105, no. 2: 141–48. https://doi.org/10.1080/00358533.2016.1154383.

Choo, Cynthia and Jeremy Lee. 2017. "Socio-Political Site The Middle Ground to Shut After 2.5 Years, cites Lack of Funding". *Today*, 28 October 2017. https://www.todayonline.com/singapore/socio-political-site-middle-ground-shut-after-25-years-cites-lack-of-funding (accessed 20 April 2020).

Choo, Daryl and Alvina Koh. 2020. "Pofma – But Not for WhatsApp so far". Our Class Notes, 16 May 2020. https://www.ourclassnotes.com/post/pofma-but-not-for-whatsapp-so-far (accessed 16 May 2020).

Chow, Jermyn. 2011. "SM Goh: The Tide was Very Strong". *The Straits Times*, 9 May 2011. p. A6. Retrieved from Factiva.

CNA. 2020. "WhatsApp Tightens Limit on Forwarding of Messages to Curb Spread of Misinformation". ChannelNewsAsia, 7 April 2020. https://www.channelnewsasia.com/news/business/whatsapp-forwarded-message-limit-tightened-covid-19-12617548 (accessed 10 April 2020).

Davis, Hank and Lyndsay McLeod. 2003. "Why Humans Value Sensational News: An Evolutionary Perspective". *Evolution and Human Behavior* 24, no. 3: 208–16. https://doi.org/10.1016/S1090-5138(03)00012-6.

Davis, Jenny L. and Nathan Jurgenson. 2014. "Context Collapse: Theorizing Context Collusions and Collisions". *Information, Communication & Society* 17, no. 4: 476–85. https://doi.org/10.1080/1369118X.2014.888458.

Ecker, Ullrich K., Stephan Lewandowsky, Ee Pin Chang and Rekha Pillai. 2014. "The Effects of Subtle Misinformation in News Headlines". *Journal of Experimental Psychology: Applied* 20, no. 4: 323–35. https://doi.org/10.1037/xap0000028.

Frater, Patrick. 2013. "Singapore Puts Online on a Leash". *Variety*, 25 July 2013. https://variety.com/2013/biz/asia/singapore-puts-online-on-a-leash-1200567202/ (accessed 5 April 2020).

George, Cherian. 2011. "Tin Pei Ling's Baptism of Fire: Should Bloggers Have Lit the Match?" *Freedom from the Press* (blog), 30 March 2011. http://blog.freedomfromthepress.info/2010/03/30/tin-pei-lings-baptism-of-fire-should-bloggers-have-lit-the-match/ (accessed 10 April 2020).

———. 2013. "Online Freedom: Time to Revise the Singapore Report Card". *Freedom from the Press* (blog), 10 December 2013. http://blog.freedomfromthepress.info/2013/12/10/online-freedom-time-to-revise-the-singapore-report-card/ (accessed 6 April 2020).

Goh, Debbie and Natalie Pang. 2016. "Untapped Potential: Internet Use by Political Parties". In *Battle for Hearts and Minds: New Media and Elections in Singapore*, edited by Tan Tarn How and Arun Mahizhnan, pp. 49–71. Singapore: World Scientific Publishing. https://doi.org/10.1142/9743.

Gov.sg. 2013. "What is the Licensing Framework for Online News Sites All About?" June 2013. https://www.gov.sg/article/what-is-the-licensing-framework-for-online-news-sites-all-about (accessed 1 April 2020).

Hao, Xiaoming, Nainan Wen and Cherian George. 2014. "News Consumption and Political and Civic Engagement Among Young People". *Journal of Youth Studies* 17, no. 9: 1221–38. https://doi.org/10.1080/13676261.2014.901490.

Harjani, Ansuya. 2014. "Balmy Singapore Contends with Rising Protests". CNBC, 25 August 2014. https://www.cnbc.com/2014/08/25/balmy-singapore-contends-with-rising-protests.html (accessed 21 April 2020).

Hicks, Robin. 2013. "Breakfast Network Closure Marks End of 'Light Touch' Internet Regulation in Singapore, says Academic". Mumbrella Asia, 17 December 2013. https://www.mumbrella.asia/2013/12/closure-breakfast-network-heralds-end-singapores-light-touch-internet-regulation-says-academic (accessed 1 May 2020).

Hodal, Kate. 2011. "Singapore Elections Marked by Online Buzz of Discontent". *The Guardian*, 6 May 2011. https://www.theguardian.com/world/2011/may/06/singapore-elections-internet (accessed 2 May 2020).

Ibrahim, Zuraidah. 2011. "81-6: Workers' Party wins Aljunied GRC; PAP Vote Share Dips to 60.1%". *Sunday Times*, p. 1. Retrieved from Factiva.

Kemp, Simon. 2020. "Digital 2020: Singapore". DataReportal, 13 February 2020. https://datareportal.com/reports/digital-2020-singapore (accessed 15 April 2020).

Khoo, Velda. 2019. "Ownself Check Ownself: The Role of Singlish Humour in the Rise of the Opposition Politician in Singapore". *Colorado Research in Linguistics* 24. http://dx.doi.org/10.33011/cril.24.1.5.

Koh, Fabian. 2020. "About 40 Instances of Covid-19 Fake News Debunked So Far This Year". *The Straits Times*, 5 May 2020. https://www.straitstimes.com/singapore/about-40-instances-of-covid-19-fake-news-debunked-so-far-this-year (accessed 10 May 2020).

Lam, Lydia. 2018. "PM Lee Sues Blogger Leong Sze Hian for Defamation over Sharing of Articles". ChannelNewsAsia, 7 December 2018. https://www.channelnewsasia.com/news/singapore/pm-lee-sues-blogger-leong-sze-hian-defamation-libellous-article-10999710 (accessed 18 April 2020).

Lang, Caroline and Hannah Barton. 2015. "Just Untag It: Exploring the Management of Undesirable Facebook Photos". *Computers in Human Behavior* 43: 147–55. https://doi.org/10.1016/j.chb.2014.10.051.

Lee, Terence and Kevin Y.L. Tan. 2011. *Voting in Change: The Politics of Singapore*. Singapore: Ethos Books, 2020.

Lum, Selina. 2015. "Blogger Alex Au Fined $8000 for Contempt of Court". *The Straits Times*, 5 March 2015. https://www.straitstimes.com/singapore/courts-crime/blogger-alex-au-fined-8000-for-contempt-of-court (accessed 3 March 2020).

Machado, Caio, Beatriz Kira, Vidya Narayanan, Bence Kollanyi and Philip Howard. 2019. "A Study of Misinformation in WhatsApp Groups with a Focus on the Brazilian Presidential Elections". *Companion Proceedings of The 2019 World Wide Web Conference (WWW '19)*: 1013–19. https://doi.org/10.1145/3308560.3316738.

Mokhtar, Faris. 2017. "About a Third of Socio-Political Websites in Singapore No Longer Active". *Today*, 22 September 2017. https://www.todayonline.com/singapore/about-third-socio-political-websites-singapore-no-longer-active (accessed 10 May 2020).

mrbrown.com. 2006. "Browncast: The Persistently Non-Political Podcast no. 6", 1 May 2006. https://www.mrbrown.com/blog/2006/05/browncast_the_p.html (accessed 1 March 2020).

Newman, Nic, Richard Fletcher, Antonis Kalogeropoulos, David A.L. Levy and Rasmus Kleis Nielsen. 2017. *Reuters Institute Digital News Report 2017*. Oxford: University of Oxford.

Oltermann, Philip. 2018. "Tough New German Law Puts Tech Firms and Free Speech in Spotlight". *The Guardian*, 5 January 2018. https://www.theguardian.com/world/2018/jan/05/tough-new-german-law-puts-tech-firms-and-free-speech-in-spotlight (12 March 2020).

Ong, Andrea. 2013. "Over 150 Singapore Websites and Blogs Hold 24-hour Blackout Protest". *The Straits Times*, 7 June 2013. https://www.straitstimes.com/singapore/over-150-singapore-websites-and-blogs-hold-24-hour-blackout-protest (accessed 20 April 2020).

Ortmann, Stephanie. 2009. *Routledge Contemporary Asia Series: Politics and Change in Singapore and Hong Kong (Book 21)*. London: Routledge.

Othman, Zul. 2013. "Is Govt's Light Touch Over?" *The New Paper*, 15 December 2013. https://www.asiaone.com/singapore/govts-light-touch-over (accessed 10 April 2020).

Palma, Stephania, Neil Munshi and John Reed. 2020. "Singapore 'Falsehoods' Law Shows Peril of Fake News Fight". *Financial Times*, 4 February 2020. https://www.ft.com/content/e50eb042-3db3-11ea-a01a-bae547046735 (accessed 30 April 2020).

Pang, Natalie and Debbie Goh. 2016a. "Are We All Here for the Same Purpose? Social Media and Individualized Collective Action". *Online Information Review* 40, no. 4: 544–59.

———. 2016b. "Can Blogs Function as Rhetorical Publics in Asian Democracies? An Analysis Using the Case of Singapore". *Telematics and Informatics* 33, no. 2: 504–13. https://doi.org/10.1016/j.tele.2015.08.001.

Pang, Natalie and Donald Schauder. 2007. "The Culture of Information Systems in Knowledge-Creating Contexts". *Informing Science Journal* 10: 203–35.

Pang, Natalie and Joshua Ng. 2016. "Twittering the Little India Riot: Audience Responses, Information Behaviour and the Use of Emotive Cues". *Computers in Human Behavior* 54 (January): 607–19. https://doi.org/10.1016/j.chb.2015.08.047.

———. 2017. "Misinformation in a Riot: A Two-Step Flow View". *Online Information Review* 41, no. 4: 438–53.

Pang, Natalie and Yueting Woo. 2020. "What about WhatsApp? A Systematic Review of WhatsApp and its Role in Civic and Political Engagement". *First Monday* 25, no. 12. https://doi.org/10.5210/fm.v25i12.10417 (accessed 1 May 2020).

Papacharissi, Zizi. 2012. "Without You, I'm Nothing: Performances of the Self on Twitter". *International Journal of Communication* 6: 1989–2006.

Reuters. 2020. "Reuters Expands Program to Combat Misinformation with Facebook Partnership in Singapore", 14 May 2020. https://www.reuters.com/article/rpb-singaporefactchecking/reuters-expands-programme-to-combat-misinformation-with-facebook-partnership-in-singapore-idUSKBN22Q063 (accessed 20 May 2020).

Romm, Tony. 2020. "Fake Cures and Other Coronavirus Conspiracy Theories are Flooding WhatsApp, Leaving Governments and Users with a 'Sense of Panic'". *The Washington Post*, 2 March 2020. https://www.washingtonpost.com/technology/2020/03/02/whatsapp-coronavirus-misinformation/.

Samsudin, Nadzirah. 2015. "Report on IPS Symposium on Media and Internet Use During General Election 2015". Singapore: Institute of Policy Studies. https://lkyspp.nus.edu.sg/docs/default-source/ips/report_-ips-symposium-on-media-and-internet-use-during-general-election-2015_180316.pdf (accessed 15 April 2020).

Schetzer, Alana. 2019. "Governments are Making Fake News a Crime – But It Could Stifle Free Speech". *The Conversation*, 8 July 2019. https://theconversation.com/governments-are-making-fake-news-a-crime-but-it-could-stifle-free-speech-117654 (accessed 20 April 2020).

Sim, C.Y. 2006. "Believe Those Blogs? Only 1 per cent Find Them Credible". *The Straits Times*, 17 March 2006.

Singh, Bilveer. 2016. "Singapore's 2015 General Election: Explaining PAP's Resounding Win". *The Round Table* 105, no. 2: 129–40. https://doi.org/10.1080/00358533.2016.1154387.

Skoric, Marko, Qinfeng Zhu and Natalie Pang. 2016. "Social Media, Political Expression, and Participation in Confucian Asia". *Chinese Journal of Communication* 9, no. 4: 331–47. https://doi.org/10.1080/17544750.2016.1143378.

Soh, Elizabeth. 2013. "Over 1,500 Singaporeans Protest at Rally Against New Online Rules". Yahoo! News, 8 June 2013. https://sg.news.yahoo.com/over-1-500-singaporeans-protest-at-rally-against-new-online-rules--144315176.html (accessed 25 April 2020).

Soo, Nikki. 2011. "Tweet Tweet: A Personal View of Social Media in GE2011". *IPS Update* (September). Singapore: Institute of Policy Studies. https://lkyspp.nus.edu.sg/docs/default-source/ips/nikki_a-personal-view-of-social-media-in-ge-2011_010911.pdf (accessed 1 March 2020).

Soon, Carol and Siti Nadzirah Samsudin. 2016. "General Election 2015 in Singapore: What Social Media Did and Did not Do". *The Round Table* 105, no. 2: 171–84. https://doi.org/10.1080/00358533.2016.1154388.

Soon, Carol, Tarn How Tan and Nadzirah Samsudin. 2016. "Media and Internet Use during General Election 2015". *IPS Exchange Series* 11 (December): 1–144. https://lkyspp.nus.edu.sg/docs/default-source/ips/exchange-11_media-and-internet-use-during-general-election-2015.pdf (accessed 21 April 2020).

Tan, Sumiko. 2015. "GE2015: PAP Vote Share Increases to 69.9%, Party Wins 83 of 89 Seats including WP-held Punggol East". *The Straits Times*, 12 September 2015. https://www.straitstimes.com/politics/ge2015-pap-vote-share-increases-to-699-party-wins-83-of-89-seats-including-wp-held-punggol (accessed 2 April 2020).

Tan, Tarn How. 2015. "Normalisation of New Media since the 2011 Election". IPS Commons, 25 August 2015. https://ipscommons.sg/normalisation-of-new-media-since-the-2011-election/.

Tan, Tarn How, Arun Mahizhan and Peng Hwa Ang, eds. 2015. *Battle for Hearts and Minds: New Media and Elections in Singapore*. Singapore: World Scientific Publishing. https://doi.org/10.1142/9743.

Tang, Hang Wu. 2009. "The Networked Electorate: The Internet and the Quiet Democratic Revolution in Malaysia and Singapore". *Journal of Information, Law and Technology* 2: 1–33.

Tham, Yuen-C. 2014. "Company Behind Socio-Political Website TOC Registers Under Class License Notification". *The Straits Times*, 10 November 2014. https://www.straitstimes.com/singapore/company-behind-socio-political-website-toc-registers-under-class-licence-notification (accessed 1 May 2020).

Today. 2013. "Little India Riot: Timeline of What Happened", 10 December 2013. https://www.todayonline.com/little-india-riot-timeline-what-happened (accessed 28 April 2020).

van Dijck, Jose, Thomas Poell and Martijn de Waal. 2018. *The Platform Society*. Oxford: Oxford University Press.

Vitak, Jessica. 2012. "The Impact of Context Collapse and Privacy on Social Network Site Disclosures". *Journal of Broadcasting & Electronic Media* 56: 451–70.

Wesch, Michael. 2007. "What is Web 2.0? What Does It Mean for Anthropology? Lessons from an Accidental Viral Video". *Anthropology News* 48, no. 5: 30–31.

Wineburg, Sam, Sarah McGrew, Joel Breakstone and Teresa Ortega. 2016. "Evaluating Information: The Cornerstone of Civic Online Reasoning". Stanford Digital Repository. http://purl.stanford.edu/fv751yt5934 (accessed 10 May 2020).

Wong, Tessa. 2013. "'Free My Internet' Netizens to Protest Against MDA Rule". *The Straits Times*, 2 June 2013.

Yong, Charissa. 2013. "Breakfast Network Website to Close, Will Not be Registering with MDA". *The Straits Times*, 10 December 2013. https://www.straitstimes.com/singapore/breakfast-network-website-to-close-will-not-be-registering-with-mda (accessed 5 March 2020).

Zastrow, Mark. 2019. "Singapore Passes 'Fake News' Law Following Research Outcry". *Nature*, 15 May 2019. https://www.nature.com/articles/d41586-019-01542-7 (accessed 15 May 2020).

Zhang, Weiyu. 2016. "Social Media and Elections in Singapore: Comparing 2011 and 2015". *Chinese Journal of Communication* 9, no. 4: 367–84. https://doi.org/10.1080/17544750.2016.1231129.

10

DEMOCRATIC BACKSLIDING AND AUTHORITARIAN RESILIENCE IN SOUTHEAST ASIA: THE ROLE OF SOCIAL MEDIA

Marco Bünte

A sharp rise in the use of new technologies and social media in Southeast Asia has triggered a debate about the possible effects on the political architecture in the region. Is social media leading to increased political participation? Can social media boost democratization in authoritarian states in Southeast Asia? How are Facebook, YouTube and Twitter changing political communication? This chapter uses Southeast Asia as a laboratory to test certain hypothesis of the impact of social media on democratization and authoritarian resilience. While social media were seen as instruments of liberation a decade ago, they are today considered a major threat to democracy and human freedom (Diamond 2019). Digital media are regarded as providing fertile ground for the rise of authoritarian strongmen and right-wing groups, accelerating and deepening the current wave of autocratization. Autocratization is used here as an umbrella term to cover the diverse processes of democratic backsliding (which means the loss of democratic quality in a democracy), the breakdown of an existing democracy and the worsening conditions in electoral authoritarian regimes. In electoral authoritarian regimes elections are not competitive and fair and incumbents often use various strategies of manipulation to stay in power.

In this chapter I argue that authoritarian regimes in Southeast Asia have adapted to new technologies and are increasingly using social media and the internet for their own ends. They have enhanced censorship and online repression and are employing the internet to co-opt certain social groups, repress critics and legitimize their rule. The young democracies in the region are unstable and weakly institutionalized. Social media is furthering polarization and distrust in Southeast Asian societies, often based on disinformation campaigns and growing sectarianism. Here, elections have become virtual battlegrounds between contestants and internet and social media are actively used to misinform and intimidate.

The chapter is structured as follows: first, I compare political developments in Southeast Asia with global developments. I show that the region has not experienced a region-wide wave of democratization seen elsewhere and authoritarian regimes are more or less resilient towards political change. I then briefly discuss causes of democratic instability and authoritarian resilience in Southeast Asia. In the last chapter I discuss the effects of digital media for authoritarian resilience and democratic backsliding and identify the main mechanisms how social media is influencing regime developments.

FOLLOWING GLOBAL TRENDS?

How does Southeast Asia fit into the broader picture of political changes at the global level? The world today is more democratic than any other point in the twentieth century. Whereas closed autocracies still accounted for around half the countries in the world in 1980, by 2019 their share had dropped to 14 per cent of the regimes in the world. At the same time, the "third wave of democratization" (Huntington 1993), which started with the Revolution of the Carnation in Portugal in 1974 and peaked with the fall of the communist regimes in Eastern Europe in 1990/91, has significantly increased the number of liberal and electoral democracies. Today, thirty-seven countries are liberal democracies, while fifty countries are electoral democracies (V-Dem 2020).

Despite this positive assessment, the most recent reports from Freedom House and V-Dem need to be seen as warning signals that democracies are increasingly in trouble. Based on V-Dem data, Lührmann and Lindberg (2019) argue that a "third wave of autocratisation is currently underway", bringing the third wave of democratization to an end. This new wave of autocratization follows similar reverse waves, after the First World War a wave of autocratization occurred between 1922 and 1945, while after the Second World War there was another wave of autocratization from 1960 to 1975. For the first time since 2001, the number and share of (both liberal and electoral) democracies are in evident decline. Electoral authoritarian rule is now the most common form of government in the world, practised in 67 countries or almost 40 per cent of all nations. Altogether, 92 countries (or 54 per cent) are authoritarian in one form or another. Freedom House data confirms these findings. Speaking of "democracy in retreat", Freedom House (2019) reports declining political rights and civil liberties since 2006. The most recent wave has now gained worldwide momentum and has affected some of the most populous and economic advanced countries such as Brazil, India, Turkey and the United States.

Haerpfer et al. (2019, p. ii) concur that the reverse wave of democratization, coupled with rising authoritarianism and electoral triumphs of right-wing populism, has instilled some pessimism about the prospects of democracy and a general sense of democratic crisis. Worldwide, we see limited spaces for civil society and increasing encroachment on independent media. More and more, elections—the core institution of democracies—are targeted by autocrats (V-Dem 2020). Yet, we also find some optimistic voices, which point to the exceptionally high degree of pro-democracy protests worldwide. With large-scale events in Hong Kong, Teheran and Santiago, 2019 was the year with the highest global average of pro-democracy protests ever, surpassing the levels of mobilization around the collapse of the Soviet Union and the Arab Spring. In the last ten years, mass protests could contribute to substantial political change and democratization in more than twenty-two countries (V-Dem 2020, p. 23). Although this has not triggered a fourth wave of democratization, it gives hope that democracy's fate is not yet sealed.

In Southeast Asia, democracy has long been an exception. Historically, the region has been dominated by authoritarian systems of government— here, especially military dictatorships and one-party regimes. Whereas the military played an important part in state and nation-building in Indonesia, Myanmar and Thailand, communist one-party regimes were established in Vietnam, Cambodia and Laos. In Singapore and Malaysia, elites could form dominant parties, which have ruled the political systems since independence.

Southeast Asia has been more of an "ebb-and-flow tide rather than a surging wave" of democratization (Shin and Tusalem 2019, p. 417). During the first wave of democratization most of the Southeast Asian people have been ruled by colonial powers, whereas the second wave of democratization resulted in the first democratic experiment in the Philippines, which ended in 1972 with Ferdinand Marcos declaring martial law and abolishing the constitution. It was only with the third wave of democratization that electoral democracies gained some ground in the region (see Table 10.1). After the People Power Revolution and the fall of Ferdinand Marcos in 1986, a fresh democratic beginning was made in the Philippines; in Thailand, large-scale protests in May 1992 led to a (temporary) retreat of the military, ushering in a fourteen-year-long period of openness and democracy. In Indonesia, democracy was established after the fall of long-term autocrat Suharto in May 1998 and free elections held in 1999. East Timor finally established an electoral democracy in 2003, after it gained independence from Indonesia in 1999 (Croissant 2019).

TABLE 10.1
Regime Types in Southeast Asia, 1985–2020

Regime Types	1985	2005	2015	2020
Monarchies	Brunei	Brunei	Brunei	Brunei
Military Regimes	Indonesia, Myanmar, Thailand	Myanmar	Thailand	–
One-Party Regimes	Cambodia, Laos, Vietnam	Laos, Vietnam	Laos, Vietnam	Laos, Vietnam
Competitive Authoritarian Regimes	Malaysia, Philippines, Singapore	Cambodia, Malaysia, Singapore	Cambodia, Malaysia, Myanmar, Singapore	Cambodia, Malaysia, Myanmar, Singapore, Thailand
Electoral Democracy	–	Indonesia, Philippines, Thailand, Timor Leste	Indonesia, Philippines, Timor Leste	Indonesia, Philippines, Timor Leste

Source: Data compiled from Magaloni, Chu and Min (2013) and V-Dem (2020).

Although democracy in Southeast Asia has gained some ground in the last three decades, it remains fragile. Faced with political polarization, a rapid political mobilization of diverse social groups and the failure of democratic structures to respond to growing pressures from below (Croissant and Bünte 2011), Southeast Asian democracies remain prone to democratic backsliding. Although Indonesia under Joko Widodo (Jokowi) and the Philippines under Rodrigo Duterte experienced episodes of democratic regression, they could avoid a complete breakdown so far (Warburton and Aspinall 2016; Aspinall and Mietzner 2019; Thompson 2016). Croissant (2019) shows that backsliding often takes the form of "executive aggrandizement", i.e. nominally democratic incumbents use their powers to reward their cronies while punishing critics, to curtail independent media and restrict spaces for civil society, to degrade the rule of law and cut the claws of independent watchdog organizations. In Thailand, democratic backsliding culminated in "promissory putsches" in 2006 and 2014—these coups "frame the ouster of an elected government as defense of democratic legality and make a promise to hold elections as soon as possible" (Bermeo 2016, p. 6); elections in Thailand were held finally in March 2019. However, these elections were not competitive but highly orchestrated by the incumbent Prayuth government to ensure the dominance of the military and conservative forces within Thai society (Ricks 2019).

Despite some democratic advances in recent decades, authoritarian forces remain deeply entrenched in Southeast Asia. Brunei, Laos and Vietnam remain closed authoritarian regimes—regimes in which no competitive elections are held to legitimize the political order. Electoral authoritarian regimes are now the most common regime form in Southeast Asia. These regimes have introduced semi-competitive elections at some point and have witnessed interesting dynamics in the past decades, though these developments have not managed to lift these countries above the democratic threshold. After ruling directly for more than two decades, Myanmar's military regime opened up and started a liberalization of the political system in 2011/12, culminating in the November 2015 elections, which were relatively free and fair and which were won by the oppositional National League for Democracy (NLD) in a landslide. Freedom House listed Myanmar as partly free from 2017 to 2019. However, the ethnic cleansing of Muslim Rohingya carried out by security forces in Rakhine state, the enormous veto-power of the military as well as the general deterioration of political freedoms and civil rights led to an autocratic regression in recent years (Bünte, Köllner and Roewer 2019).

In Malaysia, the electoral authoritarian regime is on the cusp of democratic transition. Traditionally relying on electoral manipulation such as gerrymandering and malapportionment as well as soft repression, the Barisan Nasional (BN) coalition was voted out of office for the first time since independence in May 2018. The opposition slowly gained more strength since the end of the 1990s. In 2008, BN lost its two-thirds parliamentary majority for the first time, and the opposition could take over five states. However, it was only after Prime Minister Najib Razak was embezzled in a major corruption scandal and the opposition coalesced around former BN-strongman and Prime Minister Mahathir Mohamad that BN was voted out of office (Ufen 2020). Since May 2018, however, the new Pakatan Harapan (PH) coalition under the leadership of ninety-three-year-old Mahathir could not agree to implement key institutional reforms of the election system, the internal security laws or the judiciary. Finally, the fragile coalition broke down in February 2020, when factions broke away from the PH-coalition and Mahathir was forced to step down. In short, it appears as if Malaysia is lost in transition.

Cambodia's political system has been dominated by strongman Hun Sen and his Cambodian People's Party (CPP) for the past three decades. The country held several flawed elections, in which the opposition could gain some strength. However, the dissolution of the opposition party in May 2018 and the crackdown on civil society and media organizations before the July 2018 "sham elections" (Morgenbesser 2019), in which the CPP could win an absolute majority, made clear that Hun Sen and his party remain in total control.

In Singapore, the People's Action Party (PAP) held a monopoly on power for the past five decades. Based on effective governance and economic growth the PAP could secure a majority in all elections. These elections, however, were not truly free and fair. The country's draconian legal system, which severely limits civil liberties and political liberties and restricts political opposition, makes it difficult to label Singapore an illiberal democracy. Instead, the country remains a competitive authoritarian regime for the time being (Ortmann 2011).

CAUSES OF DEMOCRATIC REGRESSION AND AUTHORITARIAN RESILIENCE

How can we explain the fragility of democratic regimes and the resilience of autocracy in Southeast Asia? Obviously, the resilience of authoritarianism and lower support of democracy tends to be found in poorer, less developed countries such as Myanmar, Laos, and Cambodia. The governments and political leaders of these countries enjoy considerable trust due to traditionalist values, the mobilization of nationalism or government propaganda (Nathan 2020). Resilient electoral-authoritarian rule in Singapore and Malaysia, however, has been attributed to the institutional strength and autonomy of their state apparatuses (Slater 2012).

Democracy in the Philippines, Indonesia and East Timor tends to be "illiberal, hollow (and) poorly institutionalised", though it has shown some resilience despite challenges (Chu et al. 2008, pp. 254–55). The most recent democratic decline in Indonesia and the Philippines is the result of social polarization and the mobilization of diverse cultural and political identities. In Indonesia, rising anti-globalization feelings and dissatisfaction with existing inequalities prepared the ground for the rise of identity politics, used by Islamic forces both inside parliament and outside in the streets since 2014. Believing that democracy was under threat, Jokowi gradually concentrated power in the executive and punished his critics by using existing defamation and electronic information laws (Mietzner 2019, p. 10). In the Philippines, liberal-reformist and populist politicians have traditionally rotated in office since 1998 (Curato 2017). Voted into office by a cross-class-coalition based on his campaign pledge to rid the country of drugs and crime, Rodrigo Duterte started to silence the press, co-opted parts of the opposition, punished his critics and dismantled constitutional checks and balances (Thompson 2016; Dressel and Bonoan 2019). Obviously, democracies in all countries are weakly institutionalized; political institutions are unable to deal with the deepening crisis. Inequalities between ethnic, sectarian or regional groups that coincide with identity-based cleavages and low levels of social cohesion also weaken democratic resilience (Croissant and Walkenhorst 2019). In Thailand, partisan civil societies and uncivil social movements mobilized in the streets against the democratic order—which has been seriously eroded under Thaksin Shinawatra. Courts and judicial institutions could not find a way out of the crises and were widely seen as lacking independence and justice, triggering the military coups of 2006 and 2014 (Kuhonta and Sinpeng 2014). The coups in Thailand and the autocratic regression in Myanmar might also be explained by the history of praetorianism. In both countries, militaries seriously undermine the rules of the democratic game, preventing democracy from taking root (Bünte 2020). In all countries, the weak support for liberal values and the serious deficit of popular trust in fundamental institutions that undergird democratic structures raise questions about the sustainability of democracy. Furthermore, according to survey data from the Asia Barometer, most of the democracies enjoy less support than their authoritarian counterparts (Nathan 2020).

Externally, China has become not only the predominant trading partner but also the provider of much needed development aid for authoritarian states such as Cambodia, Laos, Myanmar and Thailand (Schüller et al. 2010) and for illiberal democracies like the Philippines or Indonesia. Here, Chinese development is often seen as an effective aid that comes with no strings attached—contrary to Western aid, which is tied to a good governance agenda and human rights conditionalities. However, although it has also been shown that China is not actively promoting authoritarianism in mainland Southeast Asia (Bader 2015), the country serves as a role model that has the potential to undermine democracy's appeal in the region. Both Indonesian and Philippine leaders openly support the Chinese model. The Indonesian Home Minister Tito Karnavian praised the effectiveness of China's one-party state for achieving economic growth, while lamenting that Western democracy is responsible for the lack of growth in Indonesia (*Jakarta Post* 2019). In a similar vein, Duterte's presidential spokesperson Salvador Panelo hopes that China could become "a role model" for the Philippines (Rappler 2019). Under Duterte, China has become an important economic partner and source of loans for the Philippine development programme. In light of recent negative opinion polls, most probably a result of China's aggressive foreign policy and territorial claims in the South China Sea, Panelo hoped for a change of mind of the Philippine population.

It is important to emphasize, however, that Chinese policies are not the causes of democratic backsliding in Asia. Yet, China's increasing economic, political and military roles have the potential to limit Western leverage and reduce the attractiveness of the democratic model. While the United States has lost influence and appeal under Trump, China has increasingly stepped in to fill the void. We can conclude that we have not witnessed a regional uprising like the Arab Spring, though we have seen a democratization of a small number of states. However, democracy remains weak and prone to backsliding while the majority of states remain either electoral-authoritarian (Singapore, Malaysia, Myanmar, Thailand) or unambiguously closed-authoritarian (Brunei, Laos, Vietnam). We need to bear this context in mind when trying to assess the impact of social media on these diverse regimes.

WHAT IS THE ROLE OF SOCIAL MEDIA IN SOUTHEAST ASIA?

The theoretical debate about social media's impact on democratization has highlighted some important, though contradictory, effects. At the beginning of the decade, Diamond (2010) praised the liberating role of the new technologies. Summarizing debates in media and communication studies, Diamond stressed the ability of the new technologies to circumvent the information monopoly and censorship of the state. Although he also warned of the new censorship possibilities of authoritarian regimes and increasing surveillance, he highlighted the new options these technologies bring for civil society to communicate, self-organize and mobilize against autocrats. By lowering the costs for participation and communication, social groups, particularly younger citizens, are drawn into politics and political movements. Especially, social movements profit, since the organization and coordination of collective action becomes much easier (Shirky 2008). Gladwell (2010) disagrees with these findings and highlights that revolutionary action is based on deeper ties and networks of mutual trust, while the internet often creates clicktivism or slacktivism—feel good activism without social impact. Morozov (2011) argued that both revolutionaries and autocrats can profit from the new technologies. Revising some of his earlier optimism and turning the earlier effects on its head, Diamond (2019) recently warned of the great dangers for democracy and the establishment of a new digital totalitarianism. Authoritarian regimes might actually not only censor the news at home but also engage in disinformation campaigns abroad. He also warned of the negative effects of increasing polarization as a result of "echo chambers" or "filter effects" and disinformation campaigns in elections.

Drawing upon this debate, we can filter out three possible consequences of social media: the liberation effect; relying on informational gains; better networking and increased protests against the (authoritarian) regime. All three might cause a dissatisfaction with the performance of the regime and ultimately lead to democratization. The second, opposing view relies on the enhanced "coercive capacity" of the state, which leads to increased oppression. A third consequence might be the triggering of disinformation campaigns, resulting in increased polarization, weakening of trust in public media or increasing ideological divides.

What effects could we witness in the authoritarian regimes and the young democracies in Southeast Asia? Southeast Asia provides a good laboratory to test some of the theoretical assumptions outlined previously. Before discussing the impact, it is necessary to look at the context social media is operating in. Internet penetration in the region varies widely from a low 35 per cent in Timor Leste, Myanmar and Laos to more than 80 per cent in Brunei, Singapore and Malaysia (see Table 10.2). Nevertheless, the internet environment is strikingly similar, and we can witness a slow deterioration of internet freedom throughout the region. The Philippines, for a long time the only country with a "free" internet environment, has lost this status after 2016 and is now listed as partially free. The rest of the Southeast countries allow only partial to little freedom surfing the net. In all the "partly" free or "unfree" countries, citizens have been arrested for their online activities, social media has been blocked more or less regularly and user rights have been frequently violated. Vietnam stands out as the most repressive regime. It has regularly blocked social media sites such as Facebook or Instagram or has given long prison sentences to activists who use the internet to disseminate certain information detrimental to the communist party. Since bloggers are the only ones distributing independent information, the Vietnamese state has increased repression of online journalists and bloggers since 2016. Currently, there are twenty-five bloggers serving prison sentences (Reporters without Borders 2019). Generally, we can say that the internet freedom broadly correlates with regime type. In the closed political regimes such as Vietnam, Laos and Thailand (2014–19), we find the lowest scores of internet freedom.

TABLE 10.2
Internet and Social Media Usage in Southeast Asia

Country	Political and Civil Rights (Freedom House 2020)	Internet Freedom (Freedom House 2019)	Internet Penetration in %, June 2019	Facebook Users in 1000/Penetration in %, June 2019
Brunei	not free	–	94.9	350 (39.7)
Cambodia	not free	partly free	48.6	6.300 (38.2)
Indonesia	partly free	partly free	63.5	130.000 (48.2)
Laos	not free	–	34.4	2.200 (30.2)
Malaysia	partly free	partly free	81.4	22.000 (68.0)
Myanmar	not free	not free	33.1	16.000 (29.4)
Philippines	partly free	partly free	72.1	62.000 (57.4)
Singapore	partly free	partly free	88.4	4.3 (73.3)
Thailand	partly free	not free	81.7	46.000 (65.9)
Timor Leste	free	–	31.1	390 (29.5)
Vietnam	not free	not free	70.4	50.000 (51.4)

Sources: Author's compilation from Freedom House (2020), Freedom House Net Freedom Report, and Internetworldstatics.com.

Growing Internet Censorship and Authoritarian Control

In line with a global deterioration of internet freedom, we can identify a number of worrisome regional trends in the past decade, which limit the liberating and emancipating character of the internet. First, nearly all Southeast Asian countries have introduced online information controls, mostly in the form of new internet regulations or laws. These new laws undermine the liberating potential and confirms Diamond's fears of the internet as a "tool of oppression". Some examples: for instance, in January 2019 Vietnam's new cybersecurity law came into force, censoring any online criticism of the government authorities. Furthermore, online platforms in Vietnam are required to store their user data and surrender it to the authorities—if required (Reporters without Borders 2019). Section 66(d) of Myanmar's 2013 Telecommunication Law also criminalizes online defamation. Used for the first time shortly before the elections in 2015, the law has been used frequently to stifle criticism of the new civilian government (Bünte 2018). In Cambodia, social media networks face surveillance and intervention by the government, reinforced by the adoption of a new government decree in 2018, which allows for interference with online media and government censorship (Human Rights Watch Report 2020). A 2017 amendment to Thailand's Computer Crimes Act empowered the Thai authorities to arrest anyone who might be spreading information that is against the national interest. A new cyber-security law adopted in February 2019 gave the executive even more powers. In December 2019, for example, a journalist was sentenced to two years in prison because she had tweeted about the appalling conditions of migrant workers (Committee to Protect Journalists 2020). Even Indonesia, one of the more open societies in the region, issued an Electronic Information Transaction Law, which has been used by the state to curb online freedom of expression. Sinpeng (2019, p. 11) has highlighted that all cyber laws are written in vague wording and allow for a broad interpretation of the authorities to protect the state's security interests.

TABLE 10.3
Key Internet Controls in Southeast Asia

	Social media or comment platforms blocked	Political, social, religious content blocked	ICT networks deliberately disrupted	Pro-government commentators manipulate online discussions	Blogger or ICT user arrested or imprisoned or in prolonged detention for political or social content	Blogger or ICT user physically attacked or killed
Cambodia		X			X	X
Indonesia	X	X	X		X	X
Malaysia		X		X	X	
Myanmar				X	X	X
Philippines			X	X	X	
Singapore		X			X	
Thailand		X		X	X	X
Vietnam		X		X	X	X

Source: Freedom House (2019).

Second, all countries engage in several forms of content control or content manipulation beyond the legal sphere (see Table 10.3). This form of control is often paired with physical intimidation or other forms of outright repression. All regimes have arrested or imprisoned bloggers due to political reasons. In the more authoritarian regimes of Vietnam, Thailand, Myanmar and Cambodia, bloggers were also physically attacked or even killed. A significant number of regimes have also employed online troopers to manipulate online discussions. Vietnam has a military cyber department of 10,000 troops called "Force 47", this is tasked with defending the party and the government from online dissidents (Reporters without Borders 2019). Interestingly, no authoritarian state has dared to shut down social media platforms directly, fearing a backlash of increased mobilization and criticism.

Third, although practised virtually by nearly all Southeast Asian states, content censorship is not random. Censorship of the online public sphere is strategic. Sinpeng (2019, p. 12) has demonstrated that censorship is most severe when it comes to criticism against the state or ruling elites such as the military, monarchy, judiciary or the police. Follow closely behind are social commentaries and corruption issues. Examples are manifold: in Myanmar, film director Min Htin Ko Ko Gyi has been jailed for a Facebook post critical of the military constitution and the military's role in politics in August 2019. This follows an arrest of a former journalist who received a seven-year jail term in 2018 for defaming state councillor Aung San Suu Kyi (Reuters 2019). Courts in Thailand sentenced a man to a prison term of thirty-five years for a Facebook post which criticized the monarchy. In conclusion, we can see a growing censorship in the authoritarian states, which clearly inhibit the liberating potential of internet and social media.

Liberation Technology? The Interplay of Technology, (Un)-Civil Society and State Repression

Whereas the deepening repression in recent years in Southeast Asia confirms Diamond's fear of the internet as a tool for oppression, the political changes in Malaysia give us hope that the new technologies can serve as tools of liberation as well. Here, the internet and social media had a liberating effect (Tapsell 2013; Abbott 2018). However, the effect of digital media is closely related to the mobilization capacity of certain social groups and the repressive capacity of the state (Liu 2015). In Malaysia, new communication technologies were seen as a main business opportunity and, consequently, the Mahathir administration was committed to a relatively free internet environment from the beginning. The internet provided a vibrant online sphere; it helped to create a news portal that bypassed traditional print media close to the ruling party and nourished a civil society, that organized around the topic of electoral reform (Abbott 2018). Social media also helped to liberalize Malaysia (and bring down the BN government) in another, more indirect way. The mass demonstrations by the Coalition for Free and Fair Elections (BERSIH)—organized five times between 2007 and 2016—helped to unite urban civil society behind the topic of clean government and electoral reform (Liu 2015). It seriously eroded the legitimacy of the BN government and helped to bring the country on the brink of transition.

Yet, the Malaysian case remains an exception in Southeast Asia. Although similar effects as in Malaysia could be witnessed in the "battle royale" on the internet in Thailand (Abbott 2018), the final outcome was different. In Thailand, civil society was highly polarized: with the help of digital media, pro-Thaksin groups ("red-shirts") could circumvent the information monopoly established by traditional elites (i.e. military and monarchy) to air their frustrations with the regime after the 2006 coup against Thaksin. They challenged the core institution of the state (the monarchy) and the dominance of the traditional elites of army, bureaucracy and Bangkok's middle class. These had called up online mobilization before, triggering the coup against Thaksin in 2006. Yet, after 2006 Thailand's traditional elites stroke back and increased cyber repression, establishing one of the most repressive cyber regimes in the world (Sinpeng 2013). Repressive laws such as the Computer Crimes Act or the *lèse majesté* law helped traditional elites to regain control and re-establish hegemony. Online vigilante groups and cyber mobs were used to monitor and report online *lèse majesté* cases to the police. Additionally, the Thai state attempted to indoctrinate the younger generation through an ideological training programme at schools and universities. These online courses reinforce official rhetoric and Thai political culture, which tend to downplay grassroots movements' genuine efforts for democratization (Sombatpoonsiri 2018).

Disinformation, Hate Speech, Online Polarization and Democratic Backsliding

While democratic breakdown in Thailand resulted in the military consolidating its grip on power, the democracies in Indonesia and the Philippines saw serious episodes of democratic backsliding (but avoiding breakdown so far) (Croissant 2019). Digital media played their role here as well. We see that when new technologies are used in an illiberal context, political regimes are not becoming more progressive. Instead, we find the opposite effects of disinformation and polarization, often paired with physical intimidation, hate speech and intolerance. In Indonesia and the Philippines, fierce electoral competition poisoned the digital sphere and the social climate. In Indonesia, social polarization goes back to the 2014 elections and deepened with the 2017 gubernatorial elections (Tapsell 2019). The rise of fake news, black campaigning and paid trolls created a highly aggressive climate, in which sectarianism and racism flourished. Religion was highly politicized, with Islamic groups being at the forefront of the online battles. The discourse, described by Lim (2017) as "freedom to hate", undermined mutual trust and social cohesion in the country. Feeling that democracy is in danger, President Jokowi gradually concentrated power in the executive and punished his critics by using existing defamation and electronic information laws (Mietzner 2019, p. 10). In the Philippines, trolls were found to spread harassment and propaganda in support of presidential candidate Duterte, both before and after the 2016 elections. Duterte's supporters actively engaged in social media campaigns that glorified him; paid "keyboard warriors" also circulated distorted news and used cyberbullying and physical assaults against Duterte's critics (Sombatpoonsiri 2018). Disillusioned with the democratic order, which had not produced any tangible benefits for the poor population and benefitted the landed elites instead, many of Duterte's sixteen million voters believed this news to be true because it confirmed pre-existing worldviews and beliefs.

A similar effect could be witnessed in liberalizing Myanmar, where the military established an online dissemination network of media companies with more than 4.4 million followers to disseminate pro-military information, which cast the NLD government as well as Muslims in the country in an extremely negative light—constructing Muslims as "fearsome others" (Schissler, Walton and Thi 2017). Asserting that Muslim Rohingya pose an existential threat to the Burmese race and religion, an imminent danger to the community in Rakhine state, and a personal threat to women and children, ultranationalists and conservative Buddhist monks spread hatred and fears online (Bünte 2018; Schissler, Walton and Thi 2017). Hate speech was used to incite violence and prepared the ground for the ethnic cleansing of the Rohingya in 2017. The UN Independent International Fact-Finding Mission on Myanmar found Facebook to be a key player in creating an environment where extremists discourse can thrive, human rights violations are legitimized and incitement to discrimination and violence facilitated. Although local civil society organizations are now cooperating to counter disinformation campaigns and provide local expertise to Facebook, Myanmar's 2020 elections pose a great danger that disinformation campaigns might incite violence. All these examples show that disinformation campaigns, hate speech and online mobilization play a huge role in undermining free speech, democratic aspirations and social cohesion in Southeast Asia.

CONCLUSION

The chapter has highlighted social media's impact on both young democracies and authoritarian regimes in Southeast Asia. So far, Southeast Asia has shown remarkable resilience against any wave of democratization, and authoritarianism remains deeply entrenched. The democracies established in the course of the global third wave—here particularly the Philippines, Indonesia, Thailand and Timor Leste—remain weakly institutionalized and prone to democratic backsliding. In the case of Thailand, we could even see "promissory coups" and democracy breaking down in 2006 and 2014. The reasons for the weakness of democracy and resilience of authoritarian regimes in Southeast Asia are manifold: weak institutions, undemocratic civil societies and middle classes, deepening social polarization and an external environment that supports undemocratic rule.

I have shown that the introduction of digital technologies has not disrupted the architecture of authoritarianism in Southeast Asia. Authoritarian regimes have shown the ability to adapt and regime elites have used new technologies to bolster regime legitimacy, co-opt the opposition or silence their critics. I have identified the following three mechanisms at work: first, authoritarian regimes increasingly use repression and intimidation. With the help of cyber trolls and cyber armies, authoritarian regime elites are patrolling the digital sphere in order to repress evolving dissent and intimidate critics. All authoritarian regimes have introduced some forms of online controls in the forms of laws and regulations. Second, authoritarian regimes block certain sites strategically to limit the diffusion of certain ideas such as democracy, republicanism (Thailand), communism (Indonesia), gender equality and LGBT issues (Indonesia and Malaysia). Third, authoritarian regimes now increasingly use the online sphere to bolster regime stability and legitimacy. Most of the authoritarian regimes have built up cyber armies tasked to defend the ruling party against online dissidents (Vietnam) or to indoctrinate the younger generation to follow social rules (Thailand).

Social media has shown its liberating effects in Malaysia in the last decade, when it helped an urban civil society to mobilize for electoral reform and a clean government and when it created an online sphere, which helped to undermine traditional media close to the ruling party. Social media helped to undermine the legitimacy of the government and bring Malaysia on the cusp of transition. In the democracies of the Philippines and Indonesia, however, it had the opposite effects and created and deepened polarization and sectarianism. Both online and offline mobilization of diverse groups helped to destabilize illiberal democracies in Indonesia (and in Thailand 2006–14), triggering executives to concentrate political power in their hands, hollowing out democratic institutions even more. As a result, new technologies in Southeast Asia have been used by authoritarians to bolster their regimes and have helped to erode young democracies.

REFERENCES

Abbott, Jason. 2018. "Politics of the Internet and Social Media in Asia: Mobilization, Participation and Retrenchment". In *Routledge Handbook of Politics in Asia*, edited by Shiping Hua, pp. 390–414. London: Routledge.

Aspinall, Edward and Marcus Mietzner. 2019. "Indonesia's Democratic Paradox: Competitive Elections amidst Rising Illiberalism". *Bulletin of Indonesian Economic Studies* 55, no. 3: 295–317.

Bader, Julia. 2015. *China's Foreign Relations and the Survival of Autocracies*. London: Routledge.

Bermeo, Nancy. 2016. "On Democratic Backsliding". *Journal of Democracy* 27, no. 1: 5–19.

Bünte, Marco. 2018. "Policing Politics: Myanmar's Military Regime and Protest Spaces in Times of Transition". In *Political Spaces in Asia: Defining and Deploying Political Space*, edited by Meredith Weiss and Eva Hannson, pp. 188–206. London: Routledge.

———. 2020. "Religious Mobilisation, Ethnic Conflict and the Problem of Trust: Social Cohesion in Democratising Myanmar". In *Social Cohesion in Asia*, edited by Aurel Croissant and Peter Walkenhorst, pp. 169–90. London: Routledge.

Bünte, Marco, Patrick Köllner and Richard Roewer. 2019. "Taking Stock of Myanmar's Political Transformation since 2011". *Journal of Current Southeast Asian Affairs* 38, no. 3: 1–14.

Chu, Yun-han, Larry Diamond and Andrew J. Nathan. 2008. "Conclusion: Values, Regime Performance and Democratic Consolidation". In *How East Asians View Democracy*, edited by Yun-han Chu, Larry Diamond, Andrew J. Nathan, and Doh Chull Shin, pp. 238–59. New York: Columbia University Press.

Committee to Protect Journalists. 2020. "Thai Court Sentences Journalist Suchanee Cloitre to Two Years in Jail for Defamation". Press Release, 3 January 2020. https://cpj.org/2020/01/thai-court-sentences-journalist-suchanee-cloitre-t/ (accessed 10 May 2020).

Croissant, Aurel. 2019. "Beating Backsliding: Episodes and Outcomes of Democratic Backsliding in Asia Pacific in the period 1950–2018". Paper presented for the workshop *Democratic Backsliding in Asia: Resilience, Responses, Revival*, Heidelberg University, 8–9 December 2019.

Croissant, Aurel and Marco Bünte. 2011. *The Crisis of Democratic Governance in Southeast Asia*. Basingstoke: Palgrave.

Croissant, Aurel and Peter Walkenhorst. 2019. *Social Cohesion in Asia: Historical Origins, Contemporary Shapes and Future Dynamics*. London: Routledge.

Curato, Nicole. 2017. "Flirting with Authoritarian Fantasies? Rodrigo Duterte and the New Terms of Philippine Populism". *Journal of Contemporary Asia* 47, no. 1: 142–53.

Diamond, Larry. 2019. "The Rise of Postmodern Totalitarianism". *Journal of Democracy* 30, no. 1: 20–24.

———. 2010. "Liberation Technology". *Journal of Democracy* 21, no. 3: 69–83.

Dressel, Björn and Cristina Regina Bonoan. 2019. "Duterte vs. the Rule of Law". *Journal of Democracy* 30, no. 4: 134–48.

Freedom House. 2019. "Freedom of the World 2019: Democracy in Retreat". Washington. https://freedomhouse.org/report/freedom-world/2019/democracy-retreat (accessed 5 May 2020).

Gladwell, Malcolm. 2010. "Small Change". *The New Yorker*, 4 October 2010. https://www.newyorker.com/magazine/2010/10/04/small-change-malcolm-gladwell (accessed 15 May 2020).

Haerpfer, Christian, Patrick Bernhagen, Christian Welzel and Ronald F. Inglehart. 2019. *Democratization*. Oxford: Oxford University Press.

Human Rights Watch Report. 2020. "Cambodia: Events of 2019". https://www.hrw.org/world-report/2020/country-chapters/cambodia (accessed 18 May 2020).

Huntington, Samuel. 1993. *The Third Wave: Democratization in the Late 20th Century*. Norman: University of Oklahoma Press.

Jakarta Post. 2019. "'Dilemma of Democracy': Tito says Nondemocratic Countries Have Better Economic Growth", 27 November 2019. https://www.thejakartapost.com/news/2019/11/27/dilemma-of-democracy-tito-says-nondemocratic-countries-have-better-economic-growth.html (accessed 10 May 2020).

Kuhonta, Erik and Aim Sinpeng. 2014. "Democratic Regression in Thailand: The Ambivalent Role of Civil Society and Political Institutions". *Contemporary Southeast Asia* 36, no. 3: 333–55.

Lim, Merlyna. 2017. "Freedom to Hate: Social Media, Algorithmic Enclaves, and the Rise of Tribal Nationalism in Indonesia". *Critical Asian Studies* 49, no. 3: 411–27.

Liu, Yangyue. 2015. "Transgressiveness, Civil Society and Internet Control in Southeast Asia". *The Pacific Review* 27, no. 3: 383–407.

Lührmann, Anna and Stefan Lindberg. 2019. "A Third Wave of Autocratisation is Here: What is New about it?" *Democratization* 26, no. 7: 1095–13.

Magaloni, Beatriz, Jonathan Chu and Eric Min. 2013. "Autocracies of the World, 1950–2012 (Version 1.0)". Dataset, Stanford University. https://cddrl.fsi.stanford.edu/research/autocracies_of_the_world_dataset (accessed 10 May 2020).

Mietzner, Marcus. 2019. "Authoritarian Innovations in Indonesia: Electoral Narrowing, Identity Politics and Executive Illiberalism". *Democratization* 27, no. 6: 1021–36. https://doi.org/10.1080/13510347.2019.1704266.

Morgenbesser, Lee. 2019. "Cambodia's Transition to Hegemonic Authoritarianism". *Journal of Democracy* 30, no. 1: 158–71.

Morozov, Evgeny. 2011. *The Net Delusion: The Dark Side of Internet Freedom*. New York: Public Affairs.

Nathan, Andrew. 2020. "The Puzzle of Authoritarian Legitimacy". *Journal of Democracy* 31, no. 1: 158–68.

Ortmann, Stefan. 2011. "Singapore: Authoritarian But Newly Competitive". *Journal of Democracy* 22, no. 4: 153–64.

Rappler. 2019. "Least Trusted? Malacanang says China can be PH role model", 21 November 2019. https://www.rappler.com/nation/245449-panelo-downplays-trust-china-philippines-role-model (accessed 10 May 2020).

Reporters without Borders. 2019. Country Report Vietnam, Online. https://rsf.org/en/vietnam (accessed 24 May 2020).

Reuters. 2019. "Myanmar Jails Film Director for Facebook Post Critical of the Military", 29 August 2019. https://www.reuters.com/article/us-myanmar-filmmaker/myanmar-jails-filmmaker-for-facebook-posts-critical-of-military-idUSKCN1VJ0Q5 (accessed 15 May 2020).

Ricks, Jacob. 2019. "Thailand's 2019 General Election". *Pacific Affairs* 92, no. 3: 443–57.

Schissler, Matt, Matthew Walton and Phyu Phyu Thi. 2017. "Reconciling Contradictions: Buddhist-Muslim Violence, Narrative Making and Memory in Myanmar". *Journal of Contemporary Asia* 47, no. 3: 376–95.

Schüller, Margot, Marcus Brod, Daniel Neff and Marco Bünte. 2010. "China's Emergence within Southeast Asia's Aid Architecture: New Kid on the Block?" Paper prepared for the AidData Conference, University College, Oxford. https://www.researchgate.net/publication/326222551_China%27s_Emergence_within_Southeast_Asia%27s_Aid_Architecture_New_Kid_on_the_Block.

Shin, Doh Chull and Rollin F. Tusalem. 2019. "East Asia". In *Democratization*, edited by Christian Haerpfer, Patrick Bernhagen, Christian Welzel and Ronald F. Inglehart, pp. 401–21. Oxford: Oxford University Press.

Shirky, Clay. 2008. *Here Comes Everybody: The Power of Organizing without Organization*. New York, NY: Penguin Books.

Sinpeng, Aim. 2013. "State Repression in Cyberspace: The Case of Thailand". *Asian Politics & Policy* 5, no. 3: 421–40.

———. 2019. "Digital Media, Political Authoritarianism and Internet Controls in Southeast Asia". *Media, Culture & Society* 42, no. 1: 25–39. https://doi.org/10.1177%2F0163443719884052.

Slater, Dan. 2012. "Strong-State Democratization in Malaysia and Singapore". *Journal of Democracy* 23, no. 2: 19–33.

Sombatpoonsiri, Jiri. 2018. "Manipulating Civic Space: Cyber Trolling in the Philippines and Thailand". *GIGA-Focus Asia* 3 (June).

Tapsell, Ross. 2013. "Negotiating Media 'Balance' in Malaysia's 2013 General Election". *Journal of Current Southeast Asian Affairs* 32, no. 2: 39–60.

———. 2019. "The Polarization Paradox in Indonesia's 2019 Elections". *New Mandala*, 22 March 2019. https://www.newmandala.org/the-polarisation-paradox-in-indonesias-2019-elections/ (accessed 20 May 2020).

Thompson, Mark. 2016. "Bloodied Democracy: Duterte and the Death of Liberal Reformism in the Philippines". *Journal of Current Southeast Asian Affairs* 35, no. 3: 39–68.

Ufen, Andreas. 2020. "Opposition in Transition: Pre-electoral Coalitions and the 2018 Electoral Breakthrough in Malaysia". *Democratization* 27, no. 2: 167–84.

V-Dem. 2020. *Autocratisation Surges – Resistance Grows*. Democracy Report 2020. University of Gothenburg. https://www.v-dem.net/media/filer_public/f0/5d/f05d46d8-626f-4b20-8e4e-53d4b134bfcb/democracy_report_2020_low.pdf (accessed 10 May 2020).

Warburton, Eve and Edward Aspinall. 2016. "Explaining Indonesia's Democratic Regression". *Contemporary Southeast Asia* 41, no. 2: 255–88.

INDEX

Note: Page numbers followed by "n" refer to endnote.

A
Abdullah Ahmad Badawi, 65, 72, 77
Abdul Rasyid, 50
activism
　blogosphere and, 147–49
　social media and, 168–75
"ADHOC 5", 138
Ahok, 12, 49, 53
Alex Au, 170, 175
Aljunied-Hougang Punggol East
　　Town Council (AHPETC), 177
Andrew Loh, 171
Anh Ba Sam, 148
"anti-Barisan Nasional", 64, 67
anti-coup activists, 109
anti-establishment forces, 116
anti-establishment sentiment, 109
Anti-Fake News Act, Malaysia, 74
Anti-Fake News Centre, Thailand,
　　105, 111
anti-Formosa movement, Vietnam,
　　154–55
Anti-Muslim, 97
　hate speech and fake news, 100
anti-Najib sentiment, 68
anti-Single Gateway proposal,
　　Thailand, 119

anti-Thaksin networks, 108
Anwar Ibrahim, 65, 67, 71, 74
Arab Spring, 66, 152, 194, 200
Architects of Networked Disinformation
　　(2018), 29
Asalkan Bukan UMNO (Anyone But
　　UMNO), 66
Aung San Suu Kyi, 88, 93, 98, 204
authoritarian control, 202–4
authoritarian regimes, 200, 207–8
authoritarian resilience
　causes of, 198–200
　in Southeast Asia, 192–93, 200–207
　democratic regression and
　　　authoritarian resilience, causes
　　　of, 198–200
　global trends, 193–97
autocratic regression, in Myanmar,
　　199
autocratization, 119, 192

B
Balik Undi (return home to vote), 67
Bangkok.com, 108
Bank Rakyat Indonesia (BRI), 52
Bannok.com, 108

Barisan Nasional (BN)
  Bersih, 66
  coalition, 80n1, 197
  cybertroopers, 77
  disinformation campaign, 78
  election, 67, 76
  electoral system, 65
  engagement in disinformation practices, 80
  fall of, 77
  GE14, 64
  GE12 in 2008, results, 71
  government, 63
  internet, 69
  national election campaign, 63–64, 67
  online disinformation strategy, 76
  responds, 69–74
  rule, 64
  ruling coalition, 12
  social media campaigning, 75
  trust deficit in, 79
Baswedan, Anies, 53
Bauxite Vietnam blog, 151
"The Beginning of Online Social Movements in Vietnam" (2017), 154
Benjamin Lee (Mr Miyagi), 170
Bersih, 66–68, 79, 80n3
  "Clean Elections" movement, 2
  rallies, 68, 71, 76
"biased" liberal media, 27
"black campaign", 10, 48
"Black Monday" campaign, 130
Blackout 505, 67
"blogfather" of Singapore, 169
bloggers, 171, 178, 201
blogging communities, 160
blogosphere, and activism, 147–49
blogs, 172
  decline of, 175–79

Bongbong Marcos, 33
Breakfast Network, 176, 178
Broadcasting Act 2013, Singapore, 13–14, 175
Buddhist extremist pages, removal from Facebook, 87
Buddhist nationalist sentiment, 93
Budi Purnomo Karjodiharjo, 52
Burma Media Association, 94
BurmaNet, 92
"Burmese Media Spring", 93
"buzzer *istana*" (the Palace's buzzers), 54
"buzzers" in Indonesia, 9, 50

C
Cambodia, 126–28
  cyberspace, 127
  "digital democracy" in, 127
  digital transformations in, 128
  emergence of digital platforms, 128–31
  political system, 197
  social media
    and decline of political opposition, 137–40
    networks, 202–3
    and political activism, 131–37
Cambodia Development Resource Institute, 134
Cambodia National Rescue Party (CNRP), 127, 131–32, 138
Cambodian People's Party (CPP)
  cyberspace, 140
  Hun Sen, 13, 127–28, 131, 197
  re-election incentives, 136
  ruling party, 126
  slogan of "change", 131
  SMS messaging, use of, 130
  social media, 132
The Cambodia Daily, 130

Cambridge Analytica, 28
celebrity endorsements, 25
censorship
   methods, 146
   of online public sphere, 204
Central Youth Union, 153
Centre of Digital Security, 112
Chatter Party, 127
China, 145–46
   aggressive foreign policy, 199
   authoritarianism in mainland Southeast Asia, 199
   ban Facebook, 155
   government's policy on, 151
Chinese-based platforms, 181
Chinese model, 199
civil society, 120n7
   cyberspaces by, 118–19
   groups, 89, 139
   nascent cyber activism, 108
   organizations, 15
   sector, 94
   Thailand, 205
clicktivism, 200
closed messenger groups, 78
Coalition for Free and Fair Elections (BERSIH), 205
coarse political discourse, amplification of, 26–28
"Coins for Prita", 45
Colours Rainbow Yangon, 2
communal violence in Myanmar, 87, 98
Communications and Multimedia Act 1998, Malaysia, 73
Communications Authority of Thailand (CAT), 107
Computer Crime Act (CCA), Thailand, 109, 114, 118, 205
Computer-Related Crimes Act, Thailand, 109, 120n3

Constitutional Court, Thailand, 105–6, 120n1
contemporary Thai politics, military in, 111
"context collapse" phenomenon, 178–79
Covid-19 pandemic, 183–84
"cures" of patient zero, 20
"cyber activists", 70
Cyber Centre, Thailand, 112
cyber defiance, 106
cyber mobs, 205
cyber repression, 205
Cyber Scouts, 115, 116
Cybersecurity Bill, Thailand, 112, 115
Cyber-Security Law, Vietnam, 145, 203
cyberspace, 111, 127
cyber terrorism, 115
cyber-*tokhang*, 30–32
cybertroopers, 70–72
   Barisan Nasional, 12, 74, 75, 77
   conversation spaces, 78
   disinformation practices, 72
   election, 79
   emergence of, 64
   in Malaysia, 9
   Najib, 76
cyber unit, 116
cyber warfare, 111

D

"Daddy Duterte" (*Tatay Digong*), 32
Declaration on a Framework to Minimise the Harmful Effects of Fake News (2018), 4
Decree 97 on the Management, Supply, and Use of Internet Services and Electronic Information on the Internet (2008), 150

democracy
  activists, 151
  autocratic rule and, 107
  Corazon Aquino, 32
  death of, 20
  in electoral authoritarian regimes, 193
  and human freedom, 192
  human rights and good governance, 26
  in Indonesia, 196
  Jokowi, 206
  lower support of, 198
  new digital totalitarianism, 200
  and political discourse, 13
  "promissory coups", 207
  prospects of, 194
  reforms for, 16
  social media, 79
  in Southeast Asia, 2, 196
  struggle for, 91
  supportive of, 44
  sustainability of, 199
  threats to, 12
  tools in, 56
  veil of, 75
democratic breakdown, in Thailand, 206
democratic regression, causes of, 198–200
Democratic Socialist Republic of Vietnam, 152
Democrat Party-led government, 109
Dengvaxia scandal, 35
Department of Health's immunization programme, Philippines, 34
de-securitizing disinformation, 118
digital activism, phase of, 91
digital authoritarianism, 127

"digital democracy" in Cambodia, 127
digital disinformation, 20
Digital Economy and Society (DE), Thailand, 111
digital era, 6
digital media, 192, 205
  grassroots activism on, 15
digital platforms, emergence of, 128–31
digital politics, turning point for, 109–10
digital public sphere in Philippines, 19–20, 35
  disinformation, 21–26
    beyond elections, 30–35
    2016 Philippine elections, 26–30
digital technologies, 22
  for political campaigns, 25
digital transformations in Cambodia, 128
digital workers, 23
disinformation
  beyond elections, 30–35
  grassroots activism to, 1–6
    diverse social media landscape, 6–9
    elections, 12–13
    laws and crackdowns, 13–16
    rise of, 9–11
  in Indonesia, 43–44
    industry and political buzzers, 47–51
    production grows, 52–55
    social media, 44–47
  industry, professionalization of, 28–30
  in Malaysia, 63–64
    Barisan Nasional, 69–74
    historic change of government, 75–78

Index   217

opposition campaigning and
    election battles, 67–69
social media activism and
    opposition politics, 64–67
in Philippines, 21–26
2016 elections, 26–30
rise of, 3, 9–11
securitization approach to, 106
"distorted information", 116
distrust, in Southeast Asian societies, 193
diverse social media landscape, 6–9
"divided disinformation", 106
"divisive" political discourse, 43
draconian laws, Malaysia, 72–74
Dung, Nguyen Tan, 152–53, 155
Duterte, R., 198, 199
    Asia's oldest democracies, 19
    campaign in Ilocos, 33
    Death Squads, 28
    drug war, 27
    election victory of, 13
    electoral outcomes, 25
    media agencies, 28
    in Philippines, 30, 196
    provincial warlords, 26
    on social media, 20
    supporters of, 31, 206

E
ecosystem of state agencies, Thailand, 112
election, 12–13
    battles, 67–69
    campaigns, 9
    disinformation, 30–35, 52–55
    2006 General Election (GE06), 169–71
    2011 General Election (GE11), 171–74
    2012 General Election (GE12), 71

2012 Jakarta gubernatorial election, 43–44, 46, 49–50
2013 General Election (GE13), 63–64, 67, 69, 71–73, 80n5
2014 General Election (GE14), 64, 68, 72, 74, 78
2015 General Election (GE15), 176–78, 184
Philippine elections, 26–30
political economy of, 47
of Rodrigo Duterte, 13
Singapore government, 13
"turning point", 12
election disinformation grows, 52–54
Elections Advertising Regulations, Singapore, 170, 172
electoral authoritarian regime, 193, 196
    Malaysia, 197
electoral authoritarian rule, 194
Electoral Commission, Malaysia, 68
electoral contestation, 45
electoral democracies, 15
electoral reform, 67
Electronic Information Transaction Law, Indonesia, 203
enhanced censorship, 193
environmental activism online, 160
exiled activist groups, 90
"explicitly political" content, ban on, 170, 172

F
Facebook, 86–89, 115–18, 133–40, 148–55
    Cambodia's largest LGBT organizations, 129
    citizens and activists, political parties, 173
    co-opting Facebook, 155–59
    disinformation campaigns, 146

dominant social media platform, 128
Filipino internet users, 21
"free basics" in Philippines, 7
and Google, 10
groups, 23
LGBT communities, 2
live streaming, 69
Ma Ba Tha, 96
Myanmar human rights groups to, 99
"patient zero", 19
silent protest on, 68
Southeast Asian countries, 8
Thinking Pinoy, 35
and Twitter, 32, 45, 172, 174, 177, 179, 180
West Papua, 55
WhatsApp and, 12, 74
and YouTube, 97, 114
Facebook Free Basics in 2015, 88
"Facebook genocide", 86
"Facebook Live" broadcasts, 25
Facebook Messenger, 8
fact-checking websites, 180
Fahmi Redza, 68
fake news, 27–28, 87, 112
  disinformation and, 21
  on Facebook, 19
  Myanmar's political transition, 86–100
  political trolling and production of, 29
  readers of, 36
  rise of, 93–97, 206
  social media and, 9, 20
  Thailand, policy responses to disinformation in, 105–20
  victims of, 139
Federal Constitution for Malaysians, 67

Filipinos, 21–24
  communities, 28
  migrant labour, 22
  online, 21
Force 47, 156, 157, 158, 159, 204
Freedom House, 9, 194
Free My Internet movement, 176
#FREETHE5KH (Free the Khmer Five) campaign, 130

G

1969 General Election, 80n2
2006 General Election (GE06), 169–71
2011 General Election (GE11), 171–74
2012 General Election (GE12), 71
2013 General Election (GE13), 63–64, 67, 69, 71–73, 80n5
2014 General Election (GE14), 64, 68, 72, 74, 78
2015 General Election (GE15), 176–78, 184
Giap, Vo Nguyen, 150
Global Day of Action for Burma, 92
Global Inventory of Organised Social Media Manipulation, 4
Google
  Facebook and, 10, 146, 157, 158, 168
  and Yahoo, 147
government officials', social media activism and, 135
Gramsci's concept of hegemony, 56
grassroots activism
  on digital media, 15
  to disinformation, 1–6
    diverse social media landscape, 6–9
    elections, 12–13
    laws and crackdowns, 13–16
    rise of, 9–11
2017 gubernatorial elections, in Indonesia, 206

Index

H
Haque, Zulkiflee Anwar (Zunar), 73–74, 78
Hari Merdeka (Independence Day), Malaysia, 68
hate speech, 87
  rise of, 93–97
health disinformation, 34–35
Hindu Rights Action Force (HINDRAF), 66
"hoax news", 9, 11
Human Rights Film Institute in Myanmar, 97
Hun Sen, 13, 127, 128, 132, 133, 135, 138, 197

I
"I am the Five" photo campaign, 130
Indonesia
  "buzzers" in, 9, 50
  civil society and pro-democracy activists, 2
  democracy in, 44, 195, 198
  disinformation, rise of, 43–44
    industry and political buzzers, 47–51
    production grows, 52–55
    social media, 44–47
  online population, 7
  political buzzers in, 50
  2014 presidential election, Indonesia, 53
  2019 presidential election, Indonesia, 44
  research in, 43
  scholarship in, 8
Indonesian Anti-Corruption Commission (KPK), 45, 54
Indonesian digital sphere, 12
Indonesian political landscape, 51

information and communication technologies (ICT), 127
Information Operation (IO), 115
information security, 114
Instagram, 201
Internal Security Operations Command (ISOC), 111, 112, 115, 116
International Fact Checking Network (IFCN), 180, 185
internet
  arrival and early digital activism, 89–93
  censorship, 202–4
  development of, 107–10
  in Indonesia, 44
  social media and, 127
  in Southeast Asia, 202
  in Thailand, 205
Internet Relay Chat (mIRC), 169
internet service providers (ISPs), 92

J
Jakarta gubernatorial election, 43, 44, 46
Jokowi, 2, 12, 43, 46, 49, 52, 54, 206
Jokowi Ahok Social Media Volunteers (JASMEV), 49, 50

K
Kem Sokha, 132, 137, 138
Khe, Nguyen Cong, 149
Ko Htike, 92
ko-htike.blogspot.com, 92
"Kon Khmer" (Facebook page), 138

L
Lee Kin Mum (mrbrown), 170
Leong Sze Hian, 175
lèse majesté (monarchy offences), 114–15, 120n2, 205

Liberal Party, 30
LINE, 8
Little India case, Singapore, 182

M
Ma Ba Tha, 95–100
Mahathir Mohamad, 65, 68, 72, 73, 77, 197, 205
mainstream media, 176, 177
Malaysia, 2
  "cybertroopers" in, 9
  disinformation in, 63–64
    Barisan Nasional, 69–74
    historic change of government, 75–78
    opposition campaigning and election battles, 67–69
    social media activism and opposition politics, 64–67
  electoral authoritarian regime, 197
  Multimedia Super Corridor, 65
  new communication technologies, 205
  resilient electoral-authoritarian rule in, 198
  scholarship in, 8
Malaysiakini, 65, 72, 76
The Malaysian Insider, 73
Marcos Cyber Warriors, 32
Martial Law, 33
"memefication" of satirical works, 78
The Middle Ground, 178
"Midnightuniv.org", 108
military, in contemporary Thai politics, 111
Min Htin Ko Ko Gyi, 204
Ministry of Information and Communication Technology (MICT), Thailand, 109
Multimedia Bill of Guarantees, Malaysia, 65
multi-user dungeons (MUDs), 169
Mulyasari, Prita, 45
"Muslim Cyber Army", 53
Muslim minorities, 98
Myanmar
  autocratic regression in, 199
  civil society, 99
  digital activism, 90
  email service in, 89
  internet penetration in, 90
  media and telecommunications sectors, 88
  military, 93
  social media in, 14, 86, 87, 98
  state-society relations online, 93
Myanmar-based dissidents, 91
Myanmar.com, 92
Myanmar Muslim community, 95
MyConsti campaign in 2009, 66

N
Najib Razak, 64, 68–70, 72–79, 197
National Broadcasting and Telecommunications Commission (NBTC), 111
National Council for Peace Order, Announcement 12/2014, 120n4
National Council for Peace Order, Announcement 17/2014, 120n4
National Cyber Security Committee (NCSC), 112
National Electronics and Computer Technology Centre (NECTEC), 107
National League for Democracy (NLD), 88–89, 94, 98–99, 196, 206
National Science and Technology Development Agency (NSTDA), 107
National Security Council (NSC), 110

Index

NATO's StratCom Centre of Excellence, 10
"negative campaigning", 9
Network Enforcement Act, Germany, 14, 180, 183
new communication technologies, Malaysia, 205
new digital totalitarianism, 200
"new" media in Malaysia, 65
Nguyen Van Hai, 149
Nguyen Viet Chien, 149
969 Buy-Buddhist campaign, 95–96
969/Ma Ba Tha monks, 96
988 FM, Malaysian Chinese Association (MCA)-owned Chinese-language station, 68
non-governmental organizations (NGOs), 94, 117
Nugraha, Pepih, 54

O

Occupy Movement, 66
1Malaysia Development Berhad (1MDB), 68
  corruption scandal, 75, 78
online blogging, 149
The Online Citizen, 170, 172
online disinformation services, 5, 28
Online Freelance Workers (OFW 2.0), 24
online public sphere, censorship of, 204
online repression, 193
online vigilante groups, 205
opposition politics, social media activism and, 64–67
opposition sympathizers, 138
overseas Filipino workers (OFWs) Facebook groups, 23, 28

P

Pakatan Harapan (PH), 69, 79, 197
Pakatan Rakyat, 67
Partai Demokrasi Indonesia Perjuangan (PDIP), 49
"patient zero", 19–20
  for disinformation, 13
  beyond elections, 30–35
  in Philippines, 21–30
People Power Revolution, 195
People's Action Party (PAP)
  mobilization by, 177
  in Singapore, 197
  Tin Pei Ling, 173
Philippines
  democracy in, 198
  development programme, 199
  digital public sphere in, 35
  disinformation in 2016 elections, 26–30
  economy, 33
  "free" internet environment, 201
  "trolls" in, 9
Philippines' Commission on Human Rights, 19–20
The Phnom Penh Post, 138
polarization, 119
  in Southeast Asian societies, 193
policies
  control, legal repression and manipulation, 113–18
  implementing bodies, 111–12
political activism, social media and, 131–37
political buzzers in Indonesia, 50
political campaigns, 43–44, 47–48
  digital technologies for, 25
  industry and political buzzers, 47–51
  production grows, 52–55
  social media, 44–47

political culture, 24–26
political disinformation, 10
political economy, 22–24
political engagement in Singapore, 167–68
  social media
    and activism, 168–75
      emerging disinformation, 179–84
      regulation and decline of blogs, 175–79
political polarization, 87, 196
post-authoritarian democracy, 56
post-authoritarian technological transformations, 46
post-2011 General Election, 176
Prabowo's campaign, 53
"Prachatai.com", 108, 114
pro-BN cybertroopers, 76
pro-BN social bots, 76
professionalization of disinformation industry, 28–30
proliferation of digital disinformation, 20
pro-regime traditional media, 117
Protection from Online Falsehoods and Manipulation Act (POFMA), 14, 183–84
pro-UMNO political bloggers, 77
Public Attorney's Office (PAO), Philippines, 35

R
Raden Nuh, 50
Radio Free Asia, 130
Rainsy, Sam, 132, 133, 139
Rakhine Buddhist mob, 94
rallies organized via social media, growth of, 174–75
Reformasi Diary (Zain), 65
Reformasi movement, 45, 66
Remy Choo Zheng Xi, 171

Reporters Without Borders, 94
repressive laws, 205
Reserve officer training corps (ROTC), 120n6
resilient electoral-authoritarian rule, 198
Ressa, Maria, 20
Reza, Fahmi, 78
Robles, Raissa, 31
Rohingya minorities, 86, 87, 98
Rohingya Muslims, 94, 97, 100, 207
Rohingyas online, 88
Rojanapruk, Praiwit, 115
Roy Ngerng, 175
Russian fake news campaigns, 9

S
Saffron Revolution, 87, 91–94
Sammyboy.com, 170
The Sarawak Report, 73
Save Malaysia movement, 68
Section 66(d) of Myanmar's 2013 Telecommunication Law, 202
securitizing disinformation, regulation and policies, 110–18
Security Offenses (Special Measures) Act 2012 (SOSMA), 73
Sedition Act, 73, 74
"Sei Ha" (Facebook page), 137
The Select Committee on Deliberate Online Falsehoods, 182
"Silent No More" (Facebook page), 31
Silicon Valley, 11
SIM cards, 89
Singapore
  government, 13
  People's Action Party (PAP) in, 197
  political engagement in social media, 167–68
    and activism, 168–75

emerging disinformation, 179–84
regulation and decline of blogs, 175–79
resilient electoral-authoritarian rule in, 198
Singapore Democratic Party (SDP), 169
Single Gateway, 119
SingNet, 168
SingTel, 168
Siregar, Denny, 54
slacktivism, 200
social media, 192–93
   anti-Barisan Nasional sentiment on, 64
   capital, 21
   "chilling effect" on, 72, 114
   democratic regression and authoritarian resilience, causes of, 198–200
   election, 171–74
   global trends, 193–97
   in Indonesia, 44–47
   and internet, 107–10, 127
   Myanmar's political transition, 86–100
   platforms, 43
   and political activism, 131–37
   political opposition, decline of, 137–40
   role of, 192–208
   Singapore, political engagement in, 167–85
   in Southeast Asia, 1–6, 202
      disinformation, rise of, 9–11
      diverse social media landscape, 6–9
      elections, 12–13
      laws and crackdowns, 13–16
   Vietnam, state information controls in, 145–60
   volunteers, 46
social media activism, 45, 168–75
   and discourse, 169–71
   and government officials', 135
   and opposition politics, 64–67
social networking sites, 108
socio-political blogs, 172
   decline of, 178–79
socio-political landscape, Singapore, 167
Sombat Boongnam-anong, 108
Southeast Asia
   authoritarian resilience in, 192–93, 200–207
      democratic regression and authoritarian resilience, causes of, 198–200
      global trends, 193–97
   internet and social media usage in, 202
   internet penetration in, 129
   key internet controls in, 203
   social media trends in, 1–6
      disinformation, rise of, 9–11
      diverse social media landscape, 6–9
      elections, 12–13
      laws and crackdowns, 13–16
Speakers' Corner, Singapore, 174, 176
Suharto's New Order government, 49

T
Telegram, 78, 183
Telephone Organisation of Thailand (TOT), 107
Temasek Review Emeritus, 172, 173
Thailand, 2, 87, 106
   case of, 118
   civil society, 205
   Computer Crimes Act, 203
   coups in, 199

cyberspace, 106
democratic breakdown in, 206
digital economy, 114
digital openness to surveillance, 109
digital repression in, 113
digital space, 107
elections in, 196
information technology, 106
internet in, 205
LINE, 8
polarization, 106
politics of, 106, 119
securitizing disinformation, 110
society, 196
Thai Rak Thai Party, 108
Thai Rath, 117
Thaksin Shinawatra, 108, 109, 198
Thanh Nien, 149
Thein Sein, 87, 93, 98
Thida Htwe, 94
Think Big Indonesia, 53
Thinking Pinoy's Facebook post, 35
Third-Party Fact-Checking Program, 168
"toxic information", 157
"trolls" in the Philippines, 9
turning point
  for digital politics, 109–10
  in social media production, 5
Twitter, 172–74
  "bots", 9
  buzzers
    in Indonesia, 50
    and Instagram, 11
  digital research industry, 6
  in disinformation studies, 8
  Facebook and, 32, 45, 55, 69–72, 172, 180
  Jokowi on social media, 54

U

UN Independent International Fact-Finding Mission on Myanmar, 207
Union Solidarity and Development Party (USDP), 87–88
United Malays National Organisation (UMNO), 80n4
  Asalkan Bukan UMNO (Anyone But UMNO), 66
  Mahathir Mohamad, 73
  New Media Unit, 70
  split in, 77
UN Special Rapporteur on the human rights situation in Myanmar, 93
U Wirathu, 96, 97

V

V-Dem data, 193–94
Vietnam, 1, 204
  social media in, 15
  state information controls in, 145–47
    blogosphere and activism, 147–49
    co-opting Facebook, 155–59
    Facebook crackdowns fail, 151–55
    traditional media crackdowns and Facebook's arrival, 149–51
Vietnamese authorities, 146, 151–52, 155–56, 159
Vietnamese Internet Service Providers, 151
Vietnamese netizens, 151
Vietnamese social media landscape, 148
Voice of America, 130

W

"weaponization" of social media, 20
weblogs, 108
Western media, 95
WhatsApp, 133, 168, 184
    and Facebook, 12, 69, 74
    in Malaysia and Indonesia, 7–8
    review of, 179
    and Telegram, 78, 183
White Paper Protest, 174
Workers' Party (WP), 173

Y

Yahoo!360 social network, 148, 150
Yawning Bread, 170, 175
YouTube, 21, 28, 30, 49, 157
    Facebook and, 97, 114
    lèse majesté, 109
    pro-BN cybertroopers, 76
    "revolution", 87
    videos on, 70

Z

Zuckerberg, Mark, 10, 99, 158

www.ingramcontent.com/pod-product-compliance
Lightning Source LLC
Chambersburg PA
CBHW052038300426
44117CB00012B/1870